How did a man's elegant **tuxedo** begin as an Algonquian Indian word?

Why are prostitutes called **hookers**?

After whom was **Peach Melba** named?

How did love pave the way to chicken **tetrazzini**?

How did Italy give birth to blue **jeans**?

What is the link between castrated sheep and **bellwether**?

Why are the origins of **bonfire** and **vermicelli** not for the squeamish?

What is the wager that resulted in the coining of **quiz**?

Why do magicians say **abracadabra** and **hocus pocus** (and why can **open sesame!** get the door ajar, but **open barley** can't?)

The answers—totally authoritative and utterly fascinating—are all in

# HUE AND CRY
# AND HUMBLE PIE
## The Stories Behind the Words

MORTON S. FREEMAN, former Director of Publications, American Law Institute–American Bar Association, writes the "Word Watcher" column, syndicated in the *Philadelphia Inquirer, St. Louis Post-Dispatch, Buffalo News, San Diego Union-Tribune,* and other newspapers. He is also the author of *Words to the Wise* and *The One-Minute Grammarian.* He lives in Wynnewood, Pennsylvania, and in Boca Raton, Florida.

# HUE AND CRY AND HUMBLE PIE

## The Stories Behind the Words

### MORTON S. FREEMAN

**Foreword by Edwin Newman**

A PLUME BOOK

For MILDRED, *sine qua non*

PLUME
Published by the Penguin Group
Penguin Books USA Inc., 375 Hudson Street, New York, New York 10014, U.S.A.
Penguin Books Ltd, 27 Wrights Lane, London W8 5TZ, England
Penguin Books Australia Ltd, Ringwood, Victoria, Australia
Penguin Books Canada Ltd, 10 Alcorn Avenue, Toronto, Ontario, Canada M4V 3B2
Penguin Books (N.Z.) Ltd, 182-190 Wairau Road, Auckland 10, New Zealand

Penguin Books Ltd, Registered Offices: Harmondsworth, Middlesex, England

Published by Plume,
an imprint of New American Library,
a division of Penguin Books USA Inc.

Previously published under the title *The Story Behind The Word*.

First Printing, January, 1993
10 9 8 7 6 5 4 3 2 1

 REGISTERED TRADEMARK—MARCA REGISTRADA

LIBRARY OF CONGRESS CATALOGING-IN-PUBLICATION DATA
Freeman, Morton S.
    [Story behind the word]
    Hue and cry and humble pie : the stories behind the words / Morton S.
Freeman : foreword by Edwin Newman.
        p.    cm.
    ISBN 0-452-26924-5
    1. English language—Etymology—Dictionaries.    I. Title.
[PE1580.F74    1993]
422′.03—dc20
                                                92-27448
                                                    CIP

Printed in the United States of America

# Contents

# Foreword

In his previous book, *A Treasury for Word Lovers,* Mr. Freeman demonstrated the basics of good English—grammar, pronunciation, and word usage.

*The Story Behind the Word* takes us another step along the road toward mastery of our rich and complex language, exploring the often romantic forebears and mysterious roots of words we take for granted and use—or misuse—every day.

English absorbs words, it almost seems indiscriminately, from place names, mythology, acronyms, the Bible, Shakespeare, family names, and many other sources. A host of cultural groups have contributed words to English, notably the French, Scandinavians, Greeks, Romans, American Indians, and even the Tongans. The process is frequently accidental and unpredictable. This makes English word origins more exciting, amusing, and educational than etymologies from more homogeneous languages. And more surprising.

If you understand the roots of your language, you are less likely to abuse it and more likely to delight in its liveliness and variety. Through the witty and readable essays in *The Story Behind the Word,* you can come by this understanding easily and with pleasure. I know of no one who gets more enjoyment from our language than Morton Freeman does—and no one who is more adept at enabling the rest of us to enjoy it, too.

EDWIN NEWMAN

# Preface

Man has long wondered about the ancestry of the words he uses. Particularly challenging has been the history of English words. It is clear that much of English has been derived from the language of Germanic tribes—the Angles, Saxons, and Jutes, who invaded England in the fifth century. This was the beginning of what has come to be known as the Old English period. During this time many Latin words, especially ecclesiastical terms, influenced English. Middle English, which began about 1100 and continued to 1500, was infiltrated with French words brought to England by the Normans, who, incidentally, made it the official language of England. Many of today's English words stem directly from French; in fact some, like *garage* and *rendezvous*, have been borrowed whole. English has reached out in many directions, not hesitating to acquire words from almost every language, including Indian dialects, Icelandic terms, and Chinese expressions.

Although the origins of some English words are indisputable because they are traceable to a distinct root, many come from unknown sources. Etymologists have conjectured and disagreed about these ancestors. Consensus has not been a hallmark of word-sleuths. This means that if one were to read about the origin of a certain word in books written by different authors, he may be perplexed to find different versions. No one can justifiably blame an etymologist for not offering substantive evidence in each case. Often no record exists that can be the basis for analysis. Also, through the generations, people have attributed the derivation of a word to a certain source, simply because it seemed logical to do so. This practice, called folk etymology, is satisfying but not accurate.

May I assure you that I have pursued what are considered the more reliable sources. But neither I nor anyone else can vouch for the authenticity of the material. I present it as I have found it. I do hope that at least you will find it enjoyable.

The preface is the place to thank those who have helped in the preparation of a manuscript. My sincerest thanks go to all those who have made worthwhile suggestions. I wish to make particular note, however, of two persons who painstakingly reviewed and copyedited my work: Dr. C. Weil, of Riehen, Switzerland, and my wife, Mildred. Both, incidentally, are classical scholars, and without them I might have been bogged down in a morass. I also thank Horace Lean, of Bala-Cynwyd, and Lorraine Wright, School of Social Service, Bryn Mawr College, who typed and retyped, so it seemed, endlessly.

I cannot close without thanking three more persons, persons not involved with the manuscript but with my health. While this book was being processed, I suffered a serious physical setback. Many people helped me, and in many ways (it's amazing how many good people there are in this world), but three physicians carried the principal onus: my family physician, who orchestrated the medical steps to be taken—Dr. Murray L. Dorfman, of Merion, Pennsylvania, a Fellow of the American Academy of Family Practice; Dr. Sidney Cohen, T. Grier Miller Professor of Medicine and Chief, Gastrointestinal Section of the Department of Medicine, Hospital of the University of Pennsylvania; and Dr. Ernest F. Rosato, Professor of Surgery, University of Pennsylvania School of Medicine.

I thank these three physicians once more, for without them, who knows, there might have been no preface.

Morton S. Freeman

Philologists who chase
A panting syllable through time and space,
Start it at home, and hunt it in the dark
To Gaul, to Greece, and into Noah's Ark.

William Cowper, *Retirement*

## ABRACADABRA

Almost everyone, when about to perform legerdermain, first utters the magical word *abracadabra,* a term which originally was not in the argot of prestidigitators, but was a holy word of a sect known as Gnostics, an early Christian group that combined religion with witchcraft. The word they used, from which *abracadabra* evolved, was *abrasadabra.* Where that word came from has not been established. But some word sleuths have guessed that it was simply an elongation of the name of their high priest, Abrasax. Others have speculated that the beginning letters of three Hebrew words were loosely assembled to create this mystic term—*ab,* "father"; *r'eb,* "son"; *cadosh,* "holy spirit."

A word seldom used today, and then only in a religious context, is *simony,* the buying of spiritual honors. This word, too, in one sense owes its beginning to magic. In *Acts* the magician Simon offered money to Peter and John for the power of the sacraments; hence the word *simony.* The full name of the sorcerer, the would-be trader in church honors, and a former Gnostic leader, was Simon Magus (in Latin *magus* means "magic"). Perhaps he had forgotten to say "abracadabra."

## ACADEMY

The subject of the greatest of all epic poems, the *Iliad* of Homer, which is the story of the Trojan War precipitated by the kidnapping of the beauteous Helen by Paris, is so well known as to need no reporting.

What is less well known is the story behind the earlier abduction of Helen by Theseus, the great legendary hero of Attica. After Helen was abducted, her twin brothers, Castor and Pollux (who later became stars that nightly gleam on Earth), went in search of her but with no success until a farmer named Akademos disclosed to them the place where she was hidden.

As a reward for this information, a spacious grove to be watched over eternally by the gods was named in his honor—*Akademia.*

Plato was said to have established a school in that grove in 387 B.C. and to have held classes while sitting under a favorite tree. (John Milton referred to it in *Paradise Regained:* "See there the olive grove of Academe, / Plato's retirement.") Long after the death of the great philospher, his pupils continued to meet there, and from the name of that place has come the name for a distinguished institution of learning—*academy,* a society of scholars.

## ACHILLES' HEEL

Everyone has a weak, unguarded spot, a figurative Achilles' heel. Achilles, the bravest and most dynamic warrior in the Trojan War and the hero of Homer's epic poem the *Iliad,* also had an unguarded spot. But his was not figurative. According to legend, Achilles' mother, Thestis, plunged him, when he was an infant, into the river Styx to make him invulnerable. Since she held him by a heel, it stayed dry—and vulnerable. Many years later, during the siege of Troy, a poisoned arrow shot from the bow of Paris pierced Achilles' heel, fatally wounding him. W. S. Merwin in *The Judgment of Paris* described the lethal arrow in these words: "In the quiver on Paris' back the head of the arrow for Achilles' heel smiled in its sleep."

The tendon at the back of the heel, which runs from the calf muscle to the heel bone, is a strong tendon known as the Achilles tendon. It was so named in 1693 by a Dutch anatomist who dissected his own amputated leg.

## ACROBAT

An *acrobat* is adept in feats of agility, especially those requiring balance. He can swing on a trapeze, turn handsprings, or walk on a tightrope. The English language borrowed the term from French *acrobate* simply by dropping the final *e.* But the word originated in Greek *akrobatos,* meaning "one who goes on a tightrope on tiptoe" (*akros,* "tip"—of the toes—and *batos,* "going"). Which is what acrobats do. The Greek *akros,* with the sense "highest" or "extreme," entered English as a prefix spelled *acro*—*acrophobia* (fear of heights), *acropolis* (high city).

The garment worn by acrobatic aerialists, made of a tight-fitting elastic material, covering the entire body from wrist to ankle but having a low neckline, was named *leotard* after its inventor, the Frenchman Jules Léotard, one of Europe's most famous tightrope dancers during the nineteenth century. Today a *leotard* is the costume that ballet dancers wear during rehearsals.

## ADAMANT

*See* DIAMOND

## ADMIRAL

An *admiral*, etymologically speaking, is not necessarily someone "to be admired." The fact is that, although he may be a distinguished personage and deserving of high regard, his title is not associated with the quoted words.

The name for this high-ranking officer came from an Arabic word, *amir* (its English variant is *emir*), meaning "a prince," "a chief," or "a lord," and appeared in the title of their commander of the sea, *amir-al-bahr* (root sense "sea lord"). In the early thirteenth century naval officers from different countries, possibly Turks or Genoese, who had had dealings with Arabs, called themselves "amirales." These self-titled "amirales" were not certain what their newly acquired title meant, but they sensed that *amir* was a word of distinction. Later, influenced by Latin *admirari*, originally "to wonder at," but ultimately "to admire," which seemed like a kissing cousin of *amiral*, they added the *d* to make *admirale*. About the year 1500 its spelling was further slightly modified and its signification radically changed. The final *e* was dropped and the title was elevated. It came to designate the chief commander of a fleet.

## ADONIS

Adonis and Aphrodite are two names from Greek mythology that have been appropriated by the English language in one form or another.

Adonis was a lad of such surpassing beauty that Aphrodite fell in love with him. Unfortunately, while hunting, Adonis was ripped apart by a wild boar. Aphrodite grieved so bitterly that the gods of the nether world (or, according to some versions, Hades's wife, Persephone, the majestic Queen of Shades) restored Adonis to life on condition that he spend six months of every year with Aphrodite on earth and the other six months in the lower world. The change of worlds by Adonis was said to symbolize the death of nature in the winter (while Adonis was down below) and its revival in the spring (while Adonis was up above). An Adonis in today's language is a preeminently handsome young man.

Aphrodite (the Roman Venus) was the goddess of love and beauty. She sprang from the foam of the sea; hence her name, from the Greek *aphros,* "foam."

The most celebrated love item of apparel in Greek mythology was Aphrodite's girdle, the Cestus, for whoever wore it immediately became an irresistible object of love and desire. Aphrodite, loath to let anyone else wear it, was inextricably involved in passionate associations, so much so that drugs which stimulate erotic desires have been named after her—aphrodisiacs.

Like her beloved—the handsome Adonis—Aphrodite has long been regarded as the acme of pulchritude.


## ADULTERY, ADULTERATE

It should first be agreed that the word *adult* does not refer specifically to a grown man and *adulteress* to a grown woman. An *adult* ("a person who has arrived at full development") can be a member of either sex.

*Adultery* is voluntary sexual activity between a married person and someone not his or her spouse. Its Latin ancestor was *adulterare,* "to make impure." This verb, in turn, came from *ad* ("to") and *alter* ("different" or "other"). Its signification was that a change to something different was a corruption. An English derivative is *adulterate,* which means "to corrupt or defile by addition of a baser substance." But during earlier times, *adulterate* meant "to commit adultery." In Shakespeare's *King John,* Constance uttered these words: "But Fortune, O, / She is corrupted, changed and won from thee; / She adulterates hourly with thine uncle John."

## AEGIS

The meaning of *aegis* is "protection" or "sponsorship of," as in "being under the aegis of the Civil Aeronautics Board." But in Greek, *aegis* meant "goatskin," the skin on Zeus's shield—a unique position for a goatskin. This came about because a goat named Amalthaea suckled Zeus while he was an infant. When Zeus grew to manhood, and became the greatest and most powerful of the Olympian gods, he covered his shield with the goat's skin, which then protected him against his enemies—especially the fearsome, destructive Titans. Anyone privileged to act "under the aegis of Zeus," since he was omnipotent, was completely protected against all harm. But regarding those who now feel secure because they are operating under the aegis of a powerful force or organization, they should realize that it is all only skin deep—and a goat's skin at that.

## AFFILIATE

A person may affiliate with a group or an acquired firm may become an affiliate of a larger company. The sense of *affiliate*, whether noun or verb, is of a close association. Considering the literal meaning of *affiliate*, however, the one associating with a group or the small company is an adopted son, and the group or the acquiring company is the parent. In Latin, *affiliatus* (past participle of *affiliare*) means "adopted" (*ad*, "to," plus *filius*, "son"). Thus the group or the parent company, figuratively, has adopted a son.

In law, to *affiliate* has the technical sense of "to trace connections." Affiliation proceedings, known as bastardy proceedings, are designed to establish the paternal origin of a child born out of wedlock and to obligate the father to maintain it. A legal statement may read: "Susan Baker affiliated her child upon James Low."

## ALLIGATOR

*See* CROCODILE

# ALLURE

To allure, everyone will agree, is to tempt or entice with something desirable. If the word *allure* is to hearken back to its original sense, however, then a girl who intentionally allures a man is treating him like a hawk (and perhaps watching him like one, too).

From Old French *aleurrer* (meaning "to bait") came English *allure*, which in falconry was a hunter's device or bait to call back the hawks. The contraption consisted of a bunch of feathers attached to a long cord. The hawks were enticed into their return because this gadget was the one used to feed them during their training period. Women who allure men, it may therefore be said, are stringing them along, but with a touch that is as light as a feather.

# AMAZON

The longest river in the Western Hemisphere is the Amazon in South America. Its name came from a mythical race of Scythian female warriors. According to the Greek historian Herodotus, the Amazons were fierce fighters in many battles with the Greeks. Legend has it that Penthesilea, their queen, leading her forces to aid the besieged Trojans, was slain on a battlefield by the mythological hero Achilles. These manlike women, it is believed, were named after a Greek word meaning "breastless" because they burnt off their right breasts so as not to hinder their accuracy with the bow. In Greek, *amazon* is a composite of *a* ("without") and *mazos* ("breast").

It is said that the discoverer of the Amazon River named it Rio Santa Maria but that a subsequent Spanish explorer, Francisco de Orellana, believing he had been attacked by a tribe in which women fought alongside men, renamed it—*Amazonas,* anglicized *Amazon.* The lower case *amazon* is used today to mean "a strong woman."

# AMBITION

*See* **CANDIDATE**

## AMBROSIA

*Ambrosia* is known as the food of the gods, just as *nectar* is known as the divine drink. What is perhaps not known is that this food and drink conferred immortality. The word *ambrosia* came from the Greek *a* ("not") and *brostos* ("mortal") and *nectar* from *nek* ("death") and *tar* ("conquering"), which means that one who ate ambrosia was not mortal and that one who drank nectar had overcome death.

Some delectable food concoctions are called *ambrosia*, the implication being that they are fit for the gods. Today ambrosia may refer to anything with a delicious flavor or fragrance; and *nectar*, to any delicious or invigorating drink. (The *nectarine* peach came by its name because it tasted so pleasant as to remind one of a drink made in heaven.)

## AMBULANCE

Everyone recognizes the word *ambulatory*, from Latin *ambulans*, as meaning "capable of walking." What is confusing to some people, however, is the name of the vehicle used to transport patients to a hospital—an *ambulance*, which certainly does not walk.

The answer lies in a military medical development. Until the Crimean War in 1854, wounded soldiers on the battlefield received no medical attention until nightfall. After Napoleon III entered the war, his men devised a means to serve injured soldiers more quickly—an itinerant hospital: a litter that contained bandages, tourniquets, and other medical supplies which could be administered at once on the field before the soldier was moved. Because the litter was carried from place to place, the French called this field hospital *hôpital ambulant*, "the walking hospital." The English borrowed the idea and the name. They dropped the first word and anglicized the second so that today the vehicle used to transport the sick or wounded is called an *ambulance*, even though neither it nor its patients are ambulatory.

## AMEN

Probably the term with the widest acceptance throughout the world is *amen*, a Hebrew word that means "certainly" or "verily." Ordinarily used at the end of a prayer to express assent or concurrence, its sense is "Thus it is," "So be it," or "May this prayer come true." No other word with such precise signification has ever been invented: only *amen* expresses this solemn thought.

The Greeks borrowed the Hebrew *amen* in 250 B.C. when scholars, at the behest of Ptolemy Philadelphus, an Egyptian king, translated the Hebrew Bible into Greek so that the king, who understood Greek, could read the Bible. Many years later *amen* was incorporated into the Latin vocabulary. Today, with the exception of French, which uses *ainsi soit-il,* meaning "and so be it," most prayers in the Western world end with *amen.*

## AMERICA

How America got its name is not much of a story; its naming, in fact, was somewhat accidental. Beginning with 1497, Florentine navigator Amerigo Vespucci made several trips to what he called Mundus Novus ("The New World" in Latin). When a German geographer, Martin Waldseemüller, prepared a map for his *Cosmographiae Introductio,* showing these journeys, he labeled the new land *America* after Amerigo Vespucci. This name was first applied to what is now South America, but ultimately to North America as well. (Americans can be grateful that Amerigo's first name, instead of his surname, was used; otherwise they all would be Vespuccians, which sounds like something from outer space.)

Although the name United States may refer to different countries, there can be only one *United States of America,* which indicates the importance of Vespucci's given name. Yet Amerigo was not a particularly important figure on the expeditions to the New World. He did not take a leading part; he was, in fact, only a pilot—or an astronomer, as pilots were called at that time.

## AMNESTY

*Amnesty,* according to Dr. Johnson, is "an act of oblivion; an act by which crimes against the government, to a certain time, are so obliterated that they can never be brought into charge." The word was first uttered by a compassionate Greek general who said he would forget the offenses of his enemies. This he would do by granting them amnesty (from the Greek *a*, "not," and *mnasthai*, "remember"); that is, he would not remember their misdeeds. An amnesty, therefore, is a purposeful forgetting, now a pardon for past offenses against a government.

Another English word that stems from the same root is *amnesia*, "loss of memory." Unlike one granting an amnesty, however, one suffering from amnesia is not forgetting on purpose.

## AMUCK

*See* **BERSERK**

## ANNIE OAKLEY

There is one surefire way to make a person happy, and that is to give him or her an Annie Oakley. An *Annie Oakley*, of course, is a complimentary ticket to a theater or other house of entertainment. The ticket has a hole punched in it to prevent its exchange for cash at the box office.

The name came from a real Annie Oakley, whose full name was Phoebe Anne Oakley Mozee. Annie was as perfect a marksman as one could find. For many years she performed as a sharpshooter in *Buffalo Bill's Wild West Show*, which traveled throughout the country. One of her stunts was to shoot the spots out of a playing card that had been tossed into the air (hence her name applied to a pass punched with a hole or a meal ticket punched whenever used). Ethel Merman, who starred in *Annie Get Your Gun*, popularized the name Annie Oakley among recent generations.

Another celebrated female marksman, at the turn of the twentieth century, was Martha Jane Burke, more commonly known as "Calamity Jane." This crack shot in effect dubbed herself with that lugubrious nickname when she warned that anyone offending her would be inviting calamity. It is said that eventually calamity became her lot. Although her nickname enriched the English language, it did not enrich her; she died in poverty.

## ANTIMACASSAR

*See* COUCH


## APHRODITE

*See* ADONIS


## APOTHECARY

An apothecary is not a druggist, and a broker does not sell stocks. At least this was true for many centuries.

The word *apothecary,* derived from Greek *apotheke* (literally "to put away"), means "a warehouse." And that is what, until recent times, an apothecary was—a storehouse for many kinds of wares, many of which were not drugs. The move to convert apothecaries into drugstores took place in England during the seventeenth century when it was agreed between the pharmacists and the grocers that only drugs would be sold in apothecaries. That a druggist was called an apothecary in Shakespeare's time is proved from the mouth of Romeo, who, when drinking the poisonous potion, cries: "O true apothecary! / Thy drugs are quick. Thus with a kiss I die." In the United States, it is all mixed up—drugstores are small supermarkets and supermarkets have small drug departments.

A broker was a person who broached or tapped a keg of wine. Figuratively this sense is used today when one speaks of broaching a subject, that is, opening up a conversation. Cardinal Wolsey used *broach* in this way in Shakespeare's *Henry VIII,* when he said: "I did broach this business to your highness." In yesteryear a wine merchant was called a *broker,* not because he was a businessman, but because he was a broacher of casks (Latin *broca* means "spike" and *brocare,* "to pierce" as though with a spike or, as is usually said, "to tap a cask"). The term *broker* has been extended to cover many people in retail and other forms of business, so that nowadays one may speak of a pawnbroker, a stockbroker, or a marriagebroker, for example, all of whom undoubtedly would like to open up or broach their favorite subject.

## APPLAUD

One might think that the verb "explode" is nothing to clap about. But there is much clapping in it. In fact, in ancient times audiences would "explode" if the performers deserved no applause. But to start at the beginning.

Roman actors were not bashful. At the end of a performance, they would command the audience to applaud by saying "Plaudite!" which is a Latin plural imperative that translates into "Applaud!" (Similarly radio audiences in the United States are told when to applaud, and commonly a master of ceremonies will plead after a "comic" has bombed out: "Let's have a big hand for our favorite comedian.") When Roman audiences were displeased with the acting, they would begin to clap, but during the performance. That clapping, however, was not a sign of approval; it was "exploding" (from Latin *explodo—ex*, "out," and *plaudo*, "clap"). What they were doing was clapping the inept actors off the stage. Americans disgusted with a showing "explode" differently; they hiss or hoot.

The expression "deserving of plaudits" literally means "deserving of applause." The word *plaudit* was appropriated directly from the Latin *plaudere*, "to break into clapping." Today *plaudits* (usually found in the plural) means "approval, praise, commendation"—"something to applaud," which is what another derivative, *plausible*, meant originally.

## APPLE

The apple has gotten around—from the Garden of Eden to the best pie on Mom's table. Yet the word *apple* (which descended from the name of an Italian province, Abella) has been loosely used and even misused.

The prominent projection in men formed by the thyroid cartilage is called the Adam's apple because a piece of this fruit was supposed to have stuck in Adam's throat. But this attribution is only fictional, since no one knows whether Adam bit into an apple. The Biblical story recounting the giving of forbidden fruit by Eve to Adam makes no mention of apples. The Bible referred to "the fruit of the tree." God said, "Ye shall not eat of it, neither shall ye touch it, lest ye die." The translation of the Hebrew tappūah hā adhām (a bodily protuberance on a man) was misinterpreted because of a double meaning.

"The apple of my eye," a centuries-old phrase, is used of any cherished thing—especially of a parent who dotes on a child. Originally, however, the reference was to the pupil of the eye, which was thought to be apple-shaped. The pupil is a very precious—and sensitive—part of the body; hence the transposition of "apple of my eye" to something treasured, something deserving special protection. It is so used in the Bible. Solomon admonished the Israelites to "keep my law as the apple of my eye," and the Lord told Zion: "He that toucheth you, toucheth the apple of my eye."

The apple, obviously, is a wonder fruit. If eaten daily, it keeps the doctor away. But not every "apple" will keep the doctor away, especially since some of them are not true apples. The French potato, for example, is called a *pomme de terre*, literally an "apple from the ground." A *pineapple* is not an apple (and it does not grow on pine trees—although, in all fairness, its outer shell resembles a pine cone). From a combination of *pomme*, "apple," plus *grenate*, "having many seeds," has come the name *pomegranate*, a fruit with a reddish rind, containing many seeds with a juicy pulp. Like the others, it is not really an apple. One may wonder, therefore, when a person says that someone is the apple of his eye, which apple is meant.

The peach came from China. But the name given it was *malum Persicum*, "Persian apple." (In Latin the noun *malum* means "apple.") Although it was known that this fruit came from the Orient, to most Europeans *Persia* was so far distant that *Persicum* seemed an appropriate name for anything coming from the Far East. With time, *malum* was dropped and *persicum* became the parent of the current names—French *pêche*, Italian *pesca*, English *peach*.

## APRON

An apron is an everyday household garment, worn at the waist to protect or adorn the front of a person's clothing. Everyone knows that. What is not so well known is that in yesteryear this apparel was not called "an apron" but "a napron." In careless speech the *a* and the initial *n* of *napron* became elided, forming the word *an* and leaving *apron* with only one *n*—*an apron.*

Attaching the initial *n* of a noun to the preceding article *a* to form *an,* so that the noun began with a vowel, was not uncommon; and the words that have evolved have continued until this day. In addition to (n)apron are (n)adder, (n)auger, and (n)umpire. A *numpire,* the anglicized form of *noumpere* (Latin *non par,* meaning "not equal"), was an impartial third party who decided a dispute between the other two. But if today a *fan* (a shortened form of *fanatic*) hollered "Kill the numpire," everyone would think he lisped, or that he was a fanatic.

## ASSASSIN

*See* THUG

## ASTROLOGY

Philologists are not certain whether the word *astrology* comes from the Latin *astrologia* ("a study of the stars") or from the Greek *astron* ("star") and *logos* ("a discoursing"). Perhaps the answer can be found in the stars.

In the Middle Ages, astrology, "the study of heavenly bodies with a view to predicting their influence on human affairs," was a predominant factor in the lives of many people because of the prevailing belief that joys and sorrows—indeed all the passions, activities, and decisions involved in human conduct and events—were directly influenced by stellar bodies.

Other celestial bodies—the planets—also contributed to astrological theory, since it was assumed that they affected the very temperament of people. A saturnine person (gloomy, melancholy), for example, was supposedly dominated by the planet Saturn. A jovial person was under the influence of Jupiter. One who was volatile or mercurial was swayed by Mercury, and so forth.

Another prevalent belief was that a person suffering from misfortune had been born under "an evil star"—a *disaster* (Latin *dis* means "against"; hence the thought that the stars were against him). Not everyone, of course, was so convinced. In Shakespeare's *King Lear,* Edmund declaimed, "We make guilty of our disasters the sun, the moon, and the stars; as if we were villains on necessity; fools by heavenly compulsion; knaves, thieves, and treachers by spherical predominance; drunkards, liars, and adulterers by an enforc'd obedience of planetary influence." And Cassius in *Julius Caesar* also believed that man's destiny lay not in astral influences but in himself, for he declared, "The fault, dear Brutus, is not in our stars / But in ourselves. . . ."

Although the original sense of misfortune implied in *disaster* continues, men by and large no longer condemn or praise the stars for their pitfalls or successes, since today astrological convictions are rare. But then again, when things go well, it is not unusual to hear someone say, "You can thank your lucky stars."

## ATLAS

An *atlas* is a book or collection of maps. In Greek mythology, Atlas, a Titan, attempted to overthrow Zeus, who then condemned him to support the pillars of the heavens. In the sixteenth century, the Flemish cartographer Gerhardus Mercator, on the first page of his collection of maps, placed a picture of Atlas bearing a globe on his shoulders. The idea caught on with other map publishers who then adopted a similar picture for their books. Subsequently the word *atlas* came to signify a bound collection of maps and, still later, a volume of systematic illustrations of any subject.

The usual plural form of *atlas* is *atlases.* Another plural form is *atlantes,* an architectural term for figures of men used in place of columns to support buildings. In *Paradise Lost,* Milton refers to "Atlantean shoulders, fit to bear the weight of mightiest monarchs." Draped female figures that in the place of pillars support an entablature are called *caryatides,* which in Greek means "a priestess of Artemis at Caryae in Laconia." One of the most famous structures graced by *caryatides* is the Erechtheum on the Acropolis, near the Parthenon.

## AUGUR

To *augur* is to foretell or presage. Although a prediction may imply the boring of a hole into the future, an *auger* (with an *er*), a hole-boring tool, is not the instrument used in an augury, even though J. R. Lowell in *A Fable for Critics* remarked that augurs were bores.

In ancient Rome, priests known as augurs (state prophets) predicted the future by interpreting flights of birds and their number. If the seers divined what they saw as promising, the undertaking or event would be under "good auspices."

These bird-watching forecasts gave rise to a related English word: *auspicious,* from the Latin *avis* ("bird") and *specere* ("to watch"). Nowadays, however, *auspicious* does not suggest a bird-watcher. It means "full of good omens," favorable or encouraging. A derivative, *auspices,* is often employed loosely to mean "under the patronage or management of." Which means that one who resents being patronized might rightly exclaim, "It's for the birds."

## AURORA BOREALIS

The Aurora Borealis is a well-known name for the "Northern Lights," the lights occasionally seen in the northern part of the sky. It is, of course, a luminous atmospheric phenomenon near the North Pole. Less widely known is the name of a similar phenomenon near the South Pole, the Aurora Australis.

Aurora was the Roman goddess of dawn and a sister of the sun god and of the moon goddess. It was she who rose from her couch at the close of every night, harnessed her horses, and ascended to heaven to announce the coming light of the sun, the dawn of a new day.

> You cannot shut the windows of the sky
> Through which Aurora shows her brightening face
> —Thomson, *Castle of Indolence*

The morning dew, poetically, is called "Aurora's tears."

According to another legend, Aurora's sons were the four winds, one of whom was Boreas, the North Wind. Boreas was regarded as the rudest of them all, since he was a ravisher of maidens and a blustering railer. Those who got wind of him stayed far away.

## A.W.O.L.

*See* **FRENCH LEAVE**

## B

## BABEL, BABBLE

Of the many biblical references that have become part of daily speech, none is more common than *babel*. It means, of course, a confusion of sounds, a hubbub.

In the Bible the word *Babel* is capitalized because it refers to a city; it is the Hebrew name for the city of Babylon. The Book of Genesis recounts the story of the people of Babel who tried to build a tower to heaven. To thwart them, the Lord decided "to confound their language, that they may not understand one another's speech." There followed a confused uproar, and from that din emerged many languages, where previously there had been only one tongue.

> God . . . comes down to see their city,
> . . . and in derision sets
> Upon their tongues a various spirit, to raze
> Quite out their native language, and instead
> To sow a jangling noise of words unknown.
> Forthwith a hideous gabble rises loud
> Among the builders; each to other calls
> Not understood . . . Thus was the building left
> Ridiculous, and the work Confusion named.
> —Milton, *Paradise Lost*

Multiplicity of languages never bothered Voltaire, a master of many of them. He once wrote Catherine the Great, perhaps facetiously: "I am not like a lady at the court of Versailles who said: 'What a dreadful pity that the bother at the tower of Babel should have got language all mixed up; but for that, everyone would always have spoken French.'"

*Babble* sounds like an offshoot of *babel,* especially since one meaning of noun *babble* is "senseless prattle." The verb *babble* means "to utter a meaningless confusion of sounds." However, its origin can be found in Middle English *babelen,* which in turn had come from *ba . . . ba* plus an intensive ending, "a mocking

**16**

imitation of those who talk on and on, with little to say"—just like a veritable babbling brook.

## BACCHANALIAN

A bacchanalian festival nowadays would be frowned upon by anyone of gentle and refined breeding. A bacchanalia is a wildly drunken party or orgy.

Nevertheless, in Roman mythology Bacchus (the equivalent of the Greek Dionysus) was the respected god of wine and vineyards. It was he who planted the vine. The triennial festivals paying homage to the harvest were characterized by propriety and sobriety and followed by dignified rituals. But with time the nature of the celebrations changed. Bacchus's worshippers succumbed to the delights and effects of the vinium, the wine, and the revelries soon became known for their drunkenness and licentiousness.

If it were not for Zeus, there might have been no Bacchus and no wine. According to this legend, Bacchus was the son of Zeus and Semele. Semele was foolish enough to ask Zeus to appear before her in all his glory, as he was wont to do before his wife Hera. Zeus complied and appeared in thunder and lightning. As Semele was being devoured by the flames, she gave birth prematurely. Zeus took the child (Bacchus) and sewed him into his thigh, where he remained until reaching maturity. Bacchus was one son who was truly raised at his father's knee.

## BAKER'S DOZEN

Did a baker's dozen—thirteen for twelve—come about to foster legitimate or illegitimate practices? No one knows for certain, but there are theories to support both views.

The more popular theory is that under English law, bakers were subject to severe penalties for short weight. Since they were often unable to determine accurately the weight of the loaves of bread, muffins, or cakes sold, they would add an extra one to an order for twelve to avoid an unwitting violation of the law and the penalty they might incur. (English bakers were better off than their Egyptian counterparts. In Egypt, a baker whose loaves were light was nailed by his ear to the doorpost of his shop.)

The other theory is that bakers gave their customers an additional loaf (called a vantage loaf) as a bonus, a practice that has survived until this day even in other businesses. Druggists are sometimes shipped a larger quantity of an order than they will be billed for, and booksellers get a "free" book with a bulk order. In any case the dealer is given an advantage.

## BANKRUPT

The origin of the word *bankrupt* is obscure. One guess is that if a bank account were drained of all its money, it could be called a bank rupture, which could logically have been the progenitor of the term *bankrupt*. Another thought advanced by some word historians is that medieval Italian financiers conducted business from benches called *bancas* on which they displayed their money. When they had disposed of all their wares, had lent all their money, they broke up or took apart their benches to cart them home. In Italian the word for "broken" is *rotta;* therefore, the moneylenders, when unable to continue their business, were called, after their dismantled benches, *bancarotte,* literally "broken benches." From that Italian word came the English *bankrupt,* meaning unable to pay one's debts as they come due. Yet another idea is that the *-rupt* in *bankrupt* came from Latin *ruptus,* which, like *rotta,* means "broken." English *rupture* comes from it, and so the first guess—bank rupture—may have been the right one.

Another Italian "bank" word borrowed into English is *mountebank,* which came from *montare in banco,* "to get up on a bench." A *mountebank* is a charlatan, one who hawks quack medicines and cheap wares, usually while standing on a bench or platform. Mountebanks have long been regarded as frauds. Massinger in *The Virgin-Martyr* put it succinctly: "Quack salving, cheating mountebanks." No word mincing there.

## BARBECUE

The word *barbecue* can refer to the cooking of meat (verb) or to the meat cooked (noun) over an open fire on a spit or gridiron. It has also come to mean, by extension, an affair held in the open in which food is cooked and meat roasted. Originally a *barbecue* was a device—a stick set on two uprights—to roast an animal whole. The word drifted into English, via Spanish, from the Haitian *barbacoa* ("a framework for roasting meat"). West Indians commonly roasted a hog whole, basted with wine. Pope in his *Satires* has this to say, "Oldfield . . . / Cries, Send me, ye gods, a whole hog barbecued!" George Washington's diary, dated September 18, 1773, noted: "Went to a Barbecue of my own giving at Accatinck."

But the belief that *barbecue* comes from the French *barbe à queue* (which means "beard to tail"), on the assumption that the first animal so treated was a goat, is without foundation. Whoever dreamed that one up was not a trained etymology sleuth and obviously followed the wrong cue.

## BARBER

Everyone agrees that a *barber* (from Latin *barba*, "beard") is a person who shaves another's beard (a Roman barber was called *tonsor;* hence the elegant name for a barbershop—"tonsorial parlor"). To find a barber, one would look for a pole decorated with red and white spiraling stripes. But that, originally, was not the only trade the pole symbolized. In fact, the pole was being used for an entirely different purpose.

In medieval times barbers practiced surgery. Dr. Johnson's *Dictionary* under the entry "barber" lists "barber-chirurgeon," defined as "a man who joins the practice of surgery to the barber's trade" (*chirurgeon* in Greek meant "surgeon"). Barbers were surgeons of a sort because the medical profession held surgery in such low esteem that they scorned it; hence the barber-surgeon. However, during the reign of Henry VIII the barber's surgery was restricted to bloodletting, a treatment designed to correct some medical disorders, primarily high blood pressure and anemia. After the blood was let (phlebotomy), the barbers would drape their blood-soaked bandages around a white pole to dry, giving the pole the alternate red and white ribbon look, which subsequently became the signpost of a barbershop. In earlier times a barber would ask his customer, "Do you want me to shave you or draw your blood?" That always put him in a lather.

## BASTARD

In the light of the increase in the number of illegitimate births, and considering how often the term *bastard* is used as an epithet, one might imagine that philologists would know how and where that word originated. But its ancestry remains doubtful, as may be the progenitors of those stigmatized.

Some lexicographers believe that *bastard* evolved from two languages about the same time, and each euphemistically. The Old French conveyed the idea of a child born out of wedlock by the term *fils de bast* (literally "son of a pack saddle"), its sense being "having been conceived on a packsaddle." Muleteers often used the *bast* as an impromptu bed. The Teutonic *bantling* had a parallel meaning, except that the German child was begotten on a bench. The only legitimate thing about all this is that *bast* probably came from Late Latin *bastum*, "packsaddle," or from Vulgar Latin *bastare*, "to carry."

## BATHOS

Although *bathos* is an uncommon term, it nevertheless is a good, precise word to convey the idea of a sudden and ludicrous descent from the sublime to the ridiculous, as in writing or in speech when a serious course of reasoning, a dignified line of thought, or a stately speech ends abruptly on a trivial note. This kind of unexpected ending, of course, may have been designed for its humor. Certainly it is anticlimactic.

*Bathos* was a coinage of Pope, who, in his celebrated poem *Dunciad*, needed a word to express false pathos but could find none. To this end, he selected the Greek word *bathos* (which meant "depth"). Today when something plunges from the top to the bottom, or appeals to excessive emotionalism, or goes from grandiloquence to the commonplace—that's bathetic!

> She was, and in my mind's eye, she still is, a thing of quivering beauty, Quivering? Undeniably. Beautiful? To me, unutterably. She was my first motor-car.
>
> —John Marshall

Valentine's Day is approaching, a time to recall that your wife still likes candy and flowers. Show her you remember, by speaking of them occasionally.

—Earl Wilson

# BEARD

Hair and its treatment have been just as important to the sense of style and grooming of men as of women. The only difference is that women are more concerned with their coiffure and men with their facial hirsuteness—until middle age, that is.

The beard has been a popular sign of masculinity (*beard* in Latin is *barba;* whence the English word *barber*). In the seventeenth century a Flemish portraitist, Anthony Van Dyck, became a painter to the English court. He wore a distinctive beard—short, trim, and pointed, and the gentlemen whose portraits he painted wore collars with scalloped edges and beards of the same cut. The beards—known by the painter's name, *vandyke* beards—became fashionable and were widely sported. Those who preferred a wisp of hair on the chin, rather than a full beard, grew a *goatee,* so-called because of its resemblance to the fuzz of a he-goat.

The odd thing about sidewhiskers (the hair that grows past the ears along the cheeks) is that they are no longer known by their original name of *burnsides.* This facial decoration came into prominence through General Ambrose Everett Burnside, commander of the Union Army of the Potomac, whose distinguishing feature was his profusive side growths. Somehow or other *burnsides* became *sideburns*—a reversed formation that no one can account for, although the shift seems justified, considering where the hair grows.

# BEDLAM

The word *bedlam*, meaning "noisy confusion" or "wild uproar," is a contraction, or a Cockney corruption, of *Bethlehem,* from the name of a London religious house, "St. Mary of Bethlehem." In the sixteenth century "St. Mary" was converted into an asylum for the insane, the first such hospital in England. Its name, lowercased *bedlam,* subsequently came to refer to the cries of the inmates, and eventually to stand for any combination of noise and utter confusion.

Wild disorder that is even more uproarious is called *pandemonium.* In *Paradise Lost,* written in 1667, Satan directed his heralds to convene a council: "A solemn Councel forthwith to be held / At Pandaemonium, the high Capital / Of Satan and his Peers." John Milton coined the word *Pandemonium,* the name of the capital of Hell, by combining *pan* ("all") and *daimon* ("demon"), referring to the abode of all the demons. Today *pandemonium* means complete confusion or a riotous place where "all hell has broken loose."

## BELFRY

No matter how wildly bats fly in a belfry, they will never strike a bell, at least according to the original meaning of *belfry.* This is because, etymologically, a *belfry* has no connection with the word *bells.* In Middle English, *belfry* was a portable siege tower. When an army attacked a walled city, the soldiers would wheel up to its wall a tower from which they could fire missiles and also look down on the beleaguered town to study its defenses.

The word *belfry* has undergone many orthographical changes since first recorded in Old French as *berfrei* ("that which watches over peace"). It arrived in English as *berfrey.* Since towers usually contain bells, the word, because of this association, came to be spelled *belfry.* Today a belfry, of course, is a spire or steeple in which bells are hung. It is no longer a siege tower or a watchtower.

## BELLWETHER

A wether is a castrated sheep. It can be located easily, since a bell fastened around its neck tinkles as the sheep moves about. The *bellwether,* as the eunuch sheep is called, acts as the leader of the flock. Sheep being sheep, they follow the leader—in all kinds of weather. It should be noted that bellwether is sometimes mistakenly used as a synonym for *harbinger.* As pointed out, a *bellwether* is a leader. It has now acquired a figurative sense of a leader in other forms of activities, such as the trend in the stock market, where it may be a harbinger of coming movements.

## BENCHMARK

Two marks—the bench and the hall—have made a mark for themselves in the English language. Nowadays a reference point in the measure of the quality or value of almost anything may be its benchmark or its hallmark. Although often interchanged, *benchmark* has a wider range of use; *hallmark* is employed only figuratively.

A *benchmark* was a surveyor's term for a marking made on a stationary object (a rock or a wall) that acted as a guide for position, like an elevation in a topographical survey. Later the term entered general usage to represent a standard of excellence or achievement in almost any field. The business world now uses it to mean an objective to be attained or a goal to be reached; in daily activities it applies to the quality of food or drink—especially wine—by which a restaurant is judged.

A *hallmark* is a mark stamped on gold and silver articles after they have been assayed. The term came from the practice of Goldsmith's Company of Goldsmith Hall, London, of using a mark on the articles it tested. When impressed on the back of an article, the mark attested to its quality—that is, that the article conformed to agreed-upon standards.

Although the guild of goldsmiths began in the twelfth century, it was not until 1721 that the designation *hallmark* first appeared. It has come to mean "high quality" or "genuine" in almost any kind of production. Or it may refer to "a distinguishing characteristic"; thus, kindness is the *hallmark* of a gentle, understanding person or penitence the *hallmark* of a contrite heart.

## BENEDICT

A *benedict* is a confirmed bachelor. The term is a generic offshoot of *Benedick,* a character in Shakespeare's *Much Ado About Nothing,* who swore to remain celibate but who (as often happens to those with such intentions) was finally entrapped into matrimony. Today, by extension, a man newly married but long a bachelor may also be called a *benedict*. The word's origin can be found in the Latin *benedictus* (meaning "blessed"), a composite of *bene,* "well," and *dict* from *dicere,* "to speak."

From the Bible has come another common name now used generically, *Benjamin,* the youngest son in a family or son of the right hand from the Hebrew *ben* ("son") and *yamin* ("right hand"). The name Benjamin harks back to the youngest of Jacob's sons, the ancestor of the twelve tribes of Israel.

## BERSERK

In Norse mythology berserkers were warriors who, after eating a trance-inducing hallucinogen, went into battle wearing a bear's skin (called a *berserker*) rather than armor. According to legend, these warriors believed that Odin, the god of war, would protect them and make them invulnerable, even though they wore only a "bear shirt." They became fierce and undaunted fighters. Supposedly they foamed at the mouth and howled or growled like animals. They fought with such fury that today (as a take-off on the shirt they wore) a person in a frenzy of rage is said to have gone berserk.

A synonym is *amuck* (variantly spelled *amok*). It, too, denotes derangement, a madness to do violence or kill. The word was associated with the Maori males in New Zealand, who, under the influence of opium, worked themselves into a frenzy and then raced through jungles and villages hollering A moq! A moq! (Kill! Kill!), slaughtering any living thing they came upon. Today one who wantonly shoots pedestrians is said to have run amuck (*run amuck* is the usual phrase). Like *berserk, amuck* is a foreign import. It did not originate in New Zealand, however; it came from Malay.

## BETWEEN THE DEVIL AND THE DEEP BLUE SEA

A person undecided which of two equally hazardous paths to take is said to be "betwixt and between" or "between the devil and the deep blue sea." This latter expression originated in the seventeenth century with Robert Monro in *His Expedition with the Worthy Scots Regiment Called MacKeyes Regiment."* He wrote:

"I, with my partie, did lie on our poste, as betwixt the devill and the deap sea." Generally the word *blue* is added, not for color, but to improve rhythm. Although *betwixt* may be used with *between* for the same reason (*betwixt and between*), it too is unnecessary, since both words convey an identical meaning.

More ancient is the phrase "between Scylla and Charybdis," which implies equal difficulties or dangers equally fatal. *Scylla*, according to Homer, was a fearsome sea monster who lived on a jutting rock in Italy opposite a similar rock in Sicily where *Charybdis* dwelt surrounded by a whirlpool. To pass through the Strait of Messina, one had to slip by both the monster Scylla and the whirlpool Charybdis. Scylla had twelve feet and six heads, each with three rows of teeth like a shark's, and attached to her waist were baying dogs. Charybdis, who lived under a fig tree, three times daily drank all the water of the sea and then belched it back. Obviously, sailing a ship between these two rocks was extremely perilous and required unusual skill. Whether to chance it was a quandary—one with no happy solution. The hapless navigator was bound to end up being sucked into a maelstrom or "thrown to the dogs."

# BIBLE

The word *bible* came into being long before the Holy Bible was written. It started with an ancient Phoenician city in the Middle East, Byblos. The Phoenicians, who were the great merchants of their time, traded with many distant countries, including Egypt, from which they imported papyrus plants. After converting the plants into writing material, the Phoenicians sold it to the country with the most prolific writers: Greece. The Greeks called the product *biblos*, after the name of the city, and ultimately *biblion*, meaning "little book." In the fourth century a Greek patriarch bestowed the name *Bible* on the holy book, intending to distinguish it as "the Book of books." A bible, lowercased, is any book considered authoritative in its field, like Gray's *Anatomy*.

*Papyrus* (Greek *papuros*), the parent of the English word *paper*, sired another everyday word—*schedule*. Its genesis can be traced to the Latin *scheda* ("a papyrus leaf") and its offspring *scedula* ("a slip of parchment"), on which were made notes of the day's programs. Eventually the same word, but anglicized, became today's schedules—train timetables, theater programs, school rosters—all of which means that contemporary man literally *leafs* through a schedule to find out what and when.

## BIKINI

Any man with eyes knows what a *bikini* is. It is the skimpiest two-piece bathing suit a woman can wear and still feign a sense of modesty. How the word took on this meaning has been a linguistic mystery since 1947 when bikinis were first seen on the beaches of the French Riviera, a year after atomic tests were held on the Bikini atoll in the Marshall Islands. One belief is that the impact of the scanty swimsuit on male beach loungers was like the effect of an atomic blast; hence the name. A simpler notion is that the swimsuit resembled the attire worn by women on the Bikini atoll. In any event, a *bikini* does not consist of two *kini's*. The *bi-* is not from the Latin "two." A girl who goes topless and calls her outfit a *monokini*—*mono-* from a Greek prefix meaning "one"—exposes her ignorance, among other things.

## BISCUIT

The word *biscuit* begins with *bis,* which in both Latin and French means "twice." The second syllable can also be found in both languages but more plainly in the French *cuit,* "cooked." Hence a biscuit is something that is twice cooked. A man whose wife is an etymologist should not expect flaky, fluffy breakfast biscuits, since she would know to cook them twice. Probably they will taste more like hardtack. (An American biscuit is baked unleavened bread. A British biscuit is a cookie.)

*Zwieback,* too, means "twice baked." It is a bread baked as a loaf that is later sliced and toasted (*zwei* in both Dutch and German means "twice").

## BISTRO

*See* CAFETERIA

# BITTER

When is bitter better? When something unbearable finally comes to an end—the so-called "seeing it to the bitter end." In this cliché, *bitter* does not refer to taste or to a trying experience, however. It is a nautical term, meaning the end of a ship's rope wound around the *bitt* or *post*. When all the rope or cable has been wound, the part closest to the bitt is called the bitter end. A person at his bitter end is, figuratively, at the end of his rope, which may be a less happy or secure position.

*Bitter* is an adjective (a bitter pill) and also an adverb (bitter cold), as is *bitterly* (bitterly cold).

That which is both bitter and sweet (pleasure alloyed with pain) is called *bittersweet,* such as a reunion between parents and a wounded son returning from war. *Bittersweet* is an oxymoron (from Greek *oxys,* "sharp," plus *moros,* "stupid"), a contradiction in words, words of opposite meaning used together.

# BIZARRE

*See* GROTESQUE

# BLACKBALL

*Blackball* and *ostracize* have a sad sense in common—rejection. A person blackballed has been denied admission to a club or fraternity; a person ostracized has been banished from companionship.

In ancient Greece, whether to admit someone to, or to exclude someone from, membership in an organization was determined by secret vote, by dropping a colored ball, usually made of stone or metal, into a receptacle. A white ball indicated approval; a black ball, disapproval. This practice has continued, figuratively, until this day. The undesirables, those voted against—by voice vote or written ballot—have been blackballed.

When the citizens of Athens regarded a person's behavior as undemocratic or dangerous to the state, they would, by vote, determine whether to send him into exile, usually for five years. The vote was made by chalk on *ostrakons,* potsherds (pronounced *pot*-sherds), which were fragments of pottery, tiles, or oyster shells. Plutarch's *Life of Aristedes* outlines the procedure: "Each voter took an ostrakon ... wrote on it the name of that citizen he wished to remove from the city ... the total number of ostraka cast (were then counted) ... the man who had received the most votes (was then) proclaimed banished. ..." Sounds like an early version of today's shell game. In any event, from this custom, and born of the word *ostrakon,* has come *ostracize,* the English verb meaning "to exclude from one's fellowship" or "to shun."

## BLACKMAIL

*Blackmail,* as is generally known today, is an extortion by threat to expose something disgraceful, a threat to prosecute criminally (an intimidation), or a tribute paid to be free from harassment (a protection). In Scotland, where it all started, there was *whitemail* as well.

The freebooters who plagued northern England and Scotland during medieval times exacted "blood money" as the price for leaving estates unmolested. What was extorted was called *blackmail,* not to reflect color or to indicate how a demand was made. *Black* meant "evil or bad or illegal," as in today's blackmarket. *Mail* (from *mal* or *mael*) was taken from the Scottish word for "rent," which was a payment agreed upon. *Whitemail* (from *whitmal*) was "white" plus "agreement." Blackmail was paid in cattle; whitemail, in silver.

For those concerned about the ancestry of *mail* (the kind a postman delivers), it can be found in Old French (*male*) and in Old High German *(mahla),* both words meaning "leather pouch." The mailman and all the other postal *mail* words come from the same source. When wondering whether a letter has gone astray, it's good to know that it's in the bag.

## BLIZZARD

The word *blizzard* sends a chill down some people's spine. And well it may, for a blizzard, according to the dictionary, is a violent snowstorm, a meaning attributed to an Iowa newspaper editor who, in 1870, used that term to describe a fierce windstorm that brought driving snow and intense cold.

But that is not what *blizzard* meant originally. It had previously been used in several senses, the closest to its present meaning being a heavy rain (reported in 1770 as "a heavy blizz of rain"). Some said that a blizzard was a prizefighter's knockout punch, but Davy Crockett used it when alluding to a volley of shots fired at a buck. Other word-detectives guessed that it meant "a loud noise," stemming from the German *Blitz*, "a flash of lightning." Still others sought its parent in "blaze" (a burst of flame)—a complete turnabout in sense. Figuratively a blizzard is "a severe attack" or "an unexpected or sudden occurrence," as, for example, a blizzard of complaints or lawsuits—or a blizzard of demands to know how the word *blizzard* originated.

## BLOOMERS

*Bloomers* are no longer stylish, but, like many other fashions, they may show up again. This outfit, composed of baggy trousers gathered about the ankles and worn under a short skirt, was named after the militant nineteenth-century advocate for women's rights, Amelia Jenks Bloomer, who habitually wore this costume as a uniform of rebellion. Although she encouraged others to do likewise, she was not successful; the shapeless garment failed to capture the imagination of the public. "Bloomers" were worn only by those women who wished to be identified with the suffragette cause.

Ironically, Mrs. Bloomer did not live to see women's suffrage adopted or to see the prominent part "bloomers" played on women's hockey fields. During her lifetime, Mrs. Bloomer insisted that she had not designed this garment, but merely adopted it. The designer, and the first person to wear this costume, was a rival reformer, Mrs. Elizabeth Smith Miller, of New York. If this story is true, the girls coming out of a gym dressing room are rightly attired in *millers,* not *bloomers.*

## BLOW

Many American idioms revolve around the word *blow*. For example, "It will soon blow over," meaning that the storm will stop shortly or that a topic will soon no longer be a subject for discussion. Or "to blow one's stack"—that is, to vent anger.

This latter expression began as a nautical term. When a boiler in an eighteenth-century riverboat became overheated, it was not unusual for the pent-up steam "to blow the stack." Hence today when people let their steam out on someone, they, too, are in a sense "blowing their stack" or, more simply put, "blowing off."

Possibly the most interesting story with "blow" concerns the phrase "blow hot and cold." In Aesop's fable, a satyr was entertaining a traveler who felt cold. To warm his hands, the traveler blew on them; when served hot broth, he again blew, but on the broth to cool it. The satyr was puzzled at this inconsistency and, not knowing what to make of it, became so vexed that he sent the traveler away because "he blew both hot and cold with the same breath." Of course nowadays the expression refers to a vacillator, one who first takes one side and then the other.

## BLUE

*Blue* (from Old French *bleu,* ultimately from Old High German *blao*) is a color. The word is used in a figurative sense in phrases ranging from despondency to exaltation.

Considering all its meanings, "blue" probably is most often employed to represent melancholy or low spirits. Where this usage came from—*to feel blue* or *to have the blues*—has never been satisfactorily established. It has, since the mid-nineteenth century, been a common element of slang, possibly reflecting the sad, funereal music of Negro jazz players still stinging from the stigma of slavery. A sister phrase—*blue funk*—also suggests emotional depression, but one in "a blue funk" is usually suffering from a disillusioning romance.

A *blue blood* was a Spanish noble who insisted that his blood (Spanish *sangre azul*) was blue, not black like that of the Moors. Today the phrase is an epithet for anyone of noble or aristocratic descent. From the same notion, and from the same Castilian families, came the phrase *true blue,* referring to the blueness of their veins as compared to those under a darker skin.

Although the origin of *once in a blue moon* is uncertain, its earliest sense was "never." Today the phrase means "very rarely." A person who says that he sees his brother "once in a blue moon" means seldom.

The stockmarket term *blue-chip stock* is indebted for its name to the blue chips used in gambling casinos. These chips come in different colors but those of the highest value are blue.

A person who screams *blue murder* ("Lord Windsor screamed blue murder at the approach of the burglar") is not hollering because he has just witnessed a homicide. He may be terror-stricken or warning others of danger. One theory holds that "blue murder" is a corruption of the French exclamation *morbleu,* which, in turn, is a contracted form of *mort de dieu* ("death of God").

On a lighter note is *blue ribbon,* a phrase defined as "the highest award of honor." And that was precisely how the expression originated. In Britain, a recipient of the blue ribbon, the badge of the Order of the Garter, has been honored with the Crown's highest order. Today, of course, blue ribbons are symbols of the best in many different fields. One may even be found on a can of beer, which may not, incidentally, be a beer to everyone's liking. It is standard to award a blue ribbon to a winning horse at a race or show. The credit for the association of blue ribbon in this case came, so it is said, from Disraeli. A friend complained that he had sold a horse which a few days later won the Derby. "You have no idea what the Derby means," said the unfortunate horse trader. "Yes, I do," replied Disraeli—and perhaps alluding to the blue garter, the highest of all orders, continued—"It is the blue ribbon of the turf."

But when a story, a conversation, a theater scene, or a "gag" is said to be *blue,* it is somewhat "indecent" or at least is garnished with risqué humor. On the other hand, it may even be downright obscene. Why is the lascivious, the prurient, "blue"? One theory associates it with the color of burning brimstone, which is blue. Another idea is that "blue," meaning "indecent," came from *bibliotèque bleue* (literally "a blue library"), books offensive to good taste. A third notion is that since harlots wore blue gowns when confined in the House of Correction, they came to be called *blues,* hence the color *blue* to represent the vulgar or the lewd.

One thing is sure, a person who has "the blues" is not looking at the world through rose-tinted glasses.

## BLUESTOCKING

A woman called a *bluestocking,* referring to her studious tastes, is not thereby complimented. Very much the opposite, she has been belittled, for a bluestocking is an eponym for a woman affectedly intellectual or literary.

Although no one disputes the meaning of *bluestocking,* the origin of the term is controversial. The story most often advanced is that in the eighteenth century Elizabeth Montagu became disheartened by the idle chatter and constant card playing of her English friends. To encourage her associates to devote more time to educational pursuits, she organized a literary society to which she invited learned persons to come and speak. One guest, Benjamin Stillingfleet, wore blue worsted stockings instead of the more formal black silks. Almost immediately the group's followers were derisively dubbed *bluestockings,* the implication being that they had pretentions to learning and erudition.

According to another story, Mrs. Montagu wore blue stockings in the hope that they would dramatize her efforts to restructure the tastes of her friends along literary lines.

Anyhow, today a bluestocking is, to borrow a statement from Rousseau, "A woman who will remain a spinster as long as there are sensible men on earth."

## BLURB

Almost anyone knows what a *blurb* is. For the record, however, a *blurb* is a glowing descriptive notice on a book's jacket.

*Blurb* was a 1907 invention of Gelett Burgess, famous for his quatrain *The Purple Cow.* Burgess first used the word *blurb* on the jacket of his *Are You a Bromide?* which contained a picture of a frail girl (named Belinda Blurb) but none of the customary fulsome praise. As he said, he "had her pictured blurbing a blurb to end all blurbs, I fondly hope." It didn't, however. Since then, *blurb* has become an established English term. (Incidentally, another word now in general usage, *bromide*—trite remarks or a person addicted to uttering them—was also borrowed from that same book.)

## BOHEMIAN

*see* GYPSY

## BONFIRE

Bonfires impart a sense of cheerfulness. Campers like to sit around them, singing songs, telling stories—and roasting marshmallows. They were a customary signal of success in America on Election Night, and no holiday was aptly celebrated without one. Yet there is a morbid side to these fires that is far from the "good" that the *bon* in *bonfire* might suggest.

The first syllable, originally from Medieval English, and influenced by the Scots, was *bane,* meaning "bone." (The English word *bane,* as in "the bane of my existence," comes from Old English, and it means "poison.") In the wake of plagues, as a precaution against the spread of disease, it was a practice to make a pyre of the corpses. These fires, literally fires of bones, were rightly called bonefires. Time has shortened and softened this word to *bonfires,* perhaps so that now they can be enjoyed without serving as a reminder of their grim history.

## BOOK

When one picks up a *book,* etymologically speaking one picks up the bark of a beechwood tree, for in very ancient times words were scratched on the bark of these trees or on the wood itself. They were the common material on which writing was inscribed. The Old English word for *beech* was *boc;* whence the word *book.* (A very large-sized book of which the pages are formed by a sheet of paper once doubled is, according to Dr. Johnson's *Dictionary,* a *folio.* That term comes from Latin *folium,* "a leaf.")

A *magazine* (from Arabic *makhzin,* "storehouse") is another breed of publication. It appears regularly and contains stories, pictures, and articles from different contributors. Long ago, books were called *magazines* because they were "storehouses" of information. The word *magazine* then came to embrace many kinds of places for storage—a building for storage of military arms, for example, or even a holder (commonly called a *clip*) of cartridges for an automatic gun. The French borrowed the word for a department store, *magasin*, a place to store and sell a variety of commodities. Today, a magazine, the kind one reads, remains a storehouse of information, and is therefore rightly named, even though it is not the sole repository of knowledge. Even the human mind can be a magazine—of wisdom.

## BOOKLET

The commonest form of printed communication, other than the newspaper, is the book, which consists of written or printed sheets bound together between covers. A *booklet* (*let* is a diminutive suffix, as in *hamlet* or *islet*) is a small book, usually made with paper covers. The pages of a book or booklet may be either glued or stitched together. But the pages of a *brochure*, a tract even smaller than a booklet, can only be, according to its root (French *brocher*, "to stitch"), sewed into a unit. The word *brochure*, it may be said, threaded its way into the English language.

The background of *pamphlet* may be entirely amatory. In the twelfth century, an erotic poem (a bawd's story on how to make love), whose author is unknown but may have been Ovid, appeared under the name *Pamphilus, seu de Amore*. This "love-making" poem was very popular, and the title *Pamphilus* became known as *Pamphilet*. After the invention of the printing press, the poem appeared in booklet form and was named a *pamphlet* after the poem. The word *pamphlet* stems from Greek *pamphilos* (meaning "beloved by all"), although Dr. Johnson believed that it came from French *par un filet* ("held by a thread"), which would be a stitched but unbound publication.

## BOONDOGGLE

*Boondoggle* is obviously a coined word. *Boon* could mean a blessing and *doggle* could allude to a dog or to a doggerel (a comical verse). Or refer to Daniel Boone's dog. But these guesses are all wrong.

Not only is the meaning of the word obscure but the signification is "puzzling." In 1925 scoutmaster R. H. Link of Rochester conceived the word as a name for leather necklaces worn by boy scouts; hence any insignificant handicraft. In this sense, used as a noun, the word was admitted into respected English, but it never attained wide usage.

During the days of Franklin Roosevelt's administration, however, its meaning and its part of speech changed. It became a verb, a slang term meaning "to perform unnecessary work; to engage in a project that is pointless, trifling, piddling." This use of the word mushroomed (as did boondoggling), and *boondoggle* became, and still is, an ordinary word—for performing less than ordinary work.

## BOOR

A *neighbor*, literally, is a farmer who lives nearby. The word is a combination of *nigh* (meaning "near") and *boor* (meaning "farmer"). The word for *farmer* in Dutch is spelled *boer* but pronounced *boor*, rhyming with *moor*. The Boer War, in which the British fought the Dutch farmers, took place in South Africa between 1899 and 1902.

Although *boor* carries within it no pejorative sense, the word in English through a process of downgrading came to mean "ill-mannered," "unrefined," or "rude" because those traits were attributed to the boers or rustics, people living out in the country who had not acquired the polish, the culture, or the refinement of city residents.

> To one well-born the affront is worse and more,
> When he's abused and baffled by a boor.
> —Dryden, *Satire on the Dutch*

Even though today in the United States, as much as in Holland, *boors* can be found almost everywhere, urbanites still continue to regard their rural cousins as provincials or "hayseeds." Calling them that, however, is bound to get one in Dutch, even if he lives in America.

## BOOZE

Booze is a barroom word not found in the vocabulary of the genteel. Yet for centuries it enjoyed credentials which had made it, in one form or another, a commonplace word in the English language. With time, however, it degenerated into slang, to the point that in the sixteenth century it was regarded as thieves' cant. Its level of acceptance has risen since then, but not enough to enter literary circles.

Although the origin of *booze* is obscure, it may be cognate with Middle Dutch *buyzen* or *busen,* meaning "to drink to excess" or "to guzzle liquor." The term has been given varying forms— *bouze, bouse, bowse* (Edmund Spenser in 1590 in *The Faerie Queen* spoke of a "bouzing can"). Some etymologists attribute its origin to the Hindustani *Booza,* "drink"; others to the Turkish *boza,* a kind of liquor favored by gypsies. One thing certain is that *booze* did not come from the name of a Philadelphia distiller E. C. Booz, a notion advanced by some word watchers. During the 1840 presidential campaign, bottles of whiskey, shaped like a log cabin and bearing the stamp "Booz's Log Cabin Whiskey," were widely distributed, the idea being to impress the electorate that General William Henry Harrison, who turned out to be the successful candidate, had been born in a log cabin. The noun *booze,* as a matter of fact, had been used in America years before and its noun and verb form used in Europe centuries before.

## BOSH

*See* PREPOSTEROUS

## BOUDOIR

*See* PARLOR

## BOWDLERIZE

In 1818, Dr. Thomas Bowdler, an English physician and editor, undertook the task of eliminating vulgar terms from the works of William Shakespeare, with the object of giving the world an expurgated version. According to Bowdler his publication, *The Family Shakespeare,* did not add anything to the text; instead "those words and expressions [were] omitted which cannot with propriety be read aloud in a family." Bowdler's purge, as might be expected, aroused vehement objections from many Shakespeare lovers. In reply to his critics, Bowdler wrote: "And shall I be classed with the Assassins of Caesar, because I have rendered these invaluable plays fit for the perusal of our virtuous females? If any word or expression is of such nature, that the first impression it excites is an impression of obscenity, that word ought not to be spoken, or written, or printed, and if printed, ought to be erased." Bowdler's name lives in the language as a derisive term meaning "to remove from someone's work arbitrarily anything considered objectionable."

Footnote: The original *bowdlerizer* was not Thomas but Henrietta Maria Bowdler, known as Harriet, Thomas's sister, a spinster who hid her authorship because, it is believed, she didn't want the public to know she understood the "obscenities" she expurgated.

Although Dr. Johnson did not include the word *bowdlerize* in his dictionary, he was familiar with it. On one occasion, so the story goes, Johnson was approached by two very proper spinsters who complimented him for omitting from his dictionary all foul words that make ladies blush when they read Shakespeare. Johnson replied, "It is interesting to note, Mesdames, that you have been looking for them."

## BOYCOTT

To *boycott* means "to join for the purpose of preventing dealings with a person, an organization, or a nation, as a means of coercion." A person who is boycotted is ignored; a store that is boycotted is not patronized; a boycotted organization has no one to deal with. This method of coercion was named after a retired English Army officer, Captain Charles Cunningham Boycott, the land agent in Ireland's County Mayo for the estates of the Earl of Erne.

In the autumn of 1880, after a crop failure struck Mayo County, the tenants found themselves unable to pay rent. Instead of lowering their rent in view of the circumstances, Boycott raised them. Whereupon the tenants, with the support of the Irish Land League, banded together and turned on him. They isolated and then harassed him, refusing to gather crops or pay rent or even talk with him. Boycott soon found his position so intolerable that he fled to England where sometime later he died in obscurity. But his name, despite its shameful past, has become a common—and useful—term in the English language as well as in other languages around the world. No other word carries precisely the same meaning.

## BRAGGADOCIO

*Braggadocio* (double *g*, single *c*) sounds like an Italian word. It's not. It is a coinage by Edmund Spenser, used by him in *The Faerie Queene* (1590) as the name of a character who personified vain boasting—Vaine Braggadocchio. The first part of his surname came from *braggart* (origin unknown but obscurely related to Middle English *braggen,* "bray"), to which was added the augmentative suffix *-occio,* giving the word its Italian flavor.

## BRAND-NEW

A person who says his car is brand-new means that it's completely new. Although he's right (if the car came fresh from the showroom), he may not know that "brand-new" literally means "fresh from the fire."

In the Middle Ages *brand,* from an Anglo-Saxon root meaning "burn," referred to glowing metal newly forged. An article that had just come out of the furnace ("fresh from the fire") was said to be brand new. Later *brand* became the term for a branch burning on one end, the equivalent of "torch," a brand snatched from the fire.

Shakespeare frequently used the phrase, but in the form "fire-new." In *Love's Labour's Lost,* for example, he had Berowne say, "A man of fire-new words, fashion's own knight," and Fabian in *Twelfth Night,* "You should have accosted her with some excellent jests, fire-new from the mint." Edgar, son of Gloucester, in *King Lear,* declared, "Despite thy victor sword and fire-new fortune."

The expression "brand-new" clearly did not grow out of the practice of putting brands or trademarks on merchandise for sale. And also quite clearly, using *bran (bran-new)* for "brand," although common, is equally erroneous.

## BRASS

Officers in top command are referred to as *brass hats* by soldiers who analogize the braid on the visors of officers' caps to brass. (The gold braid is also sometimes called *scrambled eggs* for the same reason.)

The expression, shortened to *brass*, has spilled over into civilian life. It has come to represent anyone in high authority in one's place of employment or in the business world generally. Today top-ranking executives are called *top brass* or just *the brass*.

Some sources attribute the term *brass hats* to a military custom developed during the time of Napoleon. Before entering an important office, soldiers would remove their hats and carry them under the left arm. The hats, because of this practice, came to be called *chapeaux à bras*, which in French translates to "hats under the arm." Pronouncing this *s* in *bras*, so that it sounds like *brass*, is a simple mistake for a non-Frenchman to make; hence "brass hats."

## BRIDAL

In former days wedding guests customarily toasted the bride with tankards of ale. From this practice emerged the word *bridal*, a compound of Old English *bryd* ("bride") and *eaulu* ("ale")—bride-ale, which became *bridal*, with a final *al*, analogous to that in *betrothal* and *espousal*. The practice of drinking to the bride's future has continued until this day. Only the drink has changed—instead of foaming, it now effervesces.

At the end of the wedding ceremony, the minister may say, "I now pronounce you man and wife." Why, someone may ask, does he not say "husband and wife" or "man and woman." The answer lies in convention. For many centuries one of the meanings of *man* was "husband." The custom of using "man and wife," therefore, became so firmly established that (with few exceptions) no one—neither man nor wife—saw fit to change it.

A *groom* is a boy employed to take care of horses. For those who wonder how come so many stable boys manage to get married, the answer (ignoring the intended humor) is that the *groom* in *bridegroom* came from another source—Old English *guma* ("man"), which, as a folk-altered term, became "groom."

# BROBDINGNAG

*See* LILLIPUTIAN

# BROCHURE

*See* BOOKLET

# BROKER

*See* APOTHECARY

# BUCCANEER

A *buccaneer* is a pirate. The name was specifically applied to the piratical adventurers who raided Spanish colonies and coastal areas of America. In Dr. Johnson's *Dictionary*, the word is spelled *bucanier*, which almost duplicates the French *boucanier*, the root of the English word.

It all started with French hunters who lived in the West Indies, particularly Haiti. They were called *boucaniers* (anglicized *buccaneers*) because they followed the practice of native Indians of smoking their meat on a wooden grid called a *boucan*. Some of the French settlers turned to piracy, and since they used a *boucan*, they came to be called *buccaneers*, meaning "pirates." A buccaneer, when all things are considered, is not a bad sort after all; he simply likes his meat smoked.

# BUFF, BUFFALO

Swimming in the buff means swimming naked. The expression "in the buff" refers to one's hide. Many years ago *buff* referred to the hide of buffaloes and later specifically to their color.

The association of the word *buff* with "fan" or "devotee" arose, according to one theory, during the early days of volunteer firefighters in New York City. These enthusiasts, all well-to-do men, were nicknamed *fire buffs* because their winter coats were made from buffalo skins. Another theory is that the term was taken from the color of the buff uniforms worn by the professional firemen. In any event, these original fire buffs were the parents of all the aficionados that followed.

The North American animal called a *buffalo* is really a *bison*. The animal was misnamed in 1544 by De Soto, who, when reporting his discoveries, called it a *buffalo*. The error was not corrected, and *buffalo* became the animal's popular name. In colloquial language, a person who is buffaloed has been intimidated or fooled. But for De Soto, he would have been *bisoned*.

## BUGLE

> Blow, bugle, blow. Set the wild echoes flying.
> —Tennyson

A *bugle* is a horn—literally. The origin of this word can be found in Latin *buculus*, diminutive of *bos*, "ox" (whose genitive, *bovis*, led to *bovine*). The Romans used an ox horn to blow through. This horn came to be called, naturally enough, "bugle-horn." After the invention of the bugle—a cornetlike military instrument—the word *horn* was dropped, which left *bugle* alone as the one thing that soldiers hate more than army chow.

Centuries ago the Hebrews warned their people of the approach of enemies by blowing through the horn of a ram, an instrument (called a *shophar* and also spelled *shofar*) which they use until this very day to trumpet the close of a Jewish High Holy Day. In the mid-eighteenth century the German *Flugelhorn*, adapted from the hunter's horn, a metal version of a wild ox's horn, became a military instrument because of its piercing notes. The English then decided to use the bugle similarly as a means for conveying signals to distant troops. It was a bugle that sounded the signals in the famous battle immortalized by Tennyson's "Charge of the Light Brigade," a charge that doomed the brave "Six Hundred."

## BUNK

Many words in the English language mean "nonsense" or "poppycock." One word with this meaning that is often used in colloquial speech sounds like slang but is not—*bunk*.

*Bunk* is a shortened form of *bunkum*, which, in turn, derived from *Buncombe*. In 1820 Congressman Felix Walker, who represented Buncombe County, North Carolina, addressed the House of Representatives. His talk was rambling, filled with claptrap, and completely pointless. When his colleagues in the Sixteenth Congress challenged him for wasting their time, he replied that he was not talking to them, that he "was talking only for Buncombe." The word *Buncombe* came to mean "political nonsense," but then it developed the larger sense of any kind of insincere talk. Mark Twain so used it in *Pudd'nhead Wilson.* He wrote: "He said that he believed that the reward offered for the lost knife was humbug and buncombe."

As time went on, *bunkum* lost its terminal syllable, and became plain *bunk*. Whether *bunko* ("a swindle or confidence game") was sired by *bunk* is a matter of dispute. Some say yes (the appended *o* converts nonsense into a designed ploy); others, that it came from the name of a Spanish card game, *banca.* No matter, the bunko squad thinks con men are full of bunk.

The verb *debunk* is rooted in "bunk." The word was supposedly coined by William E. Woodward, who first used it in a novel titled *Bunk.* During the period between the two World Wars, certain historians who challenged the accuracy of information concerning the deeds in the biographies of men of prominence were called *debunkers*. The *de-* was prefixed to create a word meaning "to expose the false or exaggerated claim or pretension"—that is, to divest of bunk.


# BURLESQUE

*Burlesque,* a French term, meaning a caricatured reproduction, originated in a material—wool. It descended from Italian *burlesco* from *burla,* "jest" or "ridicule," but ultimately from Late Latin *burra,* "a puff of wool," which figuratively meant "trifles" or "nonsense." The word in common speech that derives directly from *burra* is *bureau,* initially a table covered with woolen material. A partial offshoot is *bureaucracy,* a word of invidious overtones. That eighteenth-century coinage was formed by combining *bureau* with the Greek *-cracy,* which means "strength, power, or rule," to make *bureaucracy,* "government by administrative officials."

# BUS

People are in such a hurry to get where they're going that they even shorten the name of the transporting vehicle so they can spit it out, as though that will get them there sooner. For example, they hop a *bus* and grab a *cab*.

The word *bus,* a clipped form of *omnibus,* the dative case of Latin *omnes,* literally "for all," in effect was a vehicle designed to accommodate everyone. Of course, the term *omnibus* has vanished in America. Adding a word in their own language, the French people traveled on a public conveyance called *voiture omnibus,* "vehicle for all."

The English language is indebted to French for the word *taxi,* but no American would recognize its full name—*taximeter-cabriolet.* The middle part, *meter,* from *metre,* is a measuring device. *Taxi,* from *taxe,* is "a charge"; hence a *taximeter* "to measure the charge." *Cabriolet* is pure French for a two-wheeled carriage. The "cab" one hails is simply the first syllable of *cabriolet.* (Can anyone picture a philologist standing in the rain and hailing a cab by its full name?)

# BUTCHER

A butcher, almost everyone will agree, sells meat—beef, veal, pork—which he buys from an abbatoir. He cuts the meat to order, weighs it, wraps it, and hands it to the customer. But that is not what a butcher did in the distant past. The root of the word *butcher* is *bouc,* which in old French meant "goat." A butcher, therefore, was a man who slaughtered goats. But not on public property. Under French law a butcher (then called *bochier*) was not permitted to "cast the blood of goats in public ways, nor slaughter the goats in the streets." It had to be a private matter. If the police suspected a butcher of violating that law, it would "get their goat."

# BYLAWS

*Bylaws* (often spelled *by-laws* or *bye-laws*) are not laws adopted by the way or by and by. And neither are they incidental or secondary laws. They are, in today's usage, the rules governing the internal affairs of an organization. When the word came into being, however, that meaning was neither literal nor applicable.

The progenitor of *bylaw* was the Old Norse *bylog* (a compound of *byr*, "village," and *log*, "law"). In Middle English it was spelled *bilaw* and came to designate the village law—the local law—as distinguished from the general laws of the realm. That the meaning of *by* was "town" or "dwelling place" can be seen in the names of many English towns—Der*by*, Rug*by*, Whit*by* (the English can thank the Danes for those names, even though they resented the Danish occupation of their land).

In Dr. Johnson's *Dictionary, bylaw* is not defined but its meaning can be gathered through excerpts cited. Its drift to the sense of "minor" might have been occasioned by analogy with other *by* terms, such as *bypath* and *byway*.

# C

## CABAL

Dictionaries define *cabal* as "a conspiratorial group of plotters or intriguers." The word originated in ancient Hebrew *gabbal*, which then had almost the same meaning it has today except that it applied to occult theosophy, whereas it is now applicable to politics—secret plans directed against a government or a political leader.

By coincidence the initials of the infamous ministry of Charles II, which consisted of five members, acrostically formed the word *cabal*. The committee members were *C*lifford, *A*rlington, *B*uckingham, *A*shley, and *L*auderdale. In 1672 they fomented a war with Holland by surreptitiously signing an alliance with France. Although these cabinet officers did not inspire the word, their nefarious schemes popularized it, in its pejorative sense.

Another political term, whose origin is obscure, is *caucus*. It, of course, refers to "a meeting of the members of a political party to decide upon questions of policy or other related matters." *Caucus* sounds like an Indian word (somewhat imitative of a bird's mating call), and it may be. Some etymologists (relying on the records of Captain John Smith, who spelled it *caucawasu*) believe that *caucus* is an Algonquian term meaning "counselor or adviser." If so, the Indian pipe-smoking pow-wows were the breeding ground for the later politicos' smoke-filled rooms.

## CADET

Annually the cadets of West Point play the midshipmen of Annapolis in a football classic. Every spectator knows who the cadets are—the future generals—and who the midshipmen are—the future admirals. But interestingly, the words *cadet* and *midshipman* originally did not signify a student in a service academy. In fact, the terms were completely unrelated to the process of training for a military or naval career.

A *cadet* was simply a younger brother or son. The word comes from a Gascon form, *capdet*, meaning "chief" or "head," which, in turn, was derived from Latin *caput*, "head." These *capdets* came to serve in the military (a regular practice for the younger sons of nobility) and eventually, with a slight alteration in spelling, were called *cadets*. Because of their youth they were considered to be in training for a military career but not yet to have achieved that goal. English borrowed the word directly from the French with no change in meaning or spelling. A young man at a military school today in training to become an officer in the armed services is still called a *cadet*.

A *midshipman* is defined in many dictionaries as "a student naval officer ranking above a master chief petty officer and below a warrant officer." But when the term originated in the British navy, the name was applied to naval students not because of their position in the hierarchy of naval officers but because of the location of their bunks on a ship, which were amidship on the lower deck. Hence these budding executive officers were called *midshipmen*. The American colonists adopted the term and the practice of putting these trainees in the ship's center. Later the term *midshipman* was given another use—the designation for students at the United States Naval Academy at Annapolis.

## CADMEAN VICTORY

*See* PYRRHIC VICTORY

## CADUCEUS

*See* HYGIENE

## CAESAR

The Roman emperor known as Julius Caesar was named Gaius Julius at birth. He later assumed the cognomen *Caesar*, which became synonymous with "emperor." Caesar's adopted son, who succeeded him as ruler, took the name Augustus Caesar. There were, including Julius, twelve Caesars. The title was continued by Roman rulers even after the death of the despotic Nero, the last emperor who could trace his lineage to the original family. The emperors who ruled after Nero continued the tradition by prefixing "Caesar" to their names; for example, *Imperator Caesar Domitianus Augustus.*

In one form or another the title *Caesar,* meaning "leader," has passed along through generations and into different countries. It was adopted by the Russians (first by Ivan the Terrible in 1547) in the form *czar* (pronounced *zahr* and sometimes spelled *tsar* or *tzar*) and was continued as the title of their ruler until the overthrow of Czar Nicholas II during the Russian Revolution. The German emperor also called himself *caesar* but spelled it *Kaiser.* Kaiser Wilhelm II, the last of the Hohenzollern line, led the German nation into World War I and was exiled in 1918 after his defeat.

American "czars" of course are not emperors but merely persons who have acquired authority over a specific sphere of activity; for example, a baseball czar, a union czar, or a political czar.

## CAFETERIA

Everyone knows what a *cafeteria* is. It is a restaurant in which customers serve themselves from the food displayed at counters. This type of eating house is comparatively new; the term was first used in English in 1839. But its ancestry goes all the way back to the fifteenth century.

After the discovery of coffee, about 1600, houses that specialized in serving this beverage sprang up in England and France and were an overnight sensation. They became the center of social, recreational, and intellectual activity. The name given this establishment in England was *coffee house;* in France, *café,* which was also the French name of the beverage. The term *café* infiltrated into many countries, denoting a small casual restaurant, although some were not so small and some not so casual.

The *cafeteria,* born much later, initially referred to a Turkish coffee house, but its name, according to general belief, derived from the Spanish, in which language a *cafetera* was a coffeepot. Mencken suggests that Italian *caffetiere* may have been its ancestor.

A common name for a small bar or café in France is *bistro*. That name, however, is not French and in no language at all does it mean "restaurant." It is phonetic Russian for *"vee-stra,* meaning "quick." It seems that the Cossacks who spent time in Paris, after the defeat of Napoleon, upon entering a restaurant would shout what sounded like "bistro"—which actually translates to "hurry"—arrogantly demanding immediate attention. The Frenchmen mistakenly assumed that what they were hearing meant "quick food"; whence the name for a certain type of neighborhood fast-service restaurant.

The basic name for an eatery, of course, is *restaurant*. That word comes from Old French *restaurer*, meaning "to restore." A restaurant is a place to restore strength by feeding the body, a putting fuel on the fire, so to speak. The Latin *restaurare*, literally "to repair again," was the ancestor of the French term, but it referred to a restoring or a fixing of a fence (*re*, "again," plus Greek *stauros*, "stake"). The word *restaurant*, according to Klein, can be traced to Paris when in 1765 Boulanger opened the very first one. Over the entrance of his establishment appeared this Latin inscription: "Venite ad me omnes qui stomacho laboratis et ego vos restaurabo" ("Come to me ye all that suffer from the stomach and I will restore you"). The coining of *restaurant* from *restaurabo* followed.

## CALISTHENICS

That the ancient Greeks idealized the classic beauty of the human body is evidenced by their words to describe it. The word *calisthenics* is a case in point. It means "the practice of exercise, primarily exercising the muscles to gain strength." The word's two elements are *kalos* ("beautiful") and *sthenos* ("strength"), which literally mean "beautiful strength," the state of the body when developed to perfection. The Greeks even have a word for shapely buttocks—*callipygian*, in which the *pyge* means "rump." (The Callipygian Venus in Naples has extra guards around it to protect its derrière from Neapolitan rump pinchers.)

Calisthenics were often held in a *gymnasium*. Here again the body and its beauty were linguistically evident, particularly so since participants in a gymnasium performed unclothed, fully exposed. In Greek a *gymnasium* is a place to train naked (*gymnos* means "naked"). Not only is the body best trained when naked, but so is the mind, according to one belief. Alexander the Great discovered a sect of Hindu philosophers who meditated in the nude. It seems there's nothing nude under the sun—not even nudity.

## CANADA

What's in a name may truthfully be nothing. For example, according to one story concerning the naming of Canada, two Spanish explorers reached a point just south of the present Canadian border. One scaled a high bluff to see what lay northward. The other shouted up to him "¿Qué ve Vd.?" ("What do you see?"). The reply was "Aca nada" ("Nothing's there"), but, with the wind whipping away the initial *a*, what was heard was *cana'da!*

Another story, also unattested, is that an Indian chief, while talking with the explorer Jacques Cartier, pointed to his village (the word for which in his language was *kanata* or *kana'da*) and then waved his hands in a semicircle. Cartier thought he was pointing to the entire region beyond the horizon; hence, if this story is true, the Indian word for "village or settlement" is now the name of the second largest country in the world—Canada.

The Alaskan seaport on the Seward Peninsula called Nome has never been given a name. In fact, one belief is that that is exactly what Nome stands for—no name. During the early period of Alaskan development, while a chart of the Alaskan coast was being prepared, it was noted that the area had not been named. A cartographer inserted on his map "No name," meaning a name was needed. In error the English draftsman ran the words together and came up with "Nome." Another version is that the cartographer simply wrote "Name," intending that someone else supply it. However, the *a* was mistaken for an *o*, and the name of the region, ever since, has remained Nome.

## CANAPÉ

It does not seem possible that *mosquito* (in Greek *konopos*) and a delectable French treat (*canapé*) could have the same ancestor, but it's true. The word referred to is the Greek *kon-*

*opion*, a mosquito net, from which evolved, through a series of language changes, an English word easily recognizable as having come from it: *canopy* (pronounced *kan*-oh-pih), a curtain used to overhang a bed or sofa as a protection against those biting insects. The French called the sofa itself a *canopy*, but spelled it *canapé*. Then the imaginative, culinary-minded Gauls dished up another use for the word. It seemed to them that the topping on a piece of toast resembled a canopy over a bed, their *canapé* (pronounced kan-ih *pae*). Hence the name for this delicacy, now standard fare in many fine American restaurants.

Incidentally, the mosquito, whose Latin name was *musca*, was an ancient pest; it stung the Romans, too. It flew into Spain and Portugal, where it was called *mosca*, meaning "fly" or "gnat." *Hakluyt's Voyages*, published in 1583, contained this notation of M. Philips: "We are also oftentimes greatly annoyed with a kinde of fly, . . . the Spaniards called them Musketas." From this diminutive Spanish form came the English *mosquito*.

## CANARY

The Canary Islands, a group of islands in the Atlantic Ocean off the Spanish coast, were not named after birds, as supposed, but after dogs. In Latin, *canis* means "dog." (The English word *canine* derives directly from it.) The original name given the islands was *Canariae Insulae*, or "dog islands," because the first explorers found the islands abounding in wild dogs, the only mammals there. The surmise was that the dogs were left behind by Arab merchants who had made unscheduled landings.

Small birds with variously colored plumage inhabited these islands as well. Some were brought to England where they were named canaries, not because they warbled (in Latin *cantare* means "to sing") but after the island on which they were found. It may be said that canaries will be dogged with their name all their lives.

The Isle of Capri, a mountainous island in the Bay of Naples, also was named after an animal. Explorers who found packs of wild goats there named the island Capri, the Italian word for *goats*. (The name of the constellation *Capricorn* is a combining of *capri*, *caper* ("goat"), and *corn* (from Latin *cornu*, "horn.")

It was an animal that lent its name to the famous national museum and art gallery in France, the *Louvre*. The original structure, a palace, was built in a wolf-field. From Latin *lupus,* "wolf," came the French *loup* (masculine) and *louve* (feminine); whence *Louvre*.

## CANCEL

The Latin word *cancellare,* the ancestor of the English word *cancel,* which means "to draw latticelike lines across," was derived from the plural noun *cancelli,* "grille" or "lattice." Latticework resembles a series of crossbars—the X's one uses to cover written mistakes. To *X* out, in fact, or to cross off or out is a more common term than *cancel* or *delete*. Today *cancel* refers to anything obsoleted or invalidated, as are stamps on mail after processing by the post office, even though not covered with latticework.

The Latin *cancer* (its diminutive form is *cancelli*) is related, with a slight change in spelling, to *carcer,* "a grating" or "an enclosure or prison," a noun form of uncertain origin, but from which came the English word *incarcerate* ("to imprison"). The sense connection of *cancel* and *cancer* lies in the latticed barriers placed in front of prison windows. The semantic evolution is appropriate, since an imprisoned person has had all his social engagements canceled.

## CANDIDATE

A person aspiring to office, a *candidate,* presumably has *ambition*. However, those terms, *candidate* and *ambition,* are lineal descendants of Latin words that only remotely relate to their present meaning.

In ancient Rome *candidatus* meant "a person clothed in white," for aspirers to office customarily wore white togas to signify humility and purity of motive. When the contestant was picked for the office, he was then called, after the garment he wore, a *candidate*. From the same Latin word—the parent verb is *candere* ("to shine")—came the English *candid,* meaning "white, clear, pure" and hence "outspoken, frank, sincere," and *candor,* meaning "absence of hypocrisy or deception, openness, sincerity."

*Ambition,* from Latin *ambitio,* literally means "going from house to house." It was the practice of Roman candidates to visit people's homes to canvass for votes. Those who scurried about were called *ambitious.* Nowadays an ambitious person may not be going from house to house, but he's still trying to go places. Although ambition lubricates the machinery of success, those cogs and axles have not always been held in the highest esteem. Samuel Daniel in *Civil Wars* put it bluntly: "Th' aspirer, once attain'd unto the top, / cuts off those means by which himself got up." John Masefield in *Biography* was terser: "Men do not heed the rungs by which they climb."

## CANNIBAL

A cannibal is a human being who eats the flesh of other human beings. The word *cannibal* dates back to the explorations of Christopher Columbus, who, while in the West Indies in 1493, heard the natives speak of their great fears of the *caribs* or *canibas,* Indian tribes of man-eaters. (Some sources claim that Columbus mistook the word *cariba*—which meant "strong men"—for followers of the Grand Khan of China, who also, supposedly, dined on human flesh. Columbus, it will be recalled, thought he had landed on Oriental shores, west of India.) Upon his return to Spain Columbus introduced the mistaken word in explaining his discoveries. The error was perpetuated by other explorers of that era. In the 1598 *Voyages of Hakluyt* appears: "The Caribs I learned to be man-eaters or canibals." The Spanish language accepted the word *canibal,* which was later borrowed into English as *cannibal.*

The Caribs lived on islands near South America. Although the race and their language are extinct, they are still remembered by the name of the water that covers the area—the Caribbean Sea.

## CAPRICIOUS

A capricious person may act impulsively (*capricious* means "changeable, mercurial, characterized by a sudden whim"). Originally, however, *capricious* had an entirely different meaning. Its noun form, *caprice,* meant "a sudden shiver of fear," which would leave the hair standing on end like the spines of a hedgehog (from *capo*, "head," and *riccio*, "hedgehog"). The metamorphosis from "a sudden fear" to "a sudden whim" occurred through the catalyst of a similar word, *capra* ("goat"). Since goats are known for their friskiness and unpredictability, *capricious* followed the goats' lead and evolved into its present meaning of impulsiveness.

## CAPTAIN

*See* **MILITARY TITLES**

## CARDIGAN

*See* **RAGLAN SLEEVE**

## CARNIVAL

A *carnival*, any child will tell you, is a traveling show with rides, perhaps a Ferris wheel, side shows, cotton candy, balloons, and a band that keeps playing—truly a place for fun and amusement.

But the word originally applied to a festivity held under different circumstances; it was associated with a religious holiday—the season of feasting and merrymaking just before Lent. According to folk etymology, *carnival* meant "flesh goodbye," from Latin *carne vale* (Byron's *Beppo* noted: "This feast is named Carnival, which being / Interpreted, implies 'farewell to flesh'; . . ."). But the term is more accurately traceable to Italian *carnevale* from Latin *caro* and *levare* meaning "to take away meat," since the practice was to abstain from eating meat during Lent. The revelry preceding Ash Wednesday became an Italian custom, which later spread throughout Europe. In America, the festival in New Orleans called *Mardi Gras*, literally "fat Tuesday," is an import from France where the celebration is limited to Shrove Tuesday, the day before Ash Wednesday.

## CAROUSE

A *carousal* is "a noisy feast or a riotous drinking party." The word is a combining of *carouse* and the suffix *al*. To *carouse* is to get drunk or to engage in coarse, boisterous merrymaking. That verb form comes directly from the German term *gar aus* (which almost sounds like English *carouse*, meaning "completely," "all out"—that is, drink deep, the full expression being *agaraus trinken*, "to drink fully," "to drink all out." If at a German drinking fest someone hollers *garaus*, it is an open invitation to the imbibers to drain their steins without dawdling—the American version of "Bottoms up!" And of course, those who "bottomed up" too often would be carousing.

The word *carousal* (the second syllable is accented) should not be misspelled *carousel* (accent on the last syllable), an Italian derivative of *carosello*, "a tournament or pageant in which horsemen engaged in various contests and in which a chariot race was a feature." In America a carousel came to mean a form of merrymaking, but on a merry-go-round. Which also is a chariot race of sorts, except that there are no winners—and no losers.

## CATERPILLAR

A *caterpillar*, the furry larva of a butterfly (and an intriguing insect to children), was once considered a hairy cat, coming as it did from the Old French *chatte peleuse*. In Latin, "hairy cat" was *catta pilosa*. The latter word stemmed from *pilus*, "hair," which has given English such words as *depilatory* and *pile* (as in a rug). On the other hand, some etymologists see within *caterpillar* a resemblance to the word *pillage*, which came from the Old English *piller*, "a robber." Bisop Hugh Latimer once referred to "extortioners, caterpillars, usurers." What the slow-moving *caterpillar* could steal, and get away with, is anyone's guess.

The origin of the word *butterfly* is not related to its large showy wings, which often are yellow—the color of butter. The name comes from the color of its excrement, which also resembles the color of butter. In Dutch, a butterfly is called *boterschyte*, which is pronounced not too far differently from its English counterpart.

## CAUCUS

*See* CABAL

## CAVALIER

Sometimes nouns and adjectives do not see eye to eye, even though formed alike. A case in point is *cavalier*. In medieval times a cavalier was a gallant on horseback. That word, *cavalier*, was based on Latin *caballus* ("horse"); whence Italian *cavaliere* and French *chevalier*, "horseman." From the French *chevalier* came English *chivalrous*, an adjective that refers to a man courteous to members of the opposite sex, a sense not unlike that of the noun *cavalier*, "a courtly gentleman," a man who doesn't horse around.

Men on horseback literally look down on those who walk. And their attitude bespeaks a similar behavior—haughty if not actually arrogant—particularly to pedestrians who get in their way (which gave rise to the phrase—now with no equestrian references—"Why don't you come down from your high horse"). The poor pedestrian (Latin *pes, pedis*, "foot") had to plod along, which provided English with another meaning for *pedestrian*, "one who thinks slowly, as slowly as he walks," and therefore "dull and unimaginative."

But because knights and soldiers, when mounted, assumed an air of haughtiness, the adjectival sense of *cavalier* deteriorated to "disdainful, free and easy, off-handed." Which means that a cavalier may be a courteous gentleman but if he acts in a cavalier manner, he is uppity or a brusque showoff.

When *cavalier* is capitalized (*Cavalier*), it refers to a royalist—a supporter of Charles I of England in his struggle with Parliament. The Parliamentary forces, led by Oliver Cromwell, known as Roundheads, derisively called their opponents Cavaliers meaning "haughty people." (The Roundheads were so called because they wore the hair on their heads short in contrast to their opponents, the Cavaliers, who wore their hair in long curls.)

## CENT

As everyone must be aware, the American forefathers were dedicated to destroying all vestiges of British presence, beginning with the lowliest British coin, the penny. To this end Gouverneur Morris in 1762 suggested that the word *cent* replace the British *penny*. One hundred of these units would constitute one dollar. When Congress in 1786 established a system of coins, it adopted the idea by legislating that the cent should be "the highest copper piece, of which 100 shall be equal to the dollar." It is believed that Morris borrowed *cent* directly from *centime*, the French derivative of Latin *centum*, which means "hundred." Shakespeare had used *cent* earlier as a French word in *King Henry V* when a soldier, pleading for his life with Ancient Pistol ("ancient," a corruption of "ensign"—Pistol was Falstaff's ancient), said, "Je vous donnerai deux cents écus" ("I will give you two hundred crowns").

The word *penny*, however, has refused to die in America. Although merely a colloquial name for *cent*, it is more commonly heard than its official counterpart. Further, except for downgrading expressions, such as "He's not worth two cents," *penny* is the choice when a literary word for a copper coin is called for. For example, *cent* would not sound right in "A penny for your thoughts." And likewise with "penny-wise and pound-foolish," "turn an honest penny," "penny-ante," and "a pretty penny."

Many lexicons attribute the origin of *penny* to an ancient Teutonic root, *pfenning*, and many languages have a word that resembles it. All, however, were derived from Latin *pannus*, "a piece of cloth," which during the Dark Ages was a medium of exchange; rags were used for money. Perhaps that's why so many of Horatio Alger's stories went "from rags to riches."


## CEREMONY

Except for its origin there is nothing curious about the word *ceremony*, "a formal act prescribed by ritual, custom, or etiquette."

In all probability the word's forebear was *caerimonia*, which in Latin means "rite" or "ceremony," signifying primarily "a sacred usage." Its French descendant, spelled *cérémonie*, was later borrowed by Wycliffe, who introduced it into English as *ceremony*.

However, it has been speculated that the term *ceremony* had a more dramatic birth. Shortly after the Gauls captured Rome in 390 B.C., the Romans fled to an Etruscan city called Caere. One Roman, a man named Albinus, who was plodding alongside a cart carrying his family, met up with the Vestal Virgins, who could scarcely bear up under their load. Albinus made room for them in his cart and conveyed them safely to Caere, where they continued to perform their sacred rituals, later called *Caeremonia*.

A ceremony nowadays may be no more significant than the investiture of a tenderfoot boy scout. Or as Shakespeare put it in *Henry V:* "What are thou, thou idle (sometimes rendered *idol*) ceremony?"

In any event a ceremony is nothing to stand on, as the phrase "Let's not stand on ceremony"—that is, being too polite or too formal—makes abundantly clear.

## CHAFE

*See* CHAUFFEUR

## CHAPERON

A *chaperon*, an older woman who accompanies a younger unmarried woman for the sake of propriety, was so named after an article of men's clothing.

During the Middle Ages, French noblemen wore a hood, called a *chape*, which resembled one worn by priests. The Norman French, after their conquest of England, brought along with them this article of dress, renamed *chaperon*. The garment captured the fancy of many Englishmen, and it even became a part of the costume of the Knights of the Garter. Ladies, too, began to wear it, and for many years it remained fashionable. Then the hood fell out of favor, and its use was continued only by older women as a protection against the weather. And since older women were regularly assigned to watch over the younger ones, these guardians of "proper conduct" came to be known by their headgear—*chaperons*.

Funny as it sounds, another male garment was the *petticoat*, which was worn under a suit of mail (no pun intended!). After the Norman victory at the Battle of Hastings, in 1066, soldiers dressed themselves in suits of armor that covered the entire body. As might be expected, the weight of the metal caused chafing of the shoulders. An ingenious tailor designed a padded garment to be worn under the armor to cushion it. Because this undergarment was smaller than an outercoat, it was called a "petty-coat." Women adopted the idea when they found it to be a serviceable article of clothing to wear under their dresses. With time the wearing of armor was discontinued, but women continued to wear the petticoat, as it came to be spelled, for many centuries. But now, as one couturier remarked, it has "slipped away."

# CHARISMA

Charisma is said to be a politician's most potent weapon in his armory of political assets. In everyday usage it means "charm," such as the personal magnetism a salesman employs when he approaches a customer.

Interestingly, although *charisma* is now an ordinary word since its ballyhoo on television, not long ago it was relatively unknown. In fact, it is not even listed in Webster's *Second Unabridged Dictionary*. Originally *charism* (the form *charisma* was seldom used) was a theological term meaning "a special divine gift"—a God-given talent or favor. It might refer to one who performed miracles or to one who had the power of prophecy or spoke in tongues.

There is no evidence that the present use of *charisma* to mean "personal appeal to fascinate and attract others" has had divine blessing.

# CHAUFFEUR

A chauffeur behind the wheel of "a hot rod" has come by his name honestly, for a *chauffeur*, in the original French, was a fireman, a stoker of the fire in the steam engines that powered the turn-of-the-century automobiles. The word comes from *chauffer*, "to heat" (whose root, *chaud*, means "hot" or "burning"). From *chauffeur*, has come another English word: *chafe*, "to heat by rubbing." But somewhere along the way the meaning of *chafe* changed to "irritate by rubbing" and then simply to "irritate or anger." Only in the word *chafing-dish* (a vessel for heating food at the table) is the original sense of "heat" still retained. The verb *chaff* is an unrelated term. It means "to tease good-naturedly," but that can heat up, too.

## CHAUVINISM

*Chauvinism* is a word made prominent by the women's rights movement as a term of derision, signifying an exaggerated belief in the superiority of one sex over another. Hence the scornful remark," You're a male *chauvinist* pig." Only vaguely and loosely is this use of *chauvinism* related to its original meaning.

The word stems from the name of Nicolas Chauvin, a much-wounded, excessively enthusiastic patriot in the army of Napoleon Bonaparte. This legendary soldier was so demonstrably devoted to Napoleon that he was held up to ridicule. *Chauvinism* has come to mean "blind patriotism" or "an unreasoning loyalty to a person or cause." From this sense of fanaticism has evolved the meaning—albeit one not used in the best circles—of undue attachment to a particular group. Although the traditional meaning of *chauvinism* ought to be preserved, the onslaught of today's usage leaves its future in doubt.

## CHICKEN TETRAZZINI

*See* MELBA TOAST

## CHIMERA

A *chimera* is an impossible or foolish fancy. Its adjective form, *chimerical* (which means "visionary, impractical, illusory"), is more common. Any notion or scheme that is unreal or imaginary (a castle in the air) is *chimerical*.

The *Chimaera*, or *Chimera,* was a mythological fire-breathing monster whose fore part was that of a lion, the hind part that of a dragon, and the middle that of a goat. Her mother was Echidna, a half-woman and half-serpent, who also bore Cerberus and the Lernaean Hydra. According to some accounts, the Chimera had three heads. In any event, the monster Chimera was ravaging Lycia, in Asia Minor. Its king, Iobates, sought a hero to destroy the fierce Chimera. Coincidental with the king's search for a dragon-slayer was the arrival of Bellerophon of Corinth. When King Iobates subsequently learned that Bellerophon had spurned his daughter's favors, he decided to send the lad against the Chimera, fully expecting him to perish. But the ingenious youth got possession of the winged horse Pegasus, surprised the Chimera from the air, and then slew it with arrows. Which proves that someone who goes up in the air doesn't necesarily have his head in the clouds.

## CHLOROFORM

*Chloroform* is a volatile liquid used as an anesthetic. It was discovered in 1831 by a Frenchman, Jean-Baptiste Dumas, who coined the word, an abbreviation for chlorinated formic acid, a substance consisting chiefly of *chloros* (chlorine) and *formic acid.* In Greek, *chloros* means "green" and in Latin *formica* means "ant." Nevertheless, *chloroform* is not made up of green ants. The ingredient formic acid is related to ants, however, but red ones, for that acid is compounded from cooked red ants. It was in the seventeenth century that John Ray, an Englishman, cooked red ants and discovered a liquid, which was quite aptly named *formica,* since that is Latinate for "ants."

A person who has a sensation of ants crawling over him is suffering from *formication.* That word must be both spelled and pronounced carefully so as not to be misunderstood! And yet according to Greek legend *formication* and *fornication* are words that are related in that Zeus, to seduce Clytoris (another word that must be handled gingerly), changed himself into a swarm of ants. History has not made note of their color.

## CHOCOLATE

*See* VANILLA

## CHOW

Orientals find it difficult to pronounce some English words, but Caucasians have as much, if not more, trouble pronouncing Oriental words. One such that bothered many Europeans was the name of an East Indian relish consisting of chopped mixed pickles. The dish sounded like *chow,* a Cantonese word for "fried" or "cooked." The relish was therefore called *chow-chow* by the English-speaking adventurers because it was their habit to sing-song unpronounceable native words. *Chow-chow* became Pidgin English. (Incidentally, from the Chinese word *chow,* meaning "fried," and *mein,* "noodles," has come the name of the popular American dish—*chow mein.*)

Since the ingredients in *chow-chow* were mysterious—they could not be distinguished—any dish whose components were unknown came to be called *chow-chow.* With time, *chow-chow* became sailors' cant for food generally, possibly because chefs during long voyages ran out of food and were forced to make concoctions from anything still available, often from the leavings and the ends of what had been previously prepared. With more time, *chow-chow* was shortened to *chow,* now slang for any kind of food—even the best. By extension, it has also come to stand for "mealtime." The term is widespread among American soldiers, who proverbially stand in line at *chow-time* for their *chow.*

## CIRCUS

In ancient Rome the word *circus* referred to a "ring"—a circular area where festivities or public spectacles were conducted, including gladiatorial combat that ended in death for the losers. The largest Roman ring, the *Circus Maximus,* with 150,000 seats, is no longer standing, but vestiges of it still remain. (The adjective *maximus* is the superlative form of *magnus,* "large.") In Britain, a *circus* is a circular area where several streets intersect. In the United States it is neither a building nor a place; it is, thanks to Barnum, an exciting medium of entertainment, a traveling company of entertainers—acrobats, clowns, and trained animals—that perform in a ring. Thus the word has come full circle. In fact, both a ring and a circus are in the round.

## CLEAVE

*See* CONTRADICTIONS

## CLICHÉ

Hackneyed remarks, which may have sparkled when first spoken, have lost their vitality. They are trite (from Latin *terere,* "to rub"), things rubbed so much that their novelty or freshness has been "rubbed or worn out." Such timeworn expressions are now without distinction or individuality. They are a commonplace, a standardized combination of words that, since they have no glimmer of original thought, are said to be stereotyped. Or a cliché.

Both terms—*stereotype* and *cliché*—have filtered into English from the printing business in France. *Stereotype* is the older. It is a 1798 coinage of Firman Didot, a prominent French printer and playwright who assembled the word from Greek *stereos,* "solid," and *tupos,* "to strike," to designate a printing plate cast from a mold. Because this plate is used over and over again, producing many exact copies, the word *stereotype* is now applied to a phrase that is everlastingly, and boringly, repeated with no change.

*Cliché* is a French noun (from the verb *clicher,* "to stereotype"), meaning a stereotype plate. In 1892 the word cliché was adopted by the English language in its exact form as the equivalent of stereotype. Subsequently, its figurative sense came to mean "trite expression" or "platitude," referring to phrases that because of frequent repetition have become drab, unprovocative, and unappealing, like "ruby lips," "sour grapes," or "as sober as a judge," phrases that alert writers know should be avoided "like the plague."

## CLOCK

A *clock* is a timepiece, a device for measuring time and telling the hour by a stroke on a bell. The word *clock* comes from Old French *cloque,* which in turn came from Late Latin *clocca,* meaning "a bell." The early clocks consisted of bells.

Almost all clocks, at one time, used Roman numerals on dials to represent the hours. What is unusual about these numbers is that the number four instead of being IV is IIII, which is not a true Roman figure. How this came about is uncertain, but it is generally attributed to the pigheadedness of Charles V of France, known as Charles the Wise, but more a pretender to, than a possessor of, knowledge. It seems that a clockmaker delivered a clock that the king had ordered. Charles carefully examined the clock but found not a single flaw. Chagrined that he could not criticize the workmanship in any way, he complained that there was an error on the face of the clock—the number IV should be IIII. The clockmaker, considering the position of his client, could do nothing other than mildly remonstrate that IV was the proper way of putting it. But the king insisted, and so the number was changed, and that form has been customary on clocks ever since, which, incidentally, was 1370.

## CLOTH NAMES

*Gabardine,* a material made from wool or rayon or a worsted cotton, is used to make clothing, primarily suits and outercoats. Its variant spelling is *gaberdine.* But *gaberdine,* with the middle *er,* had another meaning. It was the name of a loose-fitting coat worn by merchants during medieval times. Later it referred to the customary cloak worn by pilgrims. In fact, the word *gaberdine* in Old French meant "pilgrimage."

The *oxford cloth,* a well-known shirting, was named after Oxford University. The cloth was the invention of a Scottish weaver who named cloths after other schools as well—Harvard for one. These other names, however, failed to make the grade.

*Lingerie* is a French import, but circumlocutorily. Its original meaning was "linen clothing" (the French word for "linen" is *linge,* which in turn came from the Greek *linon,* "flax"). Today, however, lingerie suggests the kind of clothing that arouses warm sensual feelings. It is defined as "intimate, feminine apparel," such as underwear or nightwear. And usually, instead of linen, it is made of silk or nylon, sometimes trimmed in satin and lace.

*Seersucker* is a cloth, not something to eat, except in Persia, where its literal meaning *(skir u sukkar)* is "milk and honey."

An *arras* is a wall-hanging made of rich tapestry fabricated in Arras, France, and originally called *drap d'Arras,* "cloth of Arras." A person wishing to conceal himself in a room, possibly to eavesdrop, could hide behind the arras and be undetected. Shakespeare made mention of it in *Hamlet* when Polonius said, "Behind the arras I'll convey myself."

Crinoline, a word derived from the Latin *crinis,* "hair," and *linum,* "linen," originally was a thread of horsehair and linen. It became the popular name for a stiff cloth used in making petticoats, a garment customarily worn by women during the Civil War years.

## CLUE

In Anglo-Saxon, a *clue* (spelled *cliwen* or *cleowen* and in Medieval English *clewe*) was a ball of thread. When Sherlock Holmes threaded his way through bits of evidence, he was, figuratively, picking up the threads—that is, following clues.

If it were not for its literal use, however, Theseus, after slaying the Minotaur, might not have found his way to safety. It all started in Crete, where the Minotaur, a fearsome half-man and half-bull monster, dwelling in a labyrinth, was waiting for the annual tribute exacted from the Athenians—seven youths and seven maidens to be devoured. The Greek hero Theseus volunteered to be one of the youths. But shortly after his arrival in Crete, Ariadne, the king's daughter, fell in love with him and gave him both a sword to slay the Minotaur and a thread (a *clewe*) to guide him out of the labyrinth. But for that skein of thread (that *clewe*), Theseus might never have reached the mouth of the cave. To show his gratitude after his successful venture, Theseus took Ariadne by the hand and sailed away with her, leaving no one a clue to their whereabouts.

Sir Richard Burton, in *Kasidah,* makes a provocative statement which stemmed from this story: "Reason is Life's sole arbitrator, the magic Labyrinth's single clue."

## COBWEB

> Whither, ah whither, ah whither so high?
> To sweep the cobwebs from the sky,
> And I'll be with you by and by.
> —Anonymous, *There Was an Old Woman*

Spiders are small animals that spin silk webs, generally called *cobwebs.* (Spiders are not insects; they are *arachnids* and have four pairs of legs. Insects have three pairs.) In Old English a *cob* was a spider. Since spiders were considered poisonous, they came to be called *attercob,* from Anglo-Saxon *attor,* "poison," and *cop* or *coppa,* "a head." A spider, therefore, literally was a "poison head." In Middle English the *web* came to be called *coppeweb* (*coppe,* "head," plus *web,* "net"). By Shakespeare's time its spelling was established as *cobweb,* although the change from *p* to *b* had no logical linguistic explanation. In *The Taming of the Shrew,* Petruchio's servant inquired whether supper was ready, "the rushes strewed, cobwebs swept." But spiders were still considered venomous. King Richard II, in Shakespeare's play of the same name, said: "But let thy spiders that suck up thy venom, / And heavy-gaited toads, lie in their way."

Many superstitions are associated with spiders. One myth holds that a feverish person could cure his malady if he placed a spider in a nutshell and then dangled it from his neck. A Scottish legend holds that Robert Bruce, broken hearted by his failures to rout the forces of Edward I, and unsure of what step to take next, was watching a spider try again and again to fasten a thread. The spider's ultimate success taught Bruce a lesson— that if one is determined enough, eventually success will be his. Bruce did go forth once again, and did, in fact, defeat the English forces.

*Arachnid* is a name derived from the myth of Arachne, a Lydian maiden who was so proud of her skill at weaving that she brazenly challenged the goddess Athena to compete with her. The maiden then produced a cloth she had woven. The goddess, since she could find no fault with it, became enraged and tore it to shreds. Arachne in despair hanged herself, but Athena untied the rope's knot and saved her life, then changed the rope into a cobweb and Arachne into a spider. From Arachne's name came the Greek word for "spider," *arakhne,* which was borrowed into English as *arachnid.*

## COCK

Cocks are known to strut about their "walk" or enclosure, which has given rise to the phrase "the cock of the walk." Applied to people, it means boastful, excessively confident— the undisputed master of his group. Such a person is said to be "cocky."

*Cocksure* means "perfectly safe" or "absolutely sure" (as William Lamb put it in *from Melbourne's Papers:* "I wish I was as cocksure of anything as Tom Macauley is of everything"). The *cock* in that word, as far as can be established, does not refer to a rooster but to a tap (a faucet), which has been inserted so tightly in a barrel of wine that undoubtedly the wine is secure. It is, in a word, "cocksure."

## COCKTAIL

Etymologists have given up trying to determine the origin of the word *cocktail*. So many theories have been advanced that to discuss them all would take pages. Mencken offers a plethora of those that he believes show plausibility. But then he concludes, "All are somewhat fishy."

A popular story attributes the origin of *cocktail* to Antoine Peychaud, a New Orleans restaurateur and the inventor of the Peychaud bitters. Another, according to Brewer, is that "the liquor was discovered by a Toltec chieftain who sent it to the king by the hand of his daughter *Xoc-til*." The king fell in love with the maiden, drank the liquor, and called it *xoc-til*, a name that has remained ever since. Another guess is that cocktail derives from *cock-tailed*, "having the tail docked so that the short stump sticks up like a cock's tail." Still another, that it comes from West African *kaketal*, "scorpion," because the drink also has a sting in it. And then there is the fanciful account of a Yonkers tavern-keeper's daughter, Peggy, known for her mixture of unusual, and sometimes potent, drinks. Her boyfriend planned one evening to ask her father for her hand in marriage. To make him nervy enough to address her father, Peggy mixed him a "stiff" one. Just as she was about to stir the drink, her fighting cock strutted by and one of his feathers fluttered into the glass. Peggy used it as a stirrer and then excitedly exclaimed, "At long last the drink has a name. Cocktail!"

## COCOA

*See* VANILLA

## COFFEE

If the question is, Where did coffee come from originally? both Arabia and berries are correct answers, even though one answer is geographical and the other botanical.

Today almost everyone knows that Brazil is the world's largest exporter of coffee and that, previously, it was Java. Years ago the word *java* (with a lower case *j*) was slang for "coffee." ("I'd like a hot cup of java.") The word *coffee*, from the French *café*, stems directly from the Arabic *qahwah*, which means "a drink made from berries." But the exhilarating effect of coffee need not be obtained from the drink; it can be gotten simply by eating the berries. And that is how coffee was discovered.

A goatherd named Kaldi, watching his goats nibble some bright red berries, was amazed to see how frisky they became. His curiosity got the best of him, and he decided to try some of the berries himself. He did and felt stimulated—and that was the beginning of the coffee industry. Today coffee is the beverage that may not exhilarate Americans all day long but it certainly gets them started in the morning.

## COLONEL

*See* **MILITARY TITLES**

## COLOSSAL

*Colossal* is an ordinary word used by ordinary people, even though it doesn't describe ordinary things. Its meaning, of course, is "enormous in size, extent, or degree." Its closest synonym is "gigantic."

In ancient times the Colossus (Latin, from the Greek *kolossos,* "large") referred to the Colossus of Rhodes, one of the Seven Wonders of the Ancient World. The Colossus was a huge statue of the sun god which bestrode the entrance of the harbor of Rhodes. It reached 120 feet heavenward and was said to be so large that ships could sail between its legs. (If the sculptor Chares had not built this statue, English might never have acquired the word *colossal,* which makes one wonder whether he was the earliest Rhodes scholar.) Disaster beset this monumental figure in 224 B.C. when an earthquake toppled it. In Shakespeare's *Julius Caesar,* Cassius describes Caesar to Brutus in these words:

> Why, man, he doth bestride the narrow world
> Like a *Colossus;* and we petty men
> Walk under his high legs, and peep about
> To find ourselves dishonourable graves.

# COMPANION

When referring to someone as a companion and comrade, it may be interesting to know that these words, at least by original source, meant an eating associate and a sleeping partner. The word *companion* comes directly from Latin *com*, "together," and *panis*, "bread." It therefore refers to "someone to break bread with"—and that is what a companion is, "a bread fellow," one who dines with another.

A *comrade* is a roommate, a bedfellow. The foundation of this word also can be found in Latin—*camera*, which means "a chamber" or "a room." On the Latin the French built their word *camarade* and the Spanish *camarada*, meaning one who shares a room with another. By extension, a comrade became one who shared someone's experiences. As soldiers, they were *comrades-in-arms*. Today a comrade may be one who lodges in the same chamber (and still be a comrade in arms), or a constant friend, or a member of the Communist Party. In any event, comrades enjoy *camaraderie*, "comradeship."

# COMPLEXION

Both *complexion* and *temperament*, according to medieval lore, stemmed from, and were controlled by, the same source—a balance of the body's humors. These fluids (choler, blood, melan khole, phlegm) combined to bestow rosy cheeks or to affect one's disposition.

The word *complexion* was fashioned from the Latin *com* ("together") and *plectere* ("to weave"). According to Aristotle the weaving or braiding of the humors gave one his complexion, which reflected the condition of the body. A disproportion or imbalance of these elements affected not only a person's appearance but also his general behavior. In fact, this interweaving was responsible for one's temper.

The words *temper* and *temperament* come from Latin *temperamentum*, which means "mixture"; whence "disposition." The ancients believed that the blending of the humors regulated these personal attributes. With the passage of time, however, the hue of *temper* turned sallow; it was always construed as bad, reflecting tendencies of anger or irritability. There came to be no such thing as a "good" temper, although occasionally one may speak of a "good-tempered" baby. Although *temperament* still means "one's manner of thinking and behaving," its adjective form, *temperamental*, remains negative—denoting excessive sensitivity or petulance. The term is frequently used to describe the high-handed tactics of high-powered entertainers, like divas or screen stars. The saving grace in this grouping is the word *temperate*. It suggests something pleasant—moderation or reasonableness, mildness or tranquility. It even refers to climate, as in "a temperate zone."

## COMPTROLLER

*See* CONTROLLER

## COMPUNCTION

> I desire to feel compunction than to know its definition.
> —Thomas à Kempis, *De Imitatione Christi*

When a person feels compunction because of something he has said or done, he feels contrite or remorseful. He has a feeling of uneasiness as though his conscience had been pricked or stung. Etymologically this is understandable because the ancestor of *compunction* is Latin *compunctus* (past participle of *compungere,* "to prick or sting"). It has been said that the anguish of compunction is to feel a wound in one's inner self. But with the passage of time, the signification of the word has been softened. It has come to mean only a slight uneasiness or passing regret. The sorrow that *compunction* now implies is temporary and usually of matters inconsequential. One wonders, in fact, whether compunction is ever felt, since it's always heard in the negative, as in "I felt no compunction about ignoring him."

*Compunction* and *remorse* are regarded as synonyms, but the latter word connotes a deeper and more persistent feeling of sorrow. It signifies such a personal reproach that the sufferer cannot be relieved of his sense of guilt. The word derives from Latin *remorsus* (past participle of *remordere,* "to bite again"). Its etymology emphasizes the idea of "gnawing" (like an animal that keeps biting). It reflects self-despair. Whereas a person might feel *compunction* for having negligently lost a child's dog, he would feel *remorse* if he had run it over and killed it.

## COMRADE

*See* COMPANION

## CONCLAVE

A conclave is "a confidential or secret meeting." Its actual meaning (from Latin *con* (*cum*), "with," and *clavis,* "key") is an inner room, a locked up place. Borrowed by the Roman Church to designate the room in which cardinals assembled to elect a pope, the room was called The Conclave because its door was kept locked until a pope was named.

What should be borne in mind when using the word *conclave* is that, although one may properly allude to a secret meeting, he may not to a secret conclave. Preceding *conclave* with "secret" is tautological because inherent in *conclave* is a sense of secrecy. Of course, in current speech *conclave* is used so loosely that it may refer to any assembly or conference, even one in which the public participates. It need not, in other words, be conducted in a room "locked with a key."

## CONSTABLE

Once upon a time the horse was the most common means of travel. In certain areas and for certain purposes, it was man's only conveyance. Obviously the horse became an exceedingly valuable possession, so much so that King Richard in Shakespeare's *Richard III* was willing to swap his kingdom for one. As almost everyone will remember, he once pleaded, "A horse! A horse! My kingdom for a horse."

From Latin *equestris* ("of a horseman") comes the English word *equestrian.* Other words associated with horses, but not in the minds of most people, are *constable* and *constabulary.* A *constable* originally was a servant who worked in a stable, in effect a stable boy—Late Latin *comes stabuli* (literally "a comrade or attendant of the stable"). Later the term was applied to an officer in the royal court of the Frankish kings. Today a constable is still a court officer—an officer in a court of law. His duty now is to execute legal process, however, not to clean stables. (A constabulary is a body of constables of a district or an armed police force.)

Another officer whose duties centered in the stable was a *marshal* (Old High German *marah* ("horse") and *scalh* ("servant"). He was a horsetender, a caretaker of horses. The first syllable is etymologically related to *mare*, a female horse. The term was later applied to the chief household officer of a royal court. In some countries a marshal holds the highest military rank (as in Great Britain) or is a federal officer or the head of a fire department (as in the United States). Or he may lead a parade. In which case, he no longer follows the horses; instead he sits astride one and leaves the cleaning up to others.

## CONTEMPLATE

The verb *contemplate* is generally used to mean "to meditate; to ponder; to consider." However, *contemplate* has another meaning, an ancient one that goes back to the time of the Romans.

During those days Roman augurs were called upon to prophesy, especially from omens. This they did by marking with a wand the area in the heavens to be consulted. The space was then declared sacred and given the name *templum*. When the diviners studied that celestial section, primarily to note the flight of birds, they were, according to Latin *con* ("together") and *templum* ("the marked off area"), contemplating. They were reading the signs to predict the future. Eventually they came to demarcate on the ground a comparable area, which was also studied for divine signs. When a prophecy was to be made through that *templum* (the forebear of the English word *temple*), an animal would be placed within it and eviscerated, and its entrails read for omens. Ultimately, on these consecrated sites holy buildings were erected, some of which still survive. The *templum* of old became today's temple where some people still go to contemplate.

## CONTRADICTIONS

Some words have two contradictory meanings. *Cleave*, for example, means "to sever or split" and, quite to the contrary, "to adhere firmly." Actually the word is not its own opposite. It consists of, as Shipley points out, two distinct words that come from ancestors who look confusingly alike. One is *cleave*, *clove, cloven, cleft,* derived from Old English *cliofan,* meaning "to cut with a blow," as a piece of wood is cut along the grain. The other is *cleave, cleaved* from Old English *clifan,* "to cling."

*Ravel* is another word that seemed as though it couldn't make up its mind. It means "to become entangled" and "to be disentangled." Klein points to its forebears—early Modern Dutch *ravelen,* "to entangle" and Dutch *rafelen* "to unravel." As an intransitive verb, *ravel* means "to become involved or confused"; as a transitive verb it means "to make plain or clear" (as Shakespeare in *Richard II* put it: "Must I ravel out / My weaved up folly," meaning "unravel").

If a person has the *sanction* of an authority to perform an act, he has its permission to do so. If, on the other hand, a *sanction* is imposed on further activity, such activity not only is now disapproved but also is subject to the imposition of a penalty. *Sanction* originally had a deeper significance than mere "approval," for it was derived from *sanctus,* a Latin word meaning "sacred," which meant a rendering that was inviolable.

## CONTROLLER

A *controller,* according to Dr. Johnson, is "one who has the power of governing or restraining," "a superintendent," and a *comptroller* is "a director, a supervisor, a governor." Shakespeare used both terms. In *Henry VI,* the Earl of Warwick said, "He dares not calm his contumelious spirit, / Nor cease to be an arrogant controller," and Lord Chamberlain in *Henry VIII,* "This night he makes a supper, and a great one, / To many lords and ladies: / I was spoke too, with Sir Henry Guilford, / This night to be comptrollers."

In today's usage, *controller* and *comptroller* are pronounced alike and have the same meaning; both designate an official who controls funds and verifies financial records. The term *controller* is more widely used, but *comptroller* is the correct designation for the Comptroller General of the United States and the Comptroller of the Currency.

Why, someone might ask, should there be two words that look so much alike and have identical meanings? According to Klein's *Etymological Dictionary, comptroller* is an erroneous spelling of *controller* due to a folk-etymological association of the first element of this word with French *compte,* "account." The progenitor of both *controller* and *comptroller* was the Latin *contra* ("against" or "counter") and *rotulus* ("roll"), meaning "to check by counter roll or duplicate register." At one time it was thought that since a controller examined and verified accounts, a better spelling would be *comptroller.* That more elegant, French-sounding title has stuck and appears, as was pointed out, in certain official usage. But not with the French. Their form for *controller* is *contrôleur,* not *comptrôleur.*

## COP

It takes a shrewd detective to sort out the many theories concerning the derivation of the word *cop* as applied to a policeman. Of one thing most people are sure, some police officers resent being called *cop,* although the term implies no offense. J. Edgar Hoover fought the word during all of his official life.

A Latin verb, *capere,* meaning "to seize," may have been its progenitor. But for a long while it was believed that *cop* was an acronym for *constabulary of police* or *constable on patrol.* All this, however, has been unattested. Also unsupported by evidence is that Robert Peel's London police wore large copper buttons on their uniforms; whence *cop* from "copper." The assumption that *cop* came from "copperhead" because those snakes were something to watch out for is also without foundation. Another notion, that the uniforms issued to Chicago policemen about 1860 were jokingly called "copper-stock" coats because Mayor Haines had made a fortune in copper stocks, is without substantive evidence.

Perhaps linguists should simply plead guilty to not knowing its origin or, as is said in criminal courts, "cop a plea."

## CORDUROY

Everyone agrees that *corduroy* is a coarse, durable, corded cotton fabric. In wearability it probably has no equal, with the possible exception of denim. But no one seems to know the word's origin. So many theories have been advanced that a list of them might fill a page. The most plausible assumption is based on the spelling of *corduroy,* since it looks suspiciously like the French *corde du roi* ("cord of the king"). The supporters of this theory assert that the fabric originally was made of silk and worn by the kings of France when they went hunting. This idea has not taken hold, however, and it is regarded as lacking etymological support. The British suggestion that initially the word was a trade name—Corderoy ("king's heart")—is also considered pure invention. Another speculation is that the word was a corruption of *couleur du roi* ("king's color").

A further controversy among etymologists is whether *corduroy* is a word of French or English origin. If it originated in England, all the "kingly" theories would be knocked into a tricorne hat. Most American dictionaries take the stand that it is a combination of *cord* and the obsolete *duroy* ("a coarse woolen fabric"). *Duroy* was a common material about the time of the American Revolution. It is said that George Washington after his marriage to Martha Custis in 1759 ordered through London "a light summer suit of Duroy." (Certainly Washington would have been averse to wearing a fabric designed for kings.) Perhaps the lexical idea is the right one, or at least the one to try on for size.

## CORNED BEEF

Some people may be disillusioned to learn that the "corn" in corned beef does not come from an ear of corn. In fact, an unrelated vegetable is more closely associated with it—the pickle. And yet there is no pickle in corned beef either, although a slice of one usually dresses up a sandwich. The relationship between *corn* and *pickle* is in the process of corning beef—pickling with salt. This process consists of sprinkling beef with coarse grains, or "corns," of salt; whence *corned beef.*

## CORNUCOPIA

The Latin term *cornucopia* was derived from two words, *cornu* ("horn") and *copia* ("plenty"). Naturally enough, in English this ornament, shaped like a horn or cone, has come to be called, from the literal Latin, "a horn of plenty."

The *cornucopia* assumed mythological importance because of a goat named Amalthea, which nursed Zeus. According to this legend, the infant Zeus plucked a horn from the goat's head and endowed it with the ability to overflow with whatever its owner wished for. In another version Zeus presented a goat's horn to the nymph who suckled him, with the promise that it would always be filled with anything she desired.

Today a favorite receptacle of florists for window displays is the cornucopia—and it is always shown overflowing with nuts and fruit. Figuratively it signifies prosperity, which is what the florist is looking for.

## CORONARY, CORONA, CORONER

*See* COURAGE

## COUCH

The noun *couch* refers to a long recliner or a seat long enough to accommodate several persons. The length of the seat makes it comfortable "to lie down on," or, as the French say, "se coucher," from which expression came the English word *couch.*

In times past the backs of couches and other upholstered pieces were covered with *antimacassars* (lace doilies) to protect them against the oil in men's hair. It was customary then for men to slick their hair down with Macassar, a popular greasy pomade. The unguent supplied for the manufacture of the hair dressing was named after its source, Macassar, a city on the Isle of Celebes in Indonesia. The protective furniture coverlet, invented by the practical-minded housewives, was so widely adopted that it became a generic term. Many dashing young blades were thankful for these antimacassars, for otherwise they might have not been allowed to "se coucher."

## COURAGE

A courageous person is stout-hearted. And this is as it should be because etymologically *courage* emanates from the heart. The Latin root for *courage* is *cor,* which means "heart." It is from the heart that a man of courage acts, facing danger or difficulty or pain without showing fear.

A cordial greeting manifests a warm heart, and the cordial one drinks is heartwarming. A couple whose spirit is in *concord* have two hearts that beat together, but if there is *discord* (*dis*, "away") the hearts evince disagreement, and they are no longer intertwined. The word *coronary*, which is defined as "pertaining to arteries supplying blood to the heart," surprisingly does not derive from *cor* but from Latin *corona*, "a crown or garland."

From that same source came *coroner*, originally an officer of the crown, whose duties were to protect the interest of the king by, among other things, collecting revenue for him. English statutes provided that the estate of a person dying without a will became the king's property. An alert *coronae*, as he was called then, naturally investigated every death to see whether a will had been written. The name of this official, in English, became *coroner* and his duty to look into deaths continued but only the unnatural ones, those caused by violence or accident. The obvious words stemming from *corona* are *coronet*, "a small crown," and *coronation*, "a crowning."

The Greek word for "heart" is *kardia*, from which has come the English element *cardio-* and from which have come *cardiac*, referring to the heart, *cardiologist*, a specialist in diseases of the heart, and *cardiograph*, a device that provides a tracing of a patient's heartbeat.

# COWARD

The tail of an animal is an appendage. Sometimes it waggles in delight. Sometimes it flicks off unwanted guests. Yet it is distinctly associated with cowardice. An animal that sneaks away with its tail between its legs is fearful. And certainly one that turns tail and flees must be afraid. Even man, a tailless animal, may figuratively do just that, which is what some soldiers do when confronted by an enemy.

The heritage of *coward* is not to be found in the word *cow* (although the verb *to cow* means "to intimidate") but in the Latin *cauda*, which means "tail." The French picked it up and called it *coue* or *coe*, from which evolved their word for "coward," *coart*. In *Reynard and the Fox*, a medieval tale of beasts, the timid hare was named *Coart* (which in Old French as *couard* meant "with tail between the legs"). Clearly for centuries "a tail" has always been behind the word *coward*.

# CRANK

A *crank* is, as anyone who drove a Model T knows, a device "for transmitting rotary motion, consisting of a handle attached at right angles to a shaft." It's what got the motor started. Some lexicographers have guessed that *crank* is a corrupt form of *crane neck*, which a crank resembles.

In Old English, the primary notion conveyed by *crank* (spelled *cranc*) was "twisted" or "bent." The influence of Dutch and German *krank*, "ill," added the sense of sick and weak and out of gear, from which, undoubtedly, has come the adjective *cranky*, now the colloquial idea "full of whims and crotchets," "ill-tempered." At one time, neither *cranky* nor *crankiness* was accepted on a literary level. Oliver Wendell Holmes, however, boosted the position of *cranky* by using that term, and James Russell Lowell employed *crankiness* in *New England, Two Centuries Ago*, in which he wrote: "There is no better ballast for keeping the mind steady on its keel, and saving it from the risk of crankiness, than business."

The use of *crank*, meaning a person governed by an obsession, was popularized after the assassination of President James A. Garfield in 1881. Charles Guiteau, the assassin, called himself "a crank." The newspaper reporters picked up the term, and it has been widely used by them to indicate "kooks" who like to telephone the city desk and confess to the headline crime. Originally *crank* was slang, of course, but it has since been elevated to general acceptability. It has, so to speak, been cranked up.

# CRAVAT

A *cravat* is, according to most dictionaries, a necktie or a scarf worn as a necktie. Originally, however, the neckcloth, called *hravatsh*, from which the word *cravat* evolved, was a silk or muslin neckpiece worn by Croatian mercenaries in the service of Austria during the seventeenth century, and it bore no resemblance to the necktie that men in the Western World wear today. French officers who served with the Croats were so attracted by this style of neckwear that they recommended its use when a cavalry regiment was organized in France. The neckcloths were imitated, and the regiment was called *The Royal*

*Cravat.* In fact, these scarves were so appealing that civilians began to wear them, eventually edging them with lace and tying them so that the ends flowed loosely. Cravats became the fashion and a standard accouterment among the elegant dressers of Paris.

Formerly cravats were wide neckties, but nowadays they may be of any width. Although the terms *necktie* and *cravat* have become synonymous, a difference between them does exist; "cravats" sell in fashionable stores at fashionable prices.

## CRESTFALLEN

A crest is the highest part of anything—the crest of a hill, of a wave, and even, in figurative speech, of pride and courage. One who is *crestfallen* is at its opposite end—depressed and disheartened.

Many animals have crests—tufts or other growths on their heads (from Latin *crista,* "top of the head"). But the best-known crest adorns a rooster, and is known as his comb. When a rooster is defeated in a cockfight, his comb droops—his crest has fallen.

## CROCODILE

The *crocodile* is an ancient reptile dating back at least to the fifth century B.C. when it was named *krokodeilos* by the Greek historian Herodotus, who chose the name, which means "pebble worm" (*kroke,* "pebble," plus *drilos,* "worm"), because this aquatic lizardlike animal had a habit of resting on pebbly banks.

The phrase "crocodile tears" is attributed to medieval lizard-watchers who claimed that crocodiles moaned in agony to lure their victims. Others believed, as Queen Margaret put it in Shakespeare's *Henry VI,* that only their tears deluded the victims: "Beguiles him as the mournful crocodile / With sorrow snares relenting passengers." Now no one knows whether a crocodile's tears entice a victim or whether the crocodile, after enjoying its meal, sheds hypocritical tears of mourning over its prey. In any event, the phrase has come to mean "pretended or insincere grief."

A reptile resembling a crocodile, but with a shorter snout, was first seen in the New World by Spanish explorers, who called it *al lagarto*, "the lizard." This reptile was not a man-eater, and in this respect differed from its African cousin. Ben Jonson named these lizards, from the Spanish, *alligators*. An interesting fact about alligators is that they inhabit only two areas in the world, and these areas are far apart—southeastern United States and the Yangtze River basin in China. Of course, when made into alligator shoes, they walk all over the world.

## CUCKOLD

> The cuckoo then on every tree
> Mocks married men; for thus sings he,
>     Cuckoo!
> Cuckoo! Cuckoo! O word of fear,
> Unpleasing to a married ear.
> —Shakespeare, *Love's Labour's Lost*

A husband becomes a *cuckold* if his wife commits adultery. Although the word *cuckold* is infrequently heard anymore, it was a common term in literary works, particularly in Shakespeare's day. *Cuckold* was derived from *cuckoo* (in Old French *cucu*), a migratory bird that, after eating other birds' eggs, laid its own eggs in the nest of those birds, leaving its young to be reared by the "host." In jest a person may be called a *cuckoo*, meaning "an idiot," but one wonders whether, after all, the bird really was such a fool. It had none of the problems of rearing its young.

Because of the cheating practice of the *cuckoo*, its name came to be applied to a man whose wife was unfaithful. He was derisively called a *cuckold*. Yet, logically, it is the adulterer who should have been named after the bird. What caused this mixup has never been explained. Dr. Johnson spoke of it but didn't clarify it. He said, "It was usual to alarm a husband at the approach of an adulterer by calling *cuckoo*, which, by mistake, was in time applied to the husband." This means, in today's parlance, that the husband was being given the bird, a turn-around that sounds cuckoo.

## CUE

A *cue*, in its theatrical use, is a direction for an actor's appearance or a signal to begin an action or speech, as was said in Shakespeare's *Midsummer Night's Dream:* "Pyramus, you begin: when you have spoken your speech, enter into that brake; and so every one according to his cue." Although the word's origin is uncertain, some etymologists believe that it was a phoneticism of the letter "q," a marking used by actors in their scripts as an abbreviation of Italian *quando* ("when"), and a word appropriated whole from Latin. Incidentally, the *cue* found in a billiard room comes from the French *queue,* "a tail." But that's another tale.

## CULPRIT

It is generally agreed that a *culprit* is a person guilty of a crime. But until the seventeenth century there was no such word. It became one—a single word—when the abridged forms *cul. prit.* were fused.

According to Blackstone the term was an outgrowth of a defendant's plea of not guilty. The clerk would respond *"culpable; prest d'averrer nostre bille,"* meaning "He is guilty and I am ready to prove our charge." This was recorded simply *culpable prest,* which was later shortened to *cul. prest.* and still later spelled *cul. prit.* (*Prit* is a variant spelling of present-day French *prêt,* "ready").

If one wonders why the pleadings in an English court were in French, the answer is that legal matters during the Norman period were conducted in French. However, centuries later a statute was enacted making English the official language in courts of law. But that did not alter the designation of a criminal; he was still a culprit.

## CUPIDITY

*Cupid,* the son of Aphrodite and the counterpart of the Greek *Eros,* was the Roman god of love. This mythological figure always carried a golden quiver of love-laced arrows to shoot into the hearts of unsuspecting mortals. *Eros,* too, enjoyed shooting love-dipped arrows, but at gods as well as mortals.

The names of these purveyors of love have given the English language two words, neither of which reflects man's better side. From *Cupid* comes *cupidity,* which means "avarice, greed, or an inordinate desire to possess something." *Eros* was the parent of a word that also suggests desire, but of only one kind—sexual. *Erotic* means "of or pertaining to sexual desire, lustful, amatory." (A more literary word is *concupiscent*, "strongly sensual in appetite" from Latin *con* (*cum*), intensive, and *capere*, "to long for.") Whatever arouses sexual desire may be classified as *erotica*. It may be people, writings, or other objects. But most often the word is applied to books and pornographic pictures.

A handmaiden of eroticism is the verb *entice*, which came from the Old French *enticier*, "to stir up a fire." A man enticed by a woman has his passion kindled, much as one would fan a fire. Although *entice* today is used in other veins, to mean "incite," "induce," or "persuade," it nevertheless is most frequently employed to suggest the arousal of passion by sexual attraction. A man enticed speaks in truth when he says, "My flame has set my heart on fire."

## CURFEW

In medieval times the danger from fire was especially great because most buildings were made of wood. With a wind blowing, a single burning house could start a conflagration. Hence the practice developed of covering fires before retiring for the night. During the reigns of William I and II a bell was sounded at sunset to give notice that the time had come to extinguish all fires and candles. This came to be called *curfew*, a word borrowed almost directly from the French *couvre feu*, which, in translation, is "cover the fire."

The word *curfew* has been extended to embrace regulations enjoining certain classes of people (juveniles, military) to retire from public places at a prescribed time, and it has nothing to do with "fire." Thomas Gray's *Elegy Written in a Country Churchyard*, for example, tolls the day's end:

> The curfew tolls the knell of parting day,
> The lowing herd wind slowly o'er the lea,
> The ploughman homeward plods his weary way,
> And leaves the world to darkness and to me.

# CURMUDGEON

A *curmudgeon* (a term made famous by Harold L. Ickes, Secretary of the Interior under FDR) is a cantankerous, crotchety old man or, as Brewer put it, "a grasping, miserly churl." It is said that Ickes, for reasons that have not been explained, adopted this label with the nebulous hope of painting a picture of himself as a kind-hearted, sympathetic person. Whether he succeeded in shifting the sense of *curmudgeon* is doubtful. Dictionaries still equate the word with testy, surly, and ill-tempered.

What is even more obscure is the origin of the word. Since *curmudgeon* means ill-tempered, someone suggested that it might have come from the French *coeur méchant*, "evil heart." Although the source of this explanation was unknown, Dr. Johnson accepted the suggestion and listed it in his dictionary as being from "*coeur méchant*, Fr. an unknown correspondent." Some years later another lexicographer, Dr. Ash, relying on the authority of Johnson, included it in his dictionary and, thinking that *Fr.* stood for French, mistakenly reported it as coming from "French *coeur*, unknown; *méchant*, correspondent." A defense that can be made on behalf of Dr. Ash, but only by those kindly disposed, is that he was an English, not a French, lexicographer.

# CURRY FAVOR

*To curry favor* is a somewhat general expression. It means, of course, "to fawn over someone," "to lick a person's boots," or "to suck about." However, *to curry,* according to its dictionary definition, is "to groom a horse with a currycomb." The meaning of *favor* of course is clear. But the odd combination, *curry* and *favor,* has no etymological basis. It came from the expression "curry favel" ("to rub down Favel or Fauvel"). In *Roman de Fauvel,* a fourteenth-century satirical poem, courtiers and others seeking to ingratiate themselves with the king would tend his favorite horse—named *Favel* (they would *curry Favel*). It was the best way of gaining the king's favor. *Curry favor* evolved simply because of the association of sounds. And with it went a complete change in the sense.

# CYCLOPS

Calling a one-eyed man a cyclops would be considered poor taste. Of course, the metaphorical reference is to a race of men in Greek mythology born with only one eye.

Although various legends have been built around these massive men called *Cyclopes* (*cycl*, "round"; *ops*, "eye"), all seem to agree that they were a race of giants with one eye in the middle of the forehead. According to Homer, Cyclopes were lawless giants who lived in Sicily, devouring human beings. In another story the Cyclopes were named as three Titans who furnished Zeus with thunderbolts and lightning with which to slay Aesculapius, the son of Apollo. For that offense Apollo killed them. Then again, it was said that the Cyclopes worked the forges for Vulcan, making armor for the gods. (John Milton in his *Paradise Lost* spoke of another race of one-eyed people— the Arimaspians. They were Scythians, who braided their hair with gold.)

The Greek fable diametrically opposed to the Cyclopean legend concerns Argus, a giant called *the all-seeing* because he had a hundred eyes. After Hermes, acting on Zeus's order, cut off Argus's head, Hera, Zeus's wife, transplanted his eyes to the tail of a peacock, and that is why today when a peacock fans out its beautiful tail, one can see a hundred eyes.

# CYNIC

Today a person called a *cynic* would probably feel insulted, for a cynic is a faultfinding critic who expects the worst in human conduct and motives. This is ironic, however, because the word originally applied to an idealist of the highest degree. The meaning of *cynic* has been turned around completely since it entered the language.

The term was first used by the followers of a school of philosophy founded by Antisthenes, an Athenian contemporary of Plato's, who taught that virtue is the highest good and constitutes true happiness. The pursuit of wealth, power, and earthly pleasure, therefore, should be scorned.

The word *cynic* came from the odd name of the gymnasium (school) outside Athens in which Antisthenes and his students met; it was called *Cynosarges* ("white dog"). Eventually the name of the school was applied to the philosophy taught there, and then later to its disciples. Some people felt that the students were cynics in the literal sense of the word (*kynikos,* "doglike"), since they ignored public customs and lived apart from other people.

As is the case with many philosophers, some cynics carried their credo—contempt for the material world and mistrust of humanity—to an extreme. (Diogenes, the most famous of the cynics, went so far as to refuse to live in a house; he slept in a tub belonging to the temple of the goddess Cybele.) The cynics eventually degenerated into a band of insolent, self-righteous critics who today, according to Oscar Wilde, "know the price of everything and the value of nothing."

## CYNOSURE

> Towers and battlements it sees
> Bosom'd high in tufted trees,
> Where perhaps some beauty lies,
> The cynosure of neighboring eyes.
> —John Milton, *L'Allegro*

The literal meaning of *cynosure* in Greek, "the dog's tail," is completely unrelated to its present English meaning, "a center of attraction." (If a famous actress, at a premiere, is "the cynosure of all eyes," she would probably resent being compared to a dog's tail.) Yet that is where the current sense of that word comes from. The Greek astronomers thought that the stars in the hind part of the constellation *Ursa Minor,* the Lesser Bear or Little Dipper, were shaped like a tail; they therefore called it *cynosure.* Legend has it that the name of the nymph who nursed Zeus was Cynosure. Upon her death the god made her into a constellation. In any event one of these stars is the Pole star, or North Star, the star nearest to the north celestial pole. Since seamen guided their ships by it, the eyes of mariners were naturally directed to that signpost, hence in one respect the center of their attention. The meaning of *cynosure* has now broadened to encompass something that attracts attention and becomes a focal point of interest and admiration. (In the case of the actress, it still refers to a star.)

## CZAR

*See* CAESAR

## DAYS OF THE WEEK

A person who complains that his days are mixed up has history on his side. The names of the days of the week are a conglomeration from unrelated sources. The first day of the week, Sunday, was named for the sun. It is the Christian analog of the Jewish Sabbath. The second day, Monday, which honors Earth's only natural satellite, the Moon, came from Old English *mona,* "moon." Tuesday was named to honor the Teutonic god of war, Tiw. The French literalized the Greek counterpart, Mars, so that its Tuesday became *mardi,* a translation of Late Latin *Martis dies* (days of Mars). The next three days owe their names to Norse mythology. Wednesday is named for *Wodin,* the king of the Norse gods, and Thursday for *Thor,* the thunderer. Friday honors the wife of *Wodin,* the Norse goddess of love, *Friya,* or *Frigg.* That leaves Saturday, the day of rest, the sabbath, named for Saturn, the Roman god of agriculture.

## DEBT

Among English words that have silent letters is a group with a silent *b.* Some examples are *doubt, subtle* (unless spelled *subtile*), *plumber,* and *debt.*

The word *plumber* originated in Latin *plumbum* ("lead"), in which the *b* was pronounced. But it was silenced when anglicized.

The word *debt* acquired its silent *b* in another way. Originally *debt* was spelled "det" but under French influence it became "dette," which was its spelling in *Visions of Piers Plowman* and in Chaucer's *Canterbury Tales.* With either spelling, however, it was pronounced as *debt* is pronounced today. The *b* was subsequently added by medieval scholars who thought they were paying a debt to the classics by making the word conform with its supposed Latin ancestor, *debitum.* By Shakespeare's time the spelling *debt* was firmly established. In *Love's Labour's Lost,* written in 1599, the pedant Holofernes facetiously recommends a pronunciation never previously heard. He said he detests "such rackers of orthography" who mistakenly say *det* when they should "pronounce debt—*d.e.b.t,* not *d.e.t.*"

## DEBUNK

*See* BUNK

## DEBUT

The curious thing about the English verb *debut* is that it is considered an informal term, as in "Quality Foods will debut its new pancake mix tomorrow." But this informality, frowned upon by strict conformists, is not so treated in France, where its parent (which sired the English word in the eighteenth century) is the acceptable verb *débuter.*

In American English, *debut,* a noun (French has a noun counterpart), means "one's first appearance," such as a movie's first public showing or a girl's formal presentation to society. Or it may be the launching of a new career or the unveiling of a new automobile. But in France, where it originally referred to matters pertinent to games—"to start off at bowling" or "to make the first stroke at billiards," or "to take the first shot at a target" (French *de,* "of," and *but,* "butt" or "target")—the verb *débuter* meant "to begin" and therefore one would correctly say in French "The popular danseuse *will debut* tomorrow." But in America, according to conservative language stylists, one should say "The popular danseuse will make her *debut* tomorrow."

*Debut* was introduced into English by Lord Chesterfield. However, Dr. Johnson did not list it in his *Dictionary.*

## DECIMATE

The word *decimate,* "to punish every tenth man," has been appropriated by the English language from the Latin *decimare,* "to decimate." As used now, *decimate* means "to destroy a great number or proportion of" or "totally," but no longer a specific percentage, even though the Latin *decem*, the word's root, is "ten."

The Latin origin of this term apart, opinions of classicists differ as to its exact meaning among the Romans. One premise is that to quell mutiny among Roman soldiers, a standard punishment was for the leaders to take one soldier out of each ten and put him to death. This method of punishment, of course, had a sobering effect upon would-be mutineers. Another belief is that decimation was reserved for enemy soldiers. Here again one out of ten chosen by lot was killed. In any case, although *decimate* is still an unhappy word, neither the number it implies nor its gruesome connotation is any longer applicable; *decimate* now means "to kill many people," as in a war, or even, as further extended, "to destroy a large area" such as the havoc caused by a tornado.

## DELIRIUM

A delirious person is in a temporary state of mental confusion from shock or serious disease. His mind is so incoherent and disordered that his mental faculties have, it may be said, deviated from a straight line. *Delirium* (its plural form is either *deliriums* or *deliria*) comes from Latin *de* ("away from") and *lira* ("furrow or track"); hence its sense of being "off the track."

Although the word *delirium* implies an apparent derangement, it is not to be equated with *insanity* (Latin *in*, "not," and *sanus*, "healthy," "sane"), a mental affliction manifested by unsoundness of mind and irrational behavior. (Violent *insanity* is *madness*—ravings and rash acts, in addition to mental irresponsibility.)

Another delirium, *delirium tremens* (*tremens* is a cousin of English *tremulous* from Latin *tremulus*, "shaking," "quivering"), is a byproduct of alcohol poisoning. It, too, can derail a person—that is, knock him off the track. In everyday language this disease is abbreviated D.T.'s.

## DEMOCRACY

*See* REPUBLIC

# DENIM

Many fabrics (from Latin *fabrica,* "an artisan's worshop") are named after the place in which they originated. For example, *cretonne* came from Creton in Normandy, and *tulle* from Tulle, France. Sometimes the name of the material was slightly altered: *gauze,* for instance, got its name from the town of Gaza, now an area in Israel; *calico,* a cotton stuff printed in bright figured patterns, from Calicut, India; and *lisle,* from Lille, France.

An odd thing about one particular fabric is that it was named after two cities, each in a different country, thus giving the material two names. What is being referred to is *denim/jean. Denim,* according to its dictionary definition, is "a coarse twilled cloth used for overalls and work uniforms." *Jean* is given the same definition. In their plural forms—*denims, jeans*—they refer to garments, but *jeans* is used only of pants and is normally called *blue jeans.* This all came about centuries ago when the cloth now known as *denim* was manufactured in the city of Nîmes, a textile center in Southern France. Originally the cloth was called *serge de Nîmes,* but later simply *de Nîmes,* meaning "a cloth of Nîmes." The English language borrowed the name but telescoped *de Nîmes* and dropped the final *s;* whence *denim.*

The manufacturing of denim into garments, primarily men's trousers, took place in the Italian city of Genoa. During those early times the Middle English name for Genoa was *Jene* or *Gene,* which came from the Middle French name for that city—Gênes. The same American phoneticized name, but with a somewhat more modern spelling, designates the ubiquitous uniform of today—*jeans.*

A further confusion arises when dungarees, a naval work uniform but now a customary working garment among farmers and "hard hats," are called *denims.* The dungaree manufacturers prefer to label the material that way (perhaps to sidestep the unpleasing first syllable), but the fact is that *dungaree* is a material in its own right. The word originated in Dungri, India, the name of a section in Bombay, and the fabric made there bore the same name. With time *dungri* became the English *dungaree.* In current, but nevertheless inaccurate, usage, *dungarees* (the word is usually found in the plural) is synonymous with *denims.*

# DERBY

*Derby* is a famous name for a classic horserace. Originally the name was applied to a British race held at Epsom Downs in Surrey. Later it was adopted in the United States as the name for the country's most prominent race, the Kentucky Derby. And France acquired it, too. (Today a *derby* is any kind of race open to all contestants, such as a soapbox derby.)

This all started in 1780 when Edward Smith Stanley, the twelfth Earl of Derby, offered a prize for an annual race of three-year-old horses, an event that came to be known as the *Derby*. The running of the Derby became so festive an occasion that the day was called *Derby Day*. Parliament adjourned, and the area surrounding the racetrack was dressed up to look like a country fair.

At these races it was not unusual to see men wearing a stiff felt hat with a dome-shaped crown and a narrow brim. The names given this hat—*derby* in the United States, *bowler* in England—are of uncertain origin. The term *derby* may be associated with the Earl's name, since he was fond of this style of headgear. The *bowler,* according to one accounting, was named after a London hatter, William Bowler, who designed this hat to accommodate a friend, William Coke, nephew of Sir Edward Coke. Another idea, that the hat resembled a bowling ball, and hence its name, has generally been discountenanced.

When a man puts on his derby, he dons it; when he tips his derby, he doffs it. But *don* and *doff* are contracted words that began as Middle English colloquialisms—*don* from "do-on," as in "put on," *doff* from the telescoped "do-off," as in "take off." Shakespeare used these crisp expressions in *King John:* "Thou wear a lion's hide! doff it for shame, / And hang a calf's skin on those recreant limbs." And in *Troilus and Cressida:* "Doff thy harness, youth / And tempt not yet the brushes of the war." But these expressions, like the derby, are not much in evidence anymore. They occasionally appear in literary works.

# DERRICK

He rides circuit with the devil, and Derrick must be his host, and Tyborne the inn at which he will light.

—Bellman of London, 1616

A *derrick* is a large crane for hoisting and moving heavy objects. It was so named because it resembled a gallows, a hangman's noose attached to a beam supported by a frame. This contraption was first used at Tyburn, England, in the seventeenth century by its inventor, Goodman Derrick, who dispatched over three thousand persons to an untimely death.

Execution by hanging fell out of favor, if one may put it that way, in the middle of the eighteenth century. A less torturous (but more efficient) method of capital punishment replaced it, one that had previously been reserved only for nobility—beheading. Dr. Joseph I. Guillotin, a French physician, proposed, from humanitarian motives, the use of a device to sever a head speedily and cleanly—a large, heavy blade that falls between two upright posts to strike the prisoner's neck placed directly below the blade. When promoting his decapitator (from Latin *de*, "off," plus *caput*, "head"), Dr. Guillotin assured the French Assembly, "With my machine, I can whisk off your head in a twinkling and you feel no pain." The machine was as good as he said it would be. As it performed the decapitations upon the victims, the revolutionaries screamed in delight. But the good doctor neither enjoyed these spectacles nor expected his name to become the eponym of that brutal instrument of death—the *guillotine*.

A story that had circulated for years, but has been debunked, is that Dr. Guillotin was a victim of this very beheading device. The fact is that the doctor died in his own bed with his head on.


## DESSERT, DESERT

A *dessert*, as everyone knows, is a course of fruit, pastries, puddings, and the like, served at the end of dinner. Originally the word did not signify something to eat. It evolved from the French *desservir*, which means "to remove what has been served, that is, to take the dishes from the table." Its literal sense, therefore, is "clear the table of the main course"—so that the final course may be brought in, and that, of course, is the dessert.

A word frequently confused with *dessert* (two *s*'s) is *desert* (one *s*), meaning "abandon." This confusion is understandable, since the words are pronounced alike. (When *desert* is used to mean "an arid land," of course it is pronounced *des*-ert.) The use that is most confusing, however, is in the phrase "just deserts," meaning "a due reward or punishment." In this usage the word derives from French *deservir* (one *s*), "to deserve." A person who gets his just deserts (one *s*), gets what he deserves—which may just be a luscious dessert (with two *s*'s).

## DEUS EX MACHINA

Playwrights whose plays cannot come to a sensible conclusion may solve the problem by introducing a novel idea—the sudden appearance of a god who then brings everything to a close. At least that was a not uncommon device employed in Greek tragedies. To accomplish this miracle ending, a god (*deus*) or goddess (*dea*), in the form of an actor, would be lowered to the stage by a derrick; hence the theatrical phrase *deus ex machina*, "god from a machine." The divine intervention quickened and quietly ended the action, and probably saved the clumsy author from further embarrassment. Now the plot need not unfold nor the actor extricate himself from an impossible situation.

This theatrical jargon is still occasionally used to describe any improbable or artificial device abruptly introduced to resolve a hopelessly snarled plot in a play or movie. If it comes just in the nick of time, it may rightly be called *deus ex machina*— a providential intervention.

## DEVIL

In everyday language, a person who argues in favor of an unpopular cause or who injures a cause by his espousal of it is called *a devil's advocate (advocatus diaboli)*. But in actuality a devil's advocate is an esteemed member of the Roman Catholic Church—its *promotor fidei*, the Defender of the Faith, whose responsibility it is to ferret out defects in the life of a person being considered for canonization. And since the derogatory information he uncovers could forestall sainthood, and since, supposedly, the devil dislikes saints, the "Defender" has come to be known as *the devil's advocate*.

Although many expressions contain the word *devil* ("The *devil* you say," "there'll be the *devil* to pay," "between the *devil* and the deep blue sea"), the devil, in the opinion of many people, is really not so bad after all. Calling a man "a devil of a fellow," for example, is meant as a compliment. And a person who "had a devil of a time" may have enjoyed himself thoroughly. But those same words, spoken in a different tone of voice, might mean the very opposite ("a devil of a time" could be a trying experience)—which shows that sometimes one can have a devil of a time figuring out what the devil is meant.

## DIAMOND

From the Greek prefix *a* ("not") and the verb *damaein* ("to tame") has come a word that refers to "a woman's best friend"—a diamond, a stone "untamed." After the discovery of this gemstone, a name was sought for it that would describe its quality of hardness. The word chosen was *adamas,* which means "unbreakable" or "invincible" and from which came *adamant,* a term that applies to any extremely hard substance. In Late Latin, a corrupted form of *adamas*—*diamas*—took hold to distinguish this precious stone from other unbreakable or impenetrably hard substances, thus giving the English language two words, *adamant* to designate the hardest known metals and stones and *diamond,* exclusively for the precious jewel. The distinction was appropriate because of the uniqueness of a diamond—incomparable hardness and incomparable value. As Thomas Fuller pointed out in his *Gnomologia,* it is "valuable tho' it lie on a dunghill."

The noun *adamant* is not in popular speech, but it has given English a figurative sense when used as an adjective, meaning "unshakable," "unyielding," "uncompromising."

## DIESEL ENGINE

But for the Franco-Prussian war of 1870, the diesel engine might never have been invented. As it was, the idea of replacing the steam engine with a more efficient one was generated in the mind of the inventor because of a fluke.

Rudolph Diesel during these times was a young boy living in Paris with his parents. Since they were Germans, they fled to England for the sake of safety. So as not to jeopardize the boy or his education, his uncle who lived in Augsburg, Germany, offered to care for the lad until the war was over. Hence, with a card of identification hanging around his neck, young Rudolph set out on a train for his uncle's home. The trip took eight days, primarily because the engine broke down several times. But of course trains were not expected to run according to schedule during wartime. When Diesel grew to manhood, he remembered this experience and decided to do something to improve the functioning of these engines.

To this end, Diesel conducted numerous experiments. He succeeded in building an engine that operated without the ignition spark. He clearly was on his way to success when the engine blew up in his face and almost killed him. Undaunted, he began all over again, having recognized the need to come up with a more suitable fuel. He tried many different kinds, from alcohol to peanut oil, until finally he discovered that a semirefined crude oil seemed to be the perfect solution to this problem. He was right and the diesel engine was born, a compression ignition engine that functioned more economically than any other engine.

Diesel's life ended in misfortune. While traveling on a German ship on September 29, 1913, bound for England, he mysteriously disappeared. He had bade goodnight to some colleagues but, after entering his stateroom, was never seen again. His bed had not been slept in and the only clue to his untimely end was his cap lying near the ship's stern. Ten days later the crew of another ship found his corpse floating in the water. The question that has never been resolved is: Was it suicide or murder?

## DISASTER

*See* ASTROLOGY

## DISMAL

Egyptians believed in unlucky days—those days when no battle should be joined, no venture undertaken, and no marriage arranged. They called this period "Egyptian Days." The idea was taken up by the Romans and was then continued through the Middle Ages. Later the French gave these days a new name, *dis mal* (from the Latin *dies mali*, "evil days"). Like the Egyptians before them, the French ascribed to these days an evil omen. They were the days when people took particular pains to avoid mischance. The English word *dismal* is a coalescing of the French *dis mal*, but the meaning has been broadened—and softened—to encompass any gloomy, rainy, or otherwise miserable day, not necessarily one fraught with danger.

## DOFF

*See* DERBY

## DOG DAYS

One might imagine that the commonly heard phrase "dog days" got its name from the sight of dogs curled up asleep during a sweltering summer's day—a day that even dogs can't stand. But this is not so, even though "dog days" are days of great heat. The phrase, originated by the Romans, was based on the assumption that, during a certain period of the summer, the brightest star in the heavens, the dog star "Sirius" (which in Greek means "scorching"), added its heat to the sun's, making these days a veritable inferno.

Another expression—*salad days*—sounds as though it refers to the coolest of days—cool as a cucumber and as cold as iceberg lettuce. But the phrase has nothing to do with temperature or with food. Rather, it signifies a period of immaturity, days of youthful inexperience.

In William Shakespeare's *Antony and Cleopatra*, the beautiful Egyptian Queen immortalized this expression when she spoke of her former love for Caesar in "my salad days, / When I was green in judgment: cold in blood...." She was explaining to her handmaiden Charmian that her youthful ardor for Caesar had wilted, but that her passion for Antony was blossoming.

## DOLLAR

The word *dollar* (the dollar is the basic monetary unit in the United States, Canada, Australia, New Zealand, and in a few smaller countries) has a history that goes back to the sixteenth century. The locale was Bohemia, now a part of Czechoslovakia. In the valley of Joachimsthal (*Joachim* translates in English to "Joseph" and *Thal* means "valley") was a mint that coined silver money called *Joachimsthalern*. Its singular form, *Joachimsthaler*, was later shortened to *thaler*. The Dutch called it *daler*, from which one can see the emergence of the English word *dollar*.

The Continental Congress, at the recommendation of Thomas Jefferson, who objected to the use of British term *pound* because of its association with England, named its basic unit of currency the *dollar*. A precedent for this term had already been established, since the Spanish "dollar" was a common medium of exchange between the United States and the West Indies. The resolution of the Continental Congress, adopted in July 1785, was simply stated: "Resolved that the money unit of the United States of America be one dollar."

The American *dollar* sign is either a capital *S* with two vertical lines superimposed on it or the letter *S* superimposed on the letter *U*. Where this symbol came from has never been fully attested. The most widely accepted belief is that it was taken from the Spanish dollar (commonly known as "a piece of eight"—so named because the figure *8* was impressed on it, the "eight" standing for eight reales (Spanish coins), the value of the dollar). The official name for the old Spanish dollar was *pillar*, from the original name of the Strait of Gibraltar, the *Pillars of Hercules,* the farthest point that seafaring men dared go. Its symbol was an *S* (for Spain) with two vertical strokes that represented the famous Pillars.

## DOLOROUS, DOLDRUMS

A person who says "Archie sounds so *dolorous* he must be in the *doldrums*" has used words of similar sounds that seem to go together but do not.

The adjective *dolorous,* which means "sorrowful, sad," and secondarily "painful," stemmed originally from the Latin verb *dolere,* "to grieve, to feel pain" (hence in Late Latin *dolorosus,* and then the Middle English *dolorous,* a word in current use). Its noun form, *dolor* ("sorrow, grief"), has disappeared from everyday language and is now only poetic. *Dolorous* still thrives but its sense of "pain" has become figurative.

The phrase "in the doldrums" originally was a nautical term referring to a ship becalmed near the equator. Nowadays it refers to a person's dull and listless state, usually reflected in a feeling of loneliness and boredom (but when business is slow it, too, is said to be in the doldrums). Although etymologists can only conjecture where the word came from, some give the poet Byron credit for it. Perhaps it was a combining of *dol,* from Old English "dull," and the second element of *tantrum.*

Returning to *dolor.* A common term, reflecting its negative sense, is *indolent,* meaning "disinclined to work." As a medical term, *indolent* means "causing little or no pain." In general usage it refers to someone constantly indulging in ease. Certainly a person who is not grieving or is not in pain is probably at ease. However, the sense of *indolent* no longer is "painless"; instead it suggests "laziness," perhaps because an indolent person finds it painful to work.

## DON

*See* **DERBY**

## DOPE

In American slang, a *dope* (among many other meanings) is a foolish or slow-witted person, one who acts as though under the influence of a narcotic. According to the literal definition of the word's ancestor, the present slang sense makes good sense. The word *dope* is traceable to Dutch *doop* (which is pronounced just like its American counterpart—"dope") and means a thick liquid, like a sauce or a lubricant. Such a pasty preparation flows slowly, if at all. The molasses-like movement of this substance can be compared to the speed at which a dope's mind works—as slow as molasses.

Opium derivatives are called *dope* because, when being readied for smoking, the heated preparation flows sluggishly. This slowness hearkens back to the Dutch *doop,* which is why it is rightly called *dope.* As any dope knows.

## DOTAGE

If one dotes, is he in his dotage? That would depend in part on his age and in part on the state of his feebleness. To dote on someone is, in the words of Dr. Johnson, "to regard with excessive fondness, to love to excess." An uncle foolishly fond of a niece (a redundancy in yesteryear when *fond* meant "foolish") may bestow affection or dote on her. In Shakespeare's *Henry IV*, the Earl of Westmoreland says: "All their prayers and love / Were set on Hereford, whom they doted on, / And blessed and graced."

The verb *to dote* came from Middle Dutch *doten,* and it begot twin meanings—"to be silly" and "to doze." The disparate current meanings, "to lavish affection on" and "to show senility," evolved logically from each other, since older people were likely to become extravagantly fond of someone, a sign of a weakened mind. As senility approaches, it is often accompanied by sleepiness (the dotard dozes), a trait associated with old age and common in one's *dotage (dote* plus *age).* But it is not always so. According to Cicero in *De Senectute:* "Senile debility, usually called 'dotage,' is a characteristic, not of all men, but only of those who are weak in mind and will."

## DRAWING ROOM

*See* PARLOR

## DUN

When it comes to the origin of the verb *dun,* many dictionaries play it safe and mark it obscure. They are wise because etymologists have disagreed for years over which of two plausible theories is the right one.

According to some word historians, *dun,* in the sense of importuning debtors for payment, was derived from Anglo-Saxon *dunan,* "to din or clamor." The thinking here is that a bill collector was bound to get into an argument with the debtor, with much resulting noise.

The theory with greater support, however, and logicality, too, is that Joseph Dun, a bailiff of Lincoln, England, was so successful in collecting debts that he became a legend. In fact, so many stories were published about him that his name entered the English language as a generic term. The *British Apollo* in 1708 wrote on the word *dun* as follows: "The word *Dun* owes its birth to one Joe Dun. . . . It became a Proverb . . . when a man refused to pay his debts, why don't you Dun him? That is, why don't you send Dun to arrest him? . . . It is now as old as since the days of King Henry the Seventh" (who reigned 1485–1509). The fact is that contemporary evidence to substantiate this second theory is lacking. Regardless, defaulters have become as sensitive to the expression "dun 'im" as criminals are to "book 'im."

## DUNCE

Traditionally a *dunce* is the pupil who sits on a high stool in the corner of the classroom, wearing a tall peaked cap. He is the one who can't learn, and so he sits, taunted by the other pupils who call him "blockhead," "dunce." Yet the meaning of this latter word comes from the middle name of John Duns Scotus, a fourteenth-century schoolman who was a brilliant but exceedingly conservative thinker. Because he was a master of theological analysis, he attracted a coterie of scholarly followers, who were called *Dunsmen* or *Duncemen*. For many years after his death, in pulpits throughout England his disciples raged in support of his teachings and against humanism and other progressive forms of scholasticism. Eventually they became so bogged down in the subtleties of their own philosophy that they were regarded as a dull and stupid lot. Those who opposed their metaphysical speculations came to mock them, calling them hair-splitters who objected merely for the sake of objecting and naming them, after the theologian, *Dunsers* or *Dunces*, from which, by extension, came today's word *dunce*, a person with little capacity for learning.

## DUNGAREES

*See* DENIM

## EASEL

*See* PALETTE

## EAVESDROPPER

One can easily imagine the meaning of *eavesdropper*. The word *eaves* (originally a singular word that has come to be treated as a plural because of its form) refers to the overhanging lower edge of a roof. The second syllable, *drop*, originally was *drip*, since before the invention of gutters and spouts the eaves were so built as to allow their drip to fall to the ground away from the foundation of the house. A person who stands under the eaves is therefore in a good position not only to stay dry but also stealthily to overhear conversation from within. Which of course he hopes is not dry.

King Richard in Shakespeare's *Richard III*, fearful that his friends will not prove true to him, decides to check on them and says, "Under our tents I'll play the eaves-dropper, / To hear if any mean to shrink from me."

## ECCENTRIC

*See* PECULIAR

## ECHO

Although Zeus was the greatest of the Greek gods, he nevertheless had to use stratagem with his wife Hera (the Queen of the heavens) when he wished to disport himself with the nymphs. To divert her attention, Zeus had a nymph, named Echo, talk to Hera incessantly. Thus engaged, the queen was unable to pay attention to her philandering husband. But one day Hera learned of the trick played on her and punished Echo by changing her into an echo—depriving her of the use of her voice, except only to repeat what others said.

According to another myth, Echo became enamored of handsome Narcissus; however, he did not return her affection, since he was in love with himself. In her grief, she pined away until nothing of her was left except her voice. Now she speaks only when spoken to and repeats only words she hears.

Milton in *Comus* describes Echo in these words:

> Sweet Echo, sweetest nymph, that liv'st unseen
>     Within thy airy shell,
> By slow Meander's margent green
> And in the violet-embroidered vale.
> Canst thou not tell me of a gentle pair
> That likest thy Narcissus are?

And from Tennyson's *Isle of Greece: Apollo:*

> What would it profit thee to be the first
> Of echoes, tho' thy tongue should live forever,
> A thing that answers, but hath not a thought
> As lasting but as senseless as a stone.

*Echo* (from Greek *ekho,* "a sound") provided the English language with a useful word that serves both as a noun (an echo is a repetition of sound) and a verb (to repeat or to imitate).

## EGREGIOUS

An *egregious* fool makes himself conspicuous by his blatant and outrageous behavior. A liar, a cheat, a hypocrite—these are all egregious, as is a blunder, for the word refers to anything that is bad.

Originally its meaning was very much the *opposite*—"prominent" or "distinguished." An egregious person was "chosen from the herd" (Latin *e,* "out of," and *gregis,* genitive of *grex,* "herd"). He was, because of superior abilities, regarded as being so exceptional that he stood out from the others. Usage, however, has turned its meaning completely around, so that it is no longer a term of commendation but has become one of condemnation. In *Cymbeline,* Shakespeare has Leonatus speak disparagingly of himself as a "most credulous fool, egregious murtherer, thief. . ." Because of this sharp turnaround in meaning, Flesch discourages its use as not likely to be understood.

A *gregarious* person (from the same Latin *grex,* "herd," plus English *-ous*) is fond of company. Originally the word applied only to animals that lived in flocks or herds. Now it refers to people who enjoy being with others, those who "flock" to places where others congregate (*con,* "with," and *grex,* "herd"), enjoying, so to speak, the sociality of the herd.

## ELIXIR

*See* PANACEA

## EMANCIPATE

*See* IMPEDE

## EMERITUS

After retirement many distinguished university professors (as well as some other highly placed academic persons) retain their title, followed by the word *emeritus.* This courtesy title is bestowed by formal order of the college or university. It might read: R. James Artman, professor emeritus; Dr. Sigmund T. Rosten, president emeritus. The Latin term *emeritus* (past participle of *emereri,* "to merit by right of service") signifies that the holder is a soldier in the army of academics, for originally *emeritus* was applied to Roman soldiers who, upon completion of their term of service, were entitled to receive a prescribed stipend. The soldier was called *emeritus* because he had earned through military service the benefits accruing to an honorable discharge. Today, of course, it refers simply to the holding of an honorary title after retirement. *Emeritus* has other, though seldom used, forms: *emerita* (feminine); *emeriti* and *emeritae* (respective masculine and feminine plurals).

## ERASE

Several English words refer to the striking out or removal of something from written matter. The words are not synonymous, however, for the methods by which the deletions are effected differ.

The most common term is *erase* (from Latin *erasus,* past participle of *eradere,* "to scratch out" or "scrape off"), a rubbing or scraping of something written or engraved until it loses its visibility. In an abstract sense *erase* refers to the disappearance of impressions from memory: "The years have *erased* from his mind the names of his schoolmates." (Its adjective form, *erasable,* should not be confused with its phonetic cousin *irascible,* which means "quick-tempered.")

The literal meaning of *expunge* (Latin *expungere,* "to prick out") is "to pick out with a sharp instrument," implying a thorough erasure as though a knife had punctured whatever had been there. Originally *to expunge* was to mark dots above or below a word to be erased. Nowadays it signifies a complete removal, one that leaves no trace, as in "to expunge testimony from the record."

*Blot out* (from middle English *blot,* of uncertain origin) and *obliterate* (Latin *ob litteras scribere,* "to strike out") are synonyms. They both mean "to efface"—with ink, chalk, paint—making the writing undecipherable. Whereas *expunge* suggests a removal, *blot out* and *obliterate* refer to a covering, a writing over, of something so as to render it illegible.

## EROTIC

*See* CUPIDITY

## ESCAPE

*See* PALLIATE

## ESOTERIC

*Esoteric,* from Greek *esotero* ("inner"), means "pertaining to those within." The term originated with Pythagoras, who offered private instruction to selected students but not to the general public. *Esoteric* has come to mean "comprehended by a select few"—that is, understood only by those within the inner circle, the initiated.

Its antonym *exoteric,* which means "those without," refers to those belonging to the outer or less initiated circle. Originally applied to the public lectures of Aristotle, it now refers to things "external," the teaching of popular subjects "that can be understood by the general public." History reports that Pythagoras lectured from behind a curtain. Those students required to sit in front of the curtain (they could not see his face) were called by him *exoteric disciples.* Those permitted behind the veil were his *esoteric.*

*Exotic* (Greek *exotikos,* literally "from the outside") means "different," "strange," or "alien." It may refer to things from a foreign source, like plants or customs, or to almost anything else not indigenous to a place. This sense of "strange," though still current, has generally been superseded by that of "the charm of the unfamiliar," "the mysterious," or "the unusual." As applied to women, which is often the case, *exotic* suggests a striking, intriguing beauty, one that is enticing and exciting. Of course, it may also apply to food, speech, dress, or whatever is considered romantic or picturesque. Travel brochures, to lure tourists, picture exotic ports of call.


## ETIQUETTE

The word *etiquette* refers to the "conventional requirements of social behavior as well as the accepted code by which ceremonies are conducted." Commonly it is associated with matters pertaining to mode of dress, style of entertaining, and manner of using eating utensils. It is the oil that lubricates the joints of polite society.

The Old French word *estiquier,* meaning "to stick on or attach," was the ancestor of *etiquette.* Originally an *etiquette* was a target attached to a post. Children used it in games. Later it was a military order prescribing the duties of the day. It, too, was "stuck on" a post for everyone to see. Then the paper or card itself became the *etiquette,* the equivalent of a "ticket" or "label." (In French this meaning has prevailed until this day.) Still later the word came to mean a card that sets out the procedures to be observed at the royal court and, with the passage of more time, the expected mode of behavior itself.

# EUROPE

Many Europeans can look to mythology for the name of their continent. The story of the naming of this continent begins with Europa, the daughter of Agenor, king of Phoenicia. According to Greek legend, Zeus became completely captivated by her charm and beauty. To ensnare her, Zeus changed himself into a gentle white bull and then mingled with her father's herd. Europa, emboldened by the tameness of the animal, ventured to mount him; whereupon the bull sped away, dashed into the sea, and swam with her to Crete, where she spent the rest of her life. (Paintings by Veronese and Titian have immortalized the so-called rape of Europa.)

Etymologists believe that, even though the myth of Europa has been well implanted in the minds of people as eponymous for the European continent, its name actually, and more prosaically, came from the Assyrian *Ereb* ("setting sun land"), which corresponds to *Asu* ("land of the rising sun"). The Greeks had a word to say about all this, nonetheless. In the *Hymn to Apollo,* the Assyrian names became *Europe* and *Asia,* and they have remained so ever since.

# EXCHEQUER

When someone says facetiously, "If you want to get paid, see my wife—the exchequer," he is being partly accurate, but not entirely so.

Although *exchequer* refers to the treasury of England, and may also refer to the treasury in a business or other organization, its sense of "money" is only distantly related. Originally *exchequer* referred to the game of chess, which is played without money. It all started during the reign of Edward I. At that time national revenues were counted on a table marked off in squares into which accountants placed colored counters as they did their figuring. They used this method of calculating revenue because figuring with Roman numerals (Arabic numbers were not yet in use) was awkward and clumsy, if not outright impossible. The table on which they worked was covered with a chequered tablecloth resembling a chessboard so much that it came to be called *eschecker,* which was Middle English for "chessboard"; hence the present term for a treasury or one's financial resources. If the Lord of the Exchequer is playing games with the country's money, perhaps it's because he's so fond of chess.

## EXOTERIC

See ESOTERIC

## EXPUNGE

See ERASE

## F

## FAN

The term *fan*, as in football or hockey fan, can be found in almost any daily newspaper. Everyone knows what it means, but perhaps everyone does not know that it is a clipped form of *fanatic*, whose original signification did not refer to the field of sports. A fanatic, from Latin *fanaticus*, is a person "inspired by a divinity." According to Dr. Johnson, who spelled it *fanatick*, he is "a man mad with wild notions of religion." Winston Churchill took a different tack. He said that a *fanatic* is "one who can't change his mind and won't change the subject," which epigrammatically defines its present meaning—an extravagantly and unreasonably zealous person.

## FARCE

*See* INFARCTION

## FERRET

It is well established that many nouns can be converted into verbs. (A person may *chair* a meeting, for example, and the matter before the meeting may be *tabled*.) From the names of two small animals, the ferret and the squirrel, come verbs that describe human activities similar to those of these animals.

The semidomesticated ferret (an animal having yellowish fur, a long snout, and red eyes), a native of Africa, was brought to Europe by the Romans to hunt rabbits. The animal's name, since those early times, has undergone a series of orthographic changes from its ultimate Latin root *fur*, meaning "a thief." It seems that the poultry-stealing ferret acquired its thieving reputation with the ancients. The term *ferret out* has come to be applied (thanks to Charles Dickens, who put these words to-

107

gether) to one who searches or hunts persistently, as does an accountant looking for errors in his client's tax return or a detective pursuing a notorious criminal.

The English word *squirrel* can be traced directly to Greek *skiouros,* which literally means "shadow tail" (*skia,* "a shadow," and *oura,* "a tail") or, in translation, "that which makes a shade with its tail." The logicality of this name is apparent, since at least a third of a squirrel is tail which, when raised, seems to become a sunshade.

The squirrels' habit of storing nuts and other edibles in holes for future use has given English the verb *to squirrel* (generally with *away*), meaning "to cache something," "to save for a future need," or, as said more prosaically, "to save for a rainy day."

## FIASCO

Many a man has *failed* because he regularly carried a *flask* in his hip pocket. Perhaps this is so because the words *fail* and *flask* have an affinity for each other. But how these words became associated is not entirely clear. According to one theory, flasks were ornamental pieces, not ordinary wine containers. Since those that were flawed could no longer serve as decorative items, they were set aside for use as common household bottles. But not ordinary bottles. These bottles, called *fiaschi* in Italian, had long necks and irregularly rounded bottoms, which meant that they could stand upright only if matted with straw. Because of this limitation, the progression of the word's idiomatic sense was that a *fiasco* (its singular form) will surely fall and that, as to other things, they will surely fail. (In Italian stage talk, to forget one's lines was *far fiasco,* "to do a bottle." The origin of this expression has never been determined.)

The word *fiasco* journeyed about many countries, landing on English shores with its figurative sense of "failure" intact. Today any ambitious undertaking that turns out to be a complete or ridiculous failure is a fiasco. In the United States a person is saddled with his fiasco; in Italy, he can put it in his pocket, take it home, and put Chianti in it.

## FILIBUSTER

The ancestor of *filibuster* journeyed through many languages (beginning with the Dutch *vrij* ("free") and *buit* ("booty")) and, having shaken off their various spellings, passed into Spanish as *filibustero*, meaning "buccaneer or pirate." The word was first used in the United States, without the final *o*, to represent American marauders who in the mid-nineteenth century fomented revolutions in Central America.

The present everyday meaning of *filibuster* is "delaying tactics." It is used of a legislator who makes long, irrelevant speeches, usually to consume so much time as to discourage other legislators from proceeding with a particular bill.

The first legitimate use of a filibuster, although its current meaning had not as yet developed, occurred in 1872 when Vice President Schuyler Colfax ruled that "under the practice of the Senate the presiding officer could not restrain a Senator in remarks which the Senator considers pertinent to the pending issue." As obstructionist tactics in Congress became more common (talking to death a bill that was not liked), the word given this maneuver was *filibuster* because its devastating effect was reminiscent of the havoc spread in countries invaded by filibusters. But any Congressman boasting of his filibustering tactics should know that, etymologically, he is just a pirate waging verbal warfare against helpless colleagues.

## FLOWER NAMES

The *dandelion* is a weed with yellow flowers and distinctive indented leaves. The toothlike edges of the leaves, according to the French, so resembled the teeth of a lion that they called the flower *dent de lion* (literally "tooth of the lion"). The English borrowed that name, slightly corrupting the first syllable.

The *gladiolus* was named after a Roman soldier's short sword, a *gladius*, because the flower's leaves were swordlike. From that Latin noun also comes the word *gladiator* (a sword-bearing captive forced to pit himself against another person, likewise equipped, for the entertainment of the public).

A *heliotrope* is a plant that turns toward the sun. And that is what its name stands for in Greek (*helios*, "sun"; *-tropos*, "turning to go into"). Legend has it that Clytie's love for Apollo, the sun god, was unrequited when he discovered the beauty of her sister. The unfortunate sea-nymph pined away; at her death Apollo changed her into a flower that kept turning toward her love, the sun.

The name *pansy*, a flower somewhat like a violet but larger, is a fanciful formation from the French *pensée*, "thought" (founded on *herbe de la pensée*), which reflects the thoughtful appearance of the flower, from whose root stems the word *pensive*). In *Hamlet*, Shakespeare expressed this attribute of pensiveness by having Ophelia say to Laertes, ". . . pray, love, remember: and there is pansies, that's for thoughts."

A *daisy* opens its flower in the morning, exposing a yellow center that resembles the sun. Because of this likeness and because the flower closed its lashes and went to sleep when the sun set, it was called, in Old English, *daeges eye*, which meant "day's eye," and which quite naturally became *daisy*.

## FOIBLE

The words *foible* and *forte* originated as terms in fencing, foible being the weaker part of a sword blade, the pointed half, and the forte, the upper or stronger part, from the middle to the hilt. Clearly a foible might lose its tip if it struck the opponent's forte.

These terms have become a part of common speech. A person's foibles are his weaknesses or his shortcomings. Although pertaining to minor weak points of character, they are nevertheless persistent faults. The genesis of *foible* was Latin *flebilis*, meaning "weak" (literally "to be wept over"). The French acquired the word (retaining its sense) and spelled if *faible*. When it entered the English language, its spelling became *foible*. In Watt's *Logick* appeared this sentence, "The witty men sometimes have sense enough to know their own foible, and therefore craftily shun the attacks of argument."

*Forte* is the antonym of *foible*. It means "the strong point," that in which a person excels. It is a word of rather recent origin; Dr. Johnson did not include it in his *Dictionary*. *Forte* consists of one syllable and is therefore pronounced *fort* (the same as a fortified place). According to Fowler, it should have been spelled that way, too. The Italian musical term, *forte*, meaning "loudly" or "with force," is pronounced *for*-tay.

# FOOLSCAP

Which came first, the dunce's cap or the foolscap? Word history recorded the term *foolscap* as early as the thirteenth century, at which time it referred to a watermark consisting of a fool's head, with cap and bells, on large-sized paper (the equivalent of the present-day legal size). The paper then took on the name of the watermark so that it became known as *foolscap*. But since this paper was originally imported from Italy, a theory has evolved that *foolscap* is a corruption of Italian *foglio capo*, meaning "a large- or full-sized sheet." This notion was given credence by the English people because during the reign of Queen Anne a statute was enacted which referred to such paper as *Genoa foolscap*. Another theory, and one with more substance, is that Oliver Cromwell, objecting to the royal arms insignia, substituted the belled cap of a court jester as the watermark for those manufacturers of paper using the stamp of Charles I.

There seems to be no record of how and where the dunce's cap (a cone-shaped cap placed on the head of a slow or lazy pupil) originated, but its name was probably suggested by *foolscap*.

# FORLORN HOPE

The most disheartening word in the English language is the adjective *forlorn*, meaning "forsaken, deserted, nearly hopeless"; its most inspirational is the noun *hope*, which means "trust, an expectation of fulfillment of something desired." But when *forlorn* and *hope* combine and become a phrase, all hope disappears, for then the sense of *forlorn hope* is "the cause or undertaking is hopeless—all is lost."

The expression arose as the English equivalent of the Dutch *verloren hoop*, which sounded like "forlorn hope" to the American ear. But its meaning was entirely different. *Verloren*, the past participle of *verliezen*, "to lose," and *hoop*, cognate with *heap*, was the Dutch term applied to assault troops, those making the initial attack and therefore not expected to survive. Literally the words meant "a lost squad" and referred to soldiers who were expendable. The French called them *enfants perdus* or lost children, and the English, "forlorn boys." The inaccuracy of the

American translation was particularly poignant because the Dutch phrase had nothing to do with "hope."

# FORNICATION

*See* HOOKER

# FORTE

*See* FOIBLE

# FORTNIGHT

The word *fort* has several meanings, but when added to the word "night" *(fortnight)*, it is a shortening of "fourteen." A fortnight is a period of fourteen nights and days (two weeks). A sister term, *sennight,* now obsolete, is a contraction of "seven nights" (one week). Both fortnight and sennight are survivals of an ancient custom of northern nations to reckon time by nights rather than by days. Tacitus in 98 A.D. wrote of the ancient Germans: "Their account of time differs from that of the Romans: instead of days, they reckon the number of nights. Their public ordinances are so dated; and their proclamations run in the same style. The night, according to them, leads the day." And so with the American Indians. They counted time by "moons," never by "suns."

# FORTY

*Forty,* in addition to introducing a person to middle age, became, because of its use in the Scriptures, a mystical number. Moses spent forty days on the Mount; the rain before the great flood lasted for forty days; and Noah kept the windows of the ark closed for another forty days.

Ali Baba had forty thieves, and Musa Dagh had forty critical days in *Die vierzig Tage des Musa Dagh,* which translates to *The Forty Days of Musa Dagh.* The Lenten period lasts for forty days. Under early law a widow was permitted to remain in the home of her late husband for forty days before relinquishing it to his heirs. And since it was believed that incubation of the black plague took forty days, a ship suspected of being infected with contagion was required to lie off port for that length of time— that is, it was quarantined.

The English word *quarantine* (from Italian *quarantina,* "a period of forty days"), meaning "a condition of isolation for one suspected of carrying a contagious disease," is no longer to be taken literally. The period has been shortened since the mysticism of *forty* has waned. A quarantine is now merely an enforced medical isolation of any duration.

## FOURFLUSHER

A *fourflusher* is a bluffer, a phony, a faker. He makes claims he can't support. Although considered slang, *fourflusher* nonetheless is a widely used term because it packs within it a lot of meaning.

The term originated in the game of poker. A *flush* (from Latin *fluxus,* "a flowing") is a strong hand consisting of five cards of the same suit. If a player has a four flush and a card from another suit, he may keep his cards, giving the impression that he has a flush, and perhaps thereby drive out the other players. In draw poker, if a player has four cards of the same suit and one from another (called a *bobtail flush*), he may draw one card and, even if it is another suit, act as though he had drawn the right card. Should the bluff succeed, the player has won legitimately, but he is, literally speaking, a *fourflusher,* for he pretended to have what he did not. He had a four flush, not a real one.

## FOURTH ESTATE

The expression "the fourth estate" is not an unusual one, but who first so dubbed the press, its reporters, and its general organization has not been confirmed. Most often it is attributed to Sir Edmund Burke from a speech delivered in 1790 when addressing the British Parliament. Fifty years later, in 1840, Thomas Carlyle declared in an essay in *Heroes and Hero Worship* that Burke had made the following statement: "Burke said that there were three Estates in Parliament; but, in the Reporters' Gallery yonder, there sat a Fourth Estate more important far than they all. It is not a figure of speech, or a witty saying; it is a literal fact—very momentous to us in these times." (Since Burke's writings make no reference to a "Fourth Estate," some phrase researchers wonder whether the term came from the pen of Carlyle. Others attribute the coinage to various sources.) In any event, the "all" referred to were the three estates of the realm: the lords spiritual, the lords temporal, and the commons. The implication was that the press, collectively, because it wields great influence upon public thinking and opinion, is a mighty power to be reckoned with. Nowadays a reference to the fourth estate is meant to be jocular, even though no one thinks its power is anything to joke about.

## FRANKENSTEIN

Almost everyone mistakenly believes that a Frankenstein is an inhuman monster too horrendous to look at. But that is certainly not the literal truth.

The monster in the story involving Frankenstein was conceived in the mind of Mary Wollstonecraft Shelley, the wife of the poet, who, together with her husband and his friend Byron, was spending time idly during a rainy day in Switzerland. To keep themselves occupied, they decided to tell ghost stories.

Mrs. Shelley's story concerned a young medical student named Victor Frankenstein, who, having learned how to infuse life into matter, fashioned a living being from bones taken from a charnel house and a dissecting laboratory. Although this creature was gentle and articulate, his appearance was so hideous that everyone feared and mistrusted him. No one would associate with him, and he was indeed treated as an outcast from society, which of course made him particularly lonely. When Frankenstein refused to create a mate for him, the monster's terrible loneliness drove him to seek revenge by murdering Frankenstein's wife, brother, and best friend. Frankenstein, now a full-fledged doctor, decided to undo what he had done. He pursued the horrible creature to destroy it, but unfortunately, he himself was destroyed. The narrative ends with the monster disappearing into the Arctic.

Mrs. Shelley published her story in 1818 in a book titled *Frankenstein,* with the subtitle *The Modern Prometheus.* In the book the monster is not named, but readers, by transference, have given it the name of its creator, Frankenstein. Almost no one calls it Frankenstein's monster. Figuratively a Frankenstein is something that gets out of control of its master who has started something he cannot stop. In a more literal sense, a person who is destroyed by his own works is said to have created a Frankenstein.

## FRENCH LEAVE

When someone uses the word *French,* he may not necessarily be referring to something that pertains to France. For example, french-fried potatoes (strips of potatoes fried in deep fat until brown and crisp) are not prepared in any Gallic manner. In fact, the *french* there is a case in point of a confusing eponym, for *frenching* is simply a method of preparing meats and vegetables before cooking them. Another misnomer is *French dressing* in that it is not a dressing concocted in France, and it is not even a favorite seasoning of the French. Their common dressing—a combination of oil and vinegar—is vinaigrette. That would be a real French dressing.

Another misleading *French* phrase is *French leave.* Although anyone anywhere may leave secretly, slip away without notice, *French leave* has come to mean to depart without bidding goodby, not even to the host or hostess. Originally it alluded to French soldiers who, after invading a foreign land, helped themselves to wares from a store and left without paying. The idea spread to other countries, where the expression came to be applied to naval or military personnel who absented themselves from their posts without permission. Later it was superseded by the phrase "absent without leave," which is the way a soldier or sailor who is missing from his unit is listed nowadays. In short, he is A.W.O.L.

Which raises another point. Why A.W.O.L.? Why not A.W.L.?—*A*bsent *W*ithout *L*eave. The "O" represents no word, and, although it is the initial letter in "out," the initial letter in the second syllable of *absent* has been ignored. The notion advanced that "O" stands for "official"—*absent without official leave*—has no merit according to the United States War Department. The fact is that the Department feared that A.W.L. might be construed to mean *absent with leave*; hence the "O" was added to disabuse anyone of that idea.

## FRITTER

Almost everyone in his lifetime has eaten a delicious, fattening fritter—perhaps an apple or a corn fritter. A *fritter,* of course, is a cake made from a small quantity of batter, often containing fruit, meat, or fish, and fried in deep fat or sautéed. Dr. Johnson defined *fritter* in his *Dictionary* first as "a small piece cut to be fried," and second, simply as "a small piece" or "a fragment." He exemplified this latter use by an excerpt from Shakespeare's *The Merry Wives of Windsor:* "Sense and putter! have I lived to stand in the taunt of one that makes fritters of English!" This use as a noun, is now obsolete. The heritage of *fritter* can be found in Old French *friture,* meaning, "something fried." Its ultimate ancestor was Latin *frictus,* past participle of *frigere,* "to roast or fry."

What may be confusing is the sense of *fritter* when used as a verb, as in "to fritter away one's inheritance is foolish." There *fritter* certainly bears no relationship to any form of food. In that phrase it means "to dissipate," "to squander," "to waste." This apparent ambiguity is due to an entirely different root word, Latin *fractura,* "a fracture." The thought in *fritter away* (*away* is a constant companion of *fritter*) evokes a person theoretically breaking or fracturing his resources into such small pieces that everything is wasted. Thoreau in *Walden* put it bluntly: "Our life is frittered away by detail . . . Simplify, simplify."

## FRONTISPIECE

At one time a *frontispiece* was an illustration facing the title page of a book. It was, to put it differently, the piece in front of the title page.

Etymologically, however, that definition is without foundation. In the first place, there is no "piece" in *frontispiece.* The word is a combination of two Latin terms: *frons, frontis* ("forehead," later meaning "front") and *spicium* (from *specere,* "to look at"). Secondly, a *frontispicium* was the "front aspect of a building"—its facade. Its sense, therefore, was purely architectural. Anglicized, it was called *frontispice.*

It is believed that the change to *frontispiece,* referring first to the title page and then to the page opposite it, came about because it was customarily decorated with columns and other architectural motifs. The last syllable may seem to have followed logically, since a front piece of the book was designated; but the history of this evolution is obscure.


## FUSSBUDGET

One may rightly ask, "What is a *fussbudget,* and why that combination of words, and especially what is the word *budget* doing there?" The answer to the first part is easy, for everyone knows what a *fussbudget* is—a person who worries about trifles. And that, by the way, is the exact definition given in many dictionaries for the noun *fuss* by itself—"unwarranted concern over unimportant matters," which seems to make the addition of "budget" superfluous.

*Fuss* is a word of unknown origin. Some etymologists think it came from Anglo-Saxon *fus,* meaning "eager" or "prompt," but all note that it is probably a sound imitative of "spluttering and puffing." Dr. Johnson defined it as "a tumult," "a bustle," and called it a low cant word.

A *budget,* of course, is a sum of money allocated for a particular purpose. The ancestor of that word was the Late Latin *bulga,* "a leather bag." *Bulga* journeyed among many languages, each one slightly altering its meaning and its spelling. In Old Irish, it was *bolg,* and in French during the Middle Ages it became *bougette,* "a little bag." The present sense of *budget* stems from the custom of carrying in a leather "bag" all papers pertaining to future income and expected expenses, from which the Chancellor of the Exchequer made a statement and recommendations to the House of Commons.

Returning to the second part of the question, no one knows for certain why a finicky or fussy person should be known as a *fussbudget.* Surely that term does not imply a fussing over a budget. Conjectures both as to sources and as to the reason for that choice of words have not alighted on firm ground. Perhaps the best thing to do is not to fret about it lest one be called by that very word—a *fussbudget.*

## GALAXY

It may be hard to believe but the words *galaxy* (meaning "a star system") and *lettuce* (the basic food in most salads) share parents with the same root sense, although their roots were nurtured in different soils. The root of *galaxy* is found in the Greek *galaxias* from *gala,* which means "milk," and the root of *lettuce,* in the Latin *lac,* which also means "milk."

The long white track of luminous stars known as the Milky Way is so called because of its whiteness, which resembles a splash of milk in the sky. The name for this kind of astral formation is *galaxy* (in Greek literally "the Milky Circle"), now a generic term and another way of saying Milky Way. Chaucer in his poem, "The House of Fame," wrote, "See yonder, loo, the Galaxie, / Which men clepeth (called) the Milky Way, / . . . ." With the elevation of entertainment personalities to stardom, *galaxy* has developed the sense of an assemblage of beautiful or prominent people. Hence the designation Milky Way is now a useful replacement for *Galaxy* to distinguish heavenly stars from those who simply look heavenly.

Lettuce is a plant with edible leaves, usually eaten in a salad. The scientific name for this kind of plant—one with succulent leaves—is *lactuca,* a Latin word stemming from *lac,* "milk." It should be pointed out that certain varieties of lettuce have a milky juice; whence *lac, lactuca* (Latin); *latuites* (Old French); *letuse* (Middle English); *lettuce*—an etymological galaxy.

## GALVANIC

From the name of an eighteenth-century Italian physiologist, Luigi Galvani, has come the term *galvanic,* "caused by, or producing, an electric current." Galvani discovered that an electric stimulus caused frogs to have muscular contractions, for which he was disdainfully labeled "the frog's dancing master."

But his findings became the basis for today's knowledge of direct-current electricity, especially when produced chemically. In a nontechnical sense *galvanize* means "to electrify" or "to spur to sudden activity."

The far-reaching discovery of Galvani began in his wife's kitchen (the Galvanis lived in Bologna). In 1790 diets were as popular as they are today. Signora Galvani, who was preparing skinned frogs in accordance with a prescribed diet, put the frogs in a vessel, which happened to be near an operating electric machine. Galvani noticed that the frogs' muscles began to twitch—manifestations of vitality. He was amazed by this strange phenomenon, which incited him to conduct further experiments. The world, for this knowledge of electricity, can thank that "kettle of frogs," which turned out to be, according to a popular phrase, "a fine kettle of fish."

## GAMUT

In the eleventh century a monk, Guido D'Arezzo, devised a musical scale (known as Guido's scale) that has since been the basis of musical notation. To the earlier six-tone scale, Guido added a low *G,* which he called *gamma* after the Greek letter. It later became known as *gamma-ut. Gamma* was later named "G," as in G-clef; *ut* was renamed *do,* as in *do-re-mi*; and *gamut* entered the English language as a generalized word designating the complete range or extent of anything—notes, prices, choices. "To run the gamut" is to run through an entire series of musical notes, a full display of figures, or a whole range of colors. It is the alphabetical A-to-Z of any subject: "Defense counsel *ran the gamut* of emotions in pleading for clemency—he laughed, he begged, he harangued, he cried."

Guido named his notes in a curious fashion—from the initial syllables of an ancient hymn to St. John.

*Ut* queant laxis
*re*sonare fibris
*Mi*ra gestorum
*fa*muli tuorum
*Sol*ve polluti
*la*bii reatum
Sancte Iohannes.

(That with full voices your servants may be able to sing the wonders of your deeds, purge the sin from their unclean lips, O holy John.)

The seventh note *si* (later changed to *ti*) is believed to be a combination of the first letters of *Sancte Iohannes*. The eight-tone notation became complete when Guido added at the top of the scale a note he called *ela* but now called *do*.

## GARGANTUA

*Gargantua,* the eponymous hero in François Rabelais's sixteenth-century satire *Gargantua and Pantagruel,* was a king of mammoth stature and enormous appetite. Despite his elephantine build, he had a kindly heart and a gentle disposition. In French folklore, he was a helpful, peace-loving giant.

His period of gestation in his mother's womb was eleven months. He was delivered after she had eaten enough to satisfy ten persons. According to legend, Gargantua was so huge that when he grew to manhood, cannon balls that struck him felt like grape kernels. Desiring a salad, he cut lettuce as big as walnut trees and ate it all up, together with six pilgrims who, unfortunately for them, were hiding inside.

Supposedly his name was related to *gargle* and *gargoyle*. This may be so, especially since his father's name was *Grandgousier,* which in French means "great gullet." In common speech *gargantuan* referes to anything huge, vast, or enormous, especially a voracious appetite.

## GAZEBO

Many slang English words have, with time, improved their image so much that they have come to be accepted even by conservative writers. One such is *gazebo,* "a summerhouse affording a fine view," now listed in most respected dictionaries. However, at its inception it was merely a humorous term, dog Latin for "I shall see" (literally "I shall gaze"), a combining of *gaze* and the Latin *-ebo* (a future tense ending).

The middle syllable of *gazebo* should be pronounced *zee,* even though some people use the long *a,* as in *zay*—guh-*zay*-boh. This latter pronunciation converts the term into another word, *gazabo,* an import from Mexico, slang for "a wise guy" in the sense "a smart alec."

A more respected word than *gazebo,* yet one with the same meaning, is Italian born *belvedere* (which translates into "a beautiful sight") from *bel,* "beautiful," and *vedere,* "to view."

## GAZETTE

A *gazette* is a newspaper. In yesteryear barbershops supplied the popular *Police Gazette* (with its pictures of sexy-looking women) to waiting customers to relieve their impatience. Although the word *gazette* probably had a Latin background (*gaza* in Latin means "treasure"), it came to mean "newspaper" in Venice, where, during the sixteenth century, the Government issued monthly papers reporting on the war between Venice and the Turks. The "newspaper" was not sold; it could be perused, however, but only for a fee—a gazetta. Sometimes it was even read aloud to a gathering of people, but those hearing it also had to pay a fee—a gazetta.

A *gazetta,* a diminutive form of *gazza,* which means "magpie," was the smallest Venetian coin. Philologists have wondered at this strange word; was the newspaper being likened to a magpie? Although there might not be an association, the fact is that about that time coins were invented and were named after birds: eagle, raven, and so forth. Hence *gazetta.* The name of this tin coin, which became the price of the newspaper, by transference was given to the paper itself. When *gazetta* moved into English, it was anglicized by a change of the final *a* to *e.*

## GERRYMANDER

Dictionaries define *gerrymander* as a method whereby a territorial unit is so divided as to give one special political party an advantage—invariably the party in power. The term came from the name of Elbridge Gerry who, in 1812 when Governor of Massachusetts, contrived with the legislature to arrange the territory into new senatorial voting districts, leaving his opponents in no position to contend for the offices at stake. The elongated shape of the territory, as it appeared on a map, with the districts rearranged, resembled a salamander (it needed only claws and a beak). In fact, it was the celebrated painter Gilbert Stuart who saw a map of the redistricted county hanging in a newspaper editor's office and added the claws and beak. "That will do for a salamander," he said. To which the witty editor replied, "Call it a gerrymander."

Despite the criticism heaped upon Gerry because of this sly stratagem, it left his political career unscathed. He shortly thereafter became the Vice President of the United States under James Madison.

## GET DOWN TO BRASS TACKS

Brass is a metal that has lent its name to many phrases but in particular to one that may have stemmed from its actual use, "to get down to brass tacks." It means, of course, to get to the root of the matter at hand, the basic issues, without further delay or, in common speech, to get to business. It is believed that this expression evolved during the heyday of dry goods stores where bolts of cloth were kept on shelves. On the counter were brass tacks set a yard apart, in effect a measuring rod, so that the amount of fabric purchased could be measured.

Another version has it that brass tacks, because they do not rust, were used in upholstered furniture. It was customary, when a chair or sofa began to sag, to open it up all the way to the brass tacks in order to find the source of the trouble. That was getting to the bottom of things.

## GLASS SLIPPER

*See* MISTRANSLATIONS

## GOBBLEDEGOOK

The trouble with *gobbledegook* is that, when one uses it, one annoys not only precisians but those who favor simple and direct expression. Gobbledegook, of course, is unintelligible inflated langauge—the hallmark of many government agencies. It was a Texas Congressman, Maury Maverick, an exponent of straight-from-the-holster talk, who vehemently denounced the long-winded, pretentious speech of his colleagues and other government spokesmen and called it *gobbledegook,* a strange-sounding word that has stuck. Although initially considered slang for "officialese," *gobbledegook* (variant spelling *gobbledygook*), which sounds like a gobbling turkey, is now a respectable term, listed in dictionaries and accepted on all levels of English. The point that Maverick made in condemning pompous, obscure bureaucratic language is clearly and tellingly conveyed in his departmental memo:

> Be short and say what you're talking about. Stop "pointing up" programs. No more "finalizing," "effectuating," or "dynamics." Anyone using the words "activation" or "implementation" will be shot.

## GOODBY

*See* WELCOME

## GOOGOL

To some people no word could sound sillier, or less academic, than *googol. Googol* sounds like an infant's cooing. Yet it is a mathematical term used throughout the world and one in good standing in dictionaries. In brief, it is a scientific notation for a large number.

The development of *googol* started with an eminent mathematician, Professor Edward Kasner. Since he occasionally used large numbers, he thought that if a name were given such a number, it would make calculations less cumbersome. According to the story in *Mathematics and the Imagination,* by Edward Kasner and James Newman, published in 1940, Kasner asked his nine-year-old nephew for a word to represent a particularly large number. He said: "Googol!" And *googol* it became. It now represents the number 10 raised to the power 100, or the number 1 followed by 100 zeros.

What is even better, or more preposterous, is another coinage from the same lad—*googolplex.* That term represents the number 10 raised to the power googol; that is, the number 1 followed by $10^{100}$ zeros, or the formula $10^{10^{100}}$. It is said that this number is so incomprehensible "that there would not be enough room to write it, if you went to the farthest star, touring all the nebulae, and putting down zeros every inch of the way."

## GORDIAN KNOT

"To cut the Gordian knot" is to solve an intricate problem with a single brilliant move—with just one stroke, so to speak. In fact, that is how the famous knot tied by the Phrygian King Gordius was opened. King Gordius dedicated his chariot to Jupiter and tied its yolk to the temple with such cunning that an oracle prophesied that whoever should untie the knot would reign over all Asia. When Alexander the Great arrived in Gordium, and found himself unable to untie the knot, he decided that the only way to open it was through a more drastic and direct approach. He withdrew his sword from its scabbard and slashed through the knot, cutting it in two. Surely enough, Alexander went on to rule the East, where he was confronted with other knotty problems.

## GOSSIP

*Siblings* (from *sib,* "a blood relation," and the substantive suffix *-ling,* meaning "having the qualities of") are persons having the same parents. In medieval times a *sib* or *sibbe* was a relative, but not necessarily a blood relative. The man and woman who served as baptismal sponsors—godparents—were then called *godsibbes* (a word that by corruption contributed the word *gossip* to the English language). The idea of gossip grew out of the regular meetings and intimate conversations of the *godsibbes.* What they talked about came to be called *godsibbes* or (as slurred) *gossip.* It was later applied to two persons seen tête à tête, chattering intimately. Its sense then took on the color of idle talk about persons and their affairs, garnished with imagination and untruths. Still later *gossip* came to refer to the talker as well as the talk. He or she—the gossip—spoke gossip, the tittle-tattle of rumormongers. The word has never been placed in a favorable light. "Gossip is," according to *Philistine* by Elbert Hubbard, "vice enjoyed vicariously."

## GRINGO

"It's Greek to me," as everyone knows, means "I don't understand it." The expression has been widely used ever since the Latin proverb "Graecum est; non potest legi" ("It's Greek;

it cannot be read") was concocted. The Spaniards, who vociferously complained about all foreign accents and dialects, labeled them simply *griego,* or Greek.

The contemptuous label popular among Mexicans for designating a foreigner, especially an American, was *gringo.* One theory concerning its origin, perhaps the one with the most substance, is that the term was not intended to be disparaging; it was derived from the Spanish *griego* and was merely the Mexican way of saying that foreign languages sounded like gibberish. *Griego,* slightly altered, became *gringo* and then it came to be applied not merely to the foreign language but also to the speaker; he became the *gringo.*

A more romantic story, but one not fully attested, is that during the Mexican War the troops of Scott and Taylor sang as they marched, as soldiers are apt to do, and their favorite song was so often repeated that the Mexican natives thought that from its first two words they had picked up an expression (*gringo*), but they were mistaken. The opening lines of the song, by Robert Burns, were

> *Green grow* the Rashes O
> The happiest hours that ere I spent
> Were spent among the lasses O.

## GROTESQUE

The murals discovered on ancient Roman grotto walls were fanciful, outlandish paintings, many consisting of human and animal forms interwoven with strange-looking fruits and exotic flowers. To describe these paintings of freakish beings, the word *grotesque* ("from a grotto" or "in grotto style") was coined. The word now has a broader meaning: that which is utterly fantastic, or lacking in good taste and judgment, or incongruous or distorted. It need not be a painting; it may be a person's style of dress.

Although *grotesque* and *bizarre* are near synonyms, their roots were not nurtured in the same soil. The Spanish *bizarro,* meaning "brave or handsome," is the ancestor of *bizarre.* It is said that, in turn, *bizarro* came from *bizar,* which in Basque meant "beard." The Basques felt that beards made them look gallant and swashbuckling. But the French did not agree. They thought the beards were so peculiar that they dubbed the bearded Basques *bizarre,* which in French means "the strange."

*Bizarre* and *bazaar* are not etymological cousins. The name of the Oriental marketplace, lined with shops and stalls and known as a *bazaar,* came from the Persian *bazar,* a market. In the United States a *bazaar* is a fair for the sale of goods, usually for charity.

# GUILLOTINE

*See* DERRICK

# GUERILLA

Guerillas can thank Spain for their name. In Spanish, *guerilla* means "a little war." At first it referred only to skirmishes and irregular military activity, but it later came to refer to the men who fought in them.

Although the word *guerilla* sounds like *gorilla,* the hairy African beast that resembles a human being, there is no relationship between the words. And the fact that both gorillas and guerillas spend time in trees (guerillas hide in them to spot the enemy; gorillas, to spot a mate) also has no bearing. The similarity in sound was accidental. In the fifth century B.C., a Carthaginian navigator named Hanno saw large anthropoid apes when he explored West Africa. He called them gorillas. How he came by this African word and its precise meaning has never been established.

# GUN

It may be just as well if a person firing a gun is not interested in the history of the word *gun,* since Dr. Johnson advised: "Of this word there is no satisfactory etymology."

The opinion of most word sleuths is that the history of *gun* began with the Old Norse *Gunnhildr,* a redundant compound, for both *gunnr* and *hildr* mean "battle" or "war." *Gunhild* was a feminine name but a logical sense development, since, according to Scandinavian mythology, women went to war with their men, sometimes carrying off the honors as the most daring fighters. *Gunhild* was later applied to a war machine, a name that continued for centuries. Windsor Castle in the fourteenth century was defended by a mammoth missle-thrower dubbed with a Latin name, *Domina Gunilda,* but generally known as *Lady Gunilda.* Perhaps soldiers in World War I had the female name Gunilda in mind when they picked another female name for the German long-range gun, *Big Bertha.*

One odd development of the word *gun* is that a "gun" man—spelled *gunman*—is someone to fear. He is a professional killer. But there is nothing alarming about any of the other "weapon" words followed by *man.* The words *swordsman* and *rifleman,* for example, refer simply to persons who handle their respective weapons with superior skill.

## GUNG-HO

Lieutenant Colonel Evans F. Carlson, who commanded a marine force that invaded Guadalcanal during World War II, is responsible for the borrowing by English of the Chinese slogan *gung-ho* (it may actually have been *kung-ho*). Regardless, as an observer with the Chinese Army between 1937 and 1939, he learned that their slogan meant "Everybody work together." Carlson's Raiders adopted the phrase, declaring themselves *gung-ho,* but with the sense "ready to go." Other marines picked up the slogan, and its meaning gradually became "extremely enthusiastic." A *gung-ho* person nowadays is wholeheartedly ready for what comes. It may be a secret government mission or just a date to go skiing.

## GUY

A guy is a boy or a man. The term is usually dressed up or down to make it complimentary ("a nice guy," "a regular guy") or insulting ("a wise guy," "a tough guy").

The origin of this word in general usage, other than as a proper name, can be pinpointed to a specific date and occasion. On November 5, 1605, a plot to blow up the House of Parliament in London was uncovered. It was learned that Guy Fawkes, as a protest against the enforcement of anti-Catholic laws, had burrowed through the walls of these buildings and planted a charge of about twenty barrels of gunpowder in the cellar. Fawkes was caught and hanged.

The failure of this conspiracy is celebrated throughout England with bonfires in which effigies of Guy Fawkes are burned. These effigies (from the French *effigie,* meaning "likeness" or "copy") are called *guys,* and children solicit money on that day, asking for "a coin for the *guy*" in order to buy fireworks. With time, any grotesque figure or odd-looking fellow came to be called a *guy.* But this, at least in the United States, is no longer so. Here a boy or a man—any fellow—is a *guy.* In fact, he might be the handsomest guy at the party, and the girls would sigh and say, "What a *guy!*"

## GYMNASIUM

*See* CALISTHENICS

## GYPSY

Gypsies are wanderers—members of a nomadic tribe that presumably was of Hindu origin. During the fifteenth century these nomads, who called themselves Romany, which also was the name of their language (some Romany words have passed into English thieves' cant and later into general usage; for example, *shiv,* meaning "knife"), wandered through much of Europe and Britain. The English thought they came from Egypt and therefore called them *Egyptians,* which eventually was shortened to *Gypsy* (but spelled *Gipsy*). (American slang for a cheat, "gip" or "gyp," is simply a clipped word.) The French had another name for them, which also entered the English language. That name was *Bohemian,* since the French believed that these bizarre-looking people originated in Bohemia. Actually, they had lived in that region for a while, but later migrated to various other countries. The word *bohemian* (with a lower case *b*) has come to mean a nonconformist, "one who lives an unconventional life." The names *bohemian* and *Gypsy* are synonymous in some usages. That those words are properly linked can be attested by the remark of a Gypsy in Sir Walter Scott's *Quentin Durward:* "I am a Zingaro, a Bohemian, an Egyptian, or whatever the Europeans . . . may choose to call me; but I have no country."

## HALCYON

Halcyon days are calm and peaceful, traditionally a time of happiness and prosperity. The phrase has come down through the centuries from Greek mythology.

According to legend, Halcyone was the wife of Ceyx, who was drowned while going to seek advice from an oracle. His body was cast upon a shore, whereupon his grieving wife threw herself into the sea. The gods admired her act of self-sacrifice and, out of compassion, transformed both Ceyx and Halcyone into birds named *halcyons*. These birds, popularly known as *kingfishers*, according to legend built floating nests on the sea, hatching their young in fourteen days. During this period (which was at the time of the winter solstice), the gods caused the winds to cease blowing and the seas to subside. Appropriately enough, these days—seven preceding the year's shortest day (December 21) and seven following it—became known as "the halcyon days." (*Halcyon* came from a Greek word, *alkyon*, meaning "brood on the sea.")

> Amidst our arms as quiet you shall be
> As halcyon brooding on a winter's sea.
> —John Dryden, *Indian Emperor*

## HALIBUT

To understand why a *halibut* is called by that name, one must start with the word *butt*. A *butt* is a flatfish, such as the sole or the fluke. The largest species of flatfish was regularly eaten on holy days during the period when what is called Middle English was spoken. The fish was accordingly dubbed haly (holy) butte. It was the "holy fish," and sometimes called "the holy flounder." By normal semantic evolution the fish came to be called by its present name, *halibut*. It may now be, as everyone

129

knows, eaten at any time. The fish no longer is reserved only for holy days, even though etymologically it is "a holy fish."

## HALLMARK

*See* BENCHMARK

## HANDICAP

A *handicap* may be either an advantage or a disadvantage. If a horse in a horserace carries more weight than is carried by the other horses, the extra weight is a disadvantage to the one carrying it but gives the others an advantage.

The term, however, had no association with horseracing or any similar sport when it originated centuries ago, although no one has pinpointed where it came from. According to one theory *handicap* was the name of a game in which forfeits were placed in a cap. It is mentioned in Pepys' *Diary,* dated September 18, 1660. A more prevalent theory is that *handicap* referred to a form of barter called *hand in the cap,* later shortened to *hand i cap.* When two persons wished to barter, they selected an umpire, who (out of sight of the parties) would inspect the goods to be bartered, describe it to the participants, and then, to make the exchange equitable, announce the additional sum that should be paid by the one submitting the inferior article. The barterers then put forfeit money into a cap. If their hands were empty when withdrawn from the cap, this signified a refusal to go along with the umpire's figure. If both barterers' hands were full, the barter was completed. Everyone then went away happy, especially the umpire, for he pocketed the forfeit money—his fee. Of course, if there had been no agreement, the barter fell through and each participant reclaimed his property—and the money. If only one of the barterers had accepted the umpire's decision, he owned the forfeit money. The other party lost his money—and the umpire, everything. It may be said that *he* was handicapped.

## HANGNAIL

Almost everyone has been annoyed by a hangnail, a piece of dead skin at the side or base of the fingernail. And yet that is not what a hangnail was in earlier times. The word is a compound of *ange*, "painful" (from Indo-European *angh*, "pain"), and *naegl*, "nail," but spelled *agnail*.

The *ange* or *ang* is easy to see, for hangnails certainly are painful (a common word combining *ang* is *angina*, as in angina pectoris, a pain in the chest). But the *nail* part raises another question. In the first place, the nail referred to in *angnaegl* was the kind one drives into a board, not like the one on a finger; secondly, the word referred not to a painful bit of torn cuticle on the edge of a fingernail but to a corn on a toe, which was thought to resemble a nail's head.

With time, popular etymology changed not only the spelling and pronunciation of *angnaegl* to *hangnail* but also (with no anatomical accreditation) its placement in the body, raising it from the toe to the finger. Anyhow, it's the cuticle that hangs, not the nail.


## HARBINGER

> Now the bright morning star, the day's harbinger
> Comes dancing from the East.
> —John Milton, *Songs On May Morning*

A harbinger is a forerunner; he or it presages what will follow or at least hints of coming events—which, incidentally, need not be favorable. Washington Irving in his *Sketch Book* spoke of "the boding cry of the tree-toad, that harbinger of storm."

During medieval times a harbinger was an army courier (not a robin or a tree-toad) whose duty was to ride in advance of the troops to arrange for their food and shelter. (Harbingers served the same purpose for royalty.) In Old High German, *heriberga* meant "a shelter or encampment for the army," from which came *herberge* in Old French, "lodging." English acquired through those sources the word *harbinger*, which first came to represent a hostelry and, later, someone who preceded travelers to find accommodations.

In general usage today a *harbinger* is "one who goes before and makes known the approach of another." As Macbeth said in Shakespeare's *Macbeth:* "I'll be myself the harbinger, and make joyful / The hearing of my wife with your approach."

# HARUM-SCARUM

The expression *harum-scarum*, a facetious formation from *hare* and *scare*, refers to a hare-brained person who enjoys scaring others. The *harum*, from Old French *harer*, meaning "to set the dogs on," is also the root of *harass*. In today's usage the phrase more often refers to a giddy person.

Words like *harum-scarum* are called reduplicated or ricochet words. The English language abounds in such combinations, whose appeal lies in their rhythm and rhyme. Among the well known are *pitter-patter, hanky-panky, mishmash, wishy-washy, willy-nilly, knicknack, mumbo-jumbo, chitter-chatter,* and *helter-skelter.* And then there is *hurly-burly,* with its sense of uproar or tumult. In the opening passage of Shakespeare's *Macbeth,* the First Witch asked, "When shall we meet again . . . ," to which the Second Witch replied, "When the hurly-burly's done, / When the battle's lost and won." Another echoic Shakespearean word is *hugger-mugger,* meaning, first, "clandestinely," and second, "disorder and confusion." In *Hamlet,* Claudius, King of Denmark, spoke to his queen about Polonius's secret burial: "For good Polonius' death; and we have done but greenly / In hugger-mugger to inter him. . . ." The king was referring to the fact that Ophelia's father had been smuggled into the grave too quickly and without ceremony.

# HAZARD

A person who says "I wouldn't hazard a guess" implies that the risk of being wrong is so great that he would not even dare to conjecture. Both the verb and the noun *hazard* mean "venture," "risk," or "peril." Originally, however, *hazard* was the name of a game played with dice. The word came from the Arabic *al-zahr,* "a die," and entered the Spanish language as *azar,* meaning "an unlucky throw of the dice." It was borrowed into Middle English, with a change in spelling, namely an added letter front and back. In Shakespeare's *Richard III,* King Richard says: "I have set my life upon a cast, / And I will stand the hazard of the die." The perils of playing dice are being compared to the hazards of everyday living.

A *die* (Old French *de,* from Latin *datum,* a thing given, by luck or good fortune) is a small cube for gaming, but the word *die* is seldom used in the singular. Ordinarily references are to *dice,* which are two or more *dies.* The expression "The die is cast" *(Alea iacta est),* made famous by Julius Caesar before crossing the Rubicon, is now a cliché; but it should be noted that it was a *die* that was cast, not a *dye* (material for staining or coloring). The casting of a die was thought to decide one's fortune or future. Today tossing the dice may do that, too.

## HEARSE

A *hearse* is a vehicle for conveying the dead. Riding behind a hearse is a harrowing experience. This, etymologically speaking, is as it should be, because originally a harrow, which contained iron prongs on which candles were set, was a triangular frame placed over a coffin at the funeral in church. In Middle English the word for harrow became *herse,* the same word as *hearse* but spelled somewhat differently. Subsequently *hearse* came to mean a "bier" and later "the carriage for a dead body."

The Latin *hirpex,* "a rake or harrow," the original ancestor of *hearse,* was responsible also for the word *rehearse.* The Latin prefix *re* means "again"; hence *to rehearse* is to harrow again. One who rakes over what he has memorized is repeating for practice. He is, like a farmer who reharrows a field, stirring up the groundwork of his memory.

## HERMAPHRODITE

A *hermaphrodite* is a living thing or being that has both male and female sex organs, such as the earthworm or certain plants. A person manifesting male and female characteristics may be termed *hermaphroditic* (or *androgynous,* a Greek word combining *andros,* "man," and *gyne,* "woman").

Hermaphroditus (his name is a combination of his parents names—Hermes and Aphrodite) was so beautiful a specimen of man that when the nymph of the fountain at Salmacis spied him bathing in her pool, she rushed in and embraced him. Hermaphroditus, much to her chagrin, rebuffed her, whereupon she prayed to the gods that their two bodies should become one—that "the twain might become one flesh" (Ovid, *Metamorphoses*). The gods granted her request. The bodies of Hermaphroditus and the nymph grew together, united, but retaining the characteristics of each sex. How this arrangement satisfied either of them has never been disclosed.


# HEROIN

*See* MORPHINE


# HOBNOB

One who hobnobs with the upper crust is said to mingle on familiar terms with wealthy or influential people. The literal meaning of *hobnob,* from Anglo-Saxon *haebbe* and *naebbe,* is "to have and have not," with the sense of "come what may."

In the eighteenth century *hobnob* came to mean "drinking alternately," as persons do who, with raised glasses, extol one another or drink to one another's health. A social practice then began of having any person who called for a round of drinks to act as the host. He, in turn, would then be treated to a round of drinks by a drinking partner. In this way each one had (and then had not) the privilege of treating—*haebbe* and *naebbe*. From this form of social drinking emerged a further sense reflecting the familiarity it breeds. *Hobnob* now refers to one who is on intimate terms with another, even if both are teetotalers.

The *upper crust* is an informal phrase, meaning "the highest social class or group." J. Fenimore Cooper used the term in *Ways of the Hour:* "Those families, you know, are our upper crust. . . ." Centuries ago it was etiquette to slice off and present the king with the *upper crust* of a loaf of bread that had been placed on his table. This ritual symbolized the importance of being on top; hence one of the elite, especially if one had the dough.


# HOBSON'S CHOICE

A Hobson's choice is one without an alternative; it says "take this or nothing." A person driven to a single course of action has only a Hobson's choice—which is no choice at all.

The phrase was an outgrowth of the practice of Thomas Hobson, a liveryman in seventeenth-century Cambridge, whose customers, especially those who were students, if unrestricted, would always select his fastest horses and ride them to exhaustion. Believing that the welfare of his horses would be best served if they were used in rotation, he established a rule that his customers could not select a horse of their own choosing but had to hire the one he had placed nearest the stable door, which was the horse that had had the most rest. The customer could accept the offer or reject it—that is, ride off or walk.

> Where to elect there is but one,
> 'Tis Hobson's choice—take that or none.
> —Thomas Ward

## HOCUS POCUS

Before performing sleight of hand, conjurors usually mutter the magical words "hocus pocus." But they never explain the significance of that nonsense phrase or where it came from. Perhaps their conjurations couldn't go that far because what they did, to borrow a phrase, was sheer hocus pocus.

A belief had formerly existed that *hocus pocus* came from Latin *hoc est corpus*, which means "Here is my body" and which was used to mock the Roman Church's mass (in which bread was changed into the body of Jesus). Word-followers now tend to believe that the phrase *hocus pocus* was false or invented Latin, fabricated by magicians to sound impressive as they worked their tricks; but the words had no meaning at all, even when made to rhyme—"hocus pocus dominocus."

Although the phrase consists of meaningless rhyming sounds, from *hocus* has come the usable words *hoax,* "a mischievous trick," and the slang term *hokum,* "nonsense," with an ending perhaps influenced by *bunkum,* a sister word.

## HOLIDAY

A *Roman holiday* is more than a festive occasion. In its historical context, it was a barbaric spectacle; it referred to physical contests in ancient Rome where gladiators fought for their lives—solely for the amusement of the spectators.

In the United States the phrase "national holiday" is a misnomer. There are no such days. The holidays which it is within the province of Congress to designate apply only to federal employees and the District of Columbia. Each state decides which holidays to observe. Few legal holidays are observed nationally—that is, by all states. They all celebrate New Year's Day and Labor Day, for example. But Columbus Day, Memorial Day, and Washington's birthday are not legal holidays throughout the fifty states. Neither are Good Friday and Election Day.

The word *holiday* stemmed from Middle English *halidai,* which meant "holy day." Holy days, of course, are days for religious worship. But, with time, common speech contracted the two elements to form a single word, *holiday.* Today a holiday is a day to relax and enjoy. In England any vacation is called a holiday, even if it falls on a holy day.


## HOMOSEXUALITY

*See* LESBIANISM


## HONEYMOON

Many a man dreams of spending his life on a continuous honeymoon. But unfortunately a honeymoon cannot last forever. The *moon* in "honeymoon" refers to the lunar month, which means that the time allotted is only one month. It is, according to Dr. Johnson, "the first month after marriage, when there is nothing but tenderness and pleasure." The *honey* does not refer to the bride, although she certainly may be one, but to a potion made of honey (mead) that was customarily drunk as an aphrodisiac during this period. History reports that Attila the Hun suffocated from guzzling too much of this stuff at his wedding celebration.

The Nordic connotation of *honeymoon* is quite cynical. It compares the blissful first month (the honeymoon) to the phases of the moon. Just as a full moon begins to wane the moment it becomes full, so does the boundless affection of the newlyweds directly after their marriage. By the end of the month, says this theory, love has waned like the moon. It is now a "blue" moon, no longer a "honey" moon.

## HOODLUM

A *hoodlum* (commonly called a *hood*) is a thug. Although the word's origin has never been established, the term was first applied to a roving band of rowdies in California who harassed Chinese laborers. Toward the end of the nineteenth century the story that made the rounds is that the leader of this gang was a Hibernian named Muldoon. A newspaper reporter assigned to cover Muldoon's felonious activities, to avoid reprisal by the gang, covered up the head man's name by reporting it backwards—*Noodlum*. But even if true, this does not account for the change in the first letter from *n* to *h*. Another theory, that a compositor was responsible for the switch, fails to explain whether it was done purposely or accidentally. Perhaps he, too, feared the swish of a shillelagh.

Another Irish name that surfaced as an eponym for "ruffian," and also about the same time, is *hooligan*. Here again the origin of this word is obscure, but it became the name of a gang of toughs. The only difference between the hoodlums and the hooligans is that the former, under Muldoon, terrified people on the American West coast, whereas Hooligan exploited Londoners.

Hoodlums and hooligans belong together in a hoosegow. Even the words seem to go together. *Hoosegow* is an English derivative of the Spanish *jusgado* (meaning "a court"), which is pronounced "hoosgado." Today a *hoosegow* is a jail, where these thugs should land after they've had their day "in court."

## HOOKER

The belief that the word *hooker*, "a prostitute," was associated with the name of General Joseph ("Fighting Joe") Hooker of Civil War fame is pure folk etymology. Although it is known that he permitted street walkers to follow his army, the term *hooker*, as confirmed by William Morris, appeared in print in the United States at least once before the Civil War, in 1859. It may have come from the other side of the Atlantic, according to Ciardi, as a bit of British slang. *London Labour and the Poor*, in 1857, reported this statement from a whore: "We hooks a white collar (a clergyman) now and then," and from another, "I've hooked many a man by showing him an ankle on a wet day," an analogy to hooking a fish. "Fighting Joe" Hooker was not considered a talented military man. His romantic episodes were more successful than his victories in battle.

*Fornication,* says Dr. Johnson in his *Dictionary,* is "concubinage or commerce with an unmarried woman." In ordinary language that means voluntary sexual intercourse between unmarried persons. The word *fornication,* however, is more closely related to an architectural design than to sexual misbehavior. A *fornix,* in Latin, is an "arch or an arched basement." During Roman times, it was the custom of prostitutes to ply their trade in underground vaults which had overhead an arch, or fornix, which mutely watched the girls performing. With a shift of the sense, from *fornix* first came the name for a brothel ("I'll meet you at the fornix"), then a verb meaning "to frequent a brothel" *(fornicari),* and then the name of the pudendous activity conducted there—fornication.

## HUE AND CRY

The expression *hue and cry* has been read or heard many times. The meaning of *cry,* as in "to cry out," is quite clear, but a question that arises is, What does *hue* mean? It means the very same thing as "cry out." *Huer* in French, from which *hue* is derived, means "to cry or call out." Hence the phrase is redundant. Beginning with the Normans, Englishmen hearing someone calling for help when chasing a felon were legally bound to join in the pursuit. If they ignored this calling—the hue and cry—they could be adjudged guilty of a misdemeanor.

In the literature of yesteryear the phrase was a common one. Shakespeare wrote, "Hue and cry, villain, go! Assist me, knight, I am undone: fly, run, hue and cry! villain, I am undone." From Sir Roger L'Estrange, English Tory journalist, "Immediately comes a hue and cry after a gang of thieves, that had taken a purse upon the road."

In the sense used here, *hue* in English appears only in this one combination of words.

## HUMBLE PIE

Whether a person who has wrongly humiliated someone should eat humble pie to express sorrow and ask forgiveness, or whether it should be eaten by someone who is obliged to come down from a high position that he has assumed, depends on what "humble pie" is believed to mean. Is it a real or only an imaginary pie?

About the time of William the Conqueror, it became the custom, after a hunt, for the lord of the manor and his guests to feast on whatever animal they had captured that day. Quite naturally, they dined on the animal's better parts. The servants and attendants also ate parts of that animal, a meat pie made from the animal's innards—heart, liver, and other less desirable organs. This dish was called *umble pie*. *Umble* came from the Latin *lumbulus*, a diminutive form of *lumbus*, "loin." Subsequently *umble* became *humble* to correct (actually to make incorrect) its spelling and pronunciation; it was believed that the Cockneys had mispronounced the word by keeping the *h* silent.

In today's usage, "to eat humble pie" means "to apologize or retract." It also means "to humiliate oneself," as a person does who is made to eat his words. But this does not mean that *humble* is a cousin of *humiliate* (which stems from the Latin *humus*, "earth" or "ground"). Although people's estimation of one who eats humble pie may be low, it would be still lower if he had been humiliated because, etymologically, he would be flat on the ground.

## HUMORS

The ancient philosophers taught that a person's well-being depended on his having the proper proportions of the four *humors* (the Latin for liquids) in his body. The predominance of any one would affect the temper of the body and mind. An overabundance of blood (Latin *sanguis*) made a person ruddy-faced, cheerful, and optimistic. He therefore was said to be *sanguine*. An excess of yellow bile (*chole* in Greek) made him *choleric*—irascible and short-tempered. Too much *phlegm* (*phlegm* is the same word in Greek) induced apathy or a phlegmatic condition—he was sluggish, unexcitable. The fourth humor was black bile, from which came the word *bilious*. *Melancholia*, it was thought, came from a heavy proportion of *melan khole*, or black bile, now known to be a nonexistent liquid.

A proper balance of these humors determined a person's temperament. It made a compound called "good humor," which is what the ice cream vendor keeps saying.

## HYACINTH

A *hyacinth* is a bulbous plant with a terminal cluster of variously colored, fragrant flowers; its native habitat is the Mediterranean region. In the beauty of this lovely flower, however, lies a tragic story.

The son of the Spartan king Amyclas was a youth named *Hyacinthus*. He was so handsome that he was beloved by both Apollo (god of the sun) and Zephyrus (god of the west wind). Hyacinthus returned the love of Apollo, whereupon Zephyrus became insanely jealous. One day while Apollo was playing quoits with Hyacinthus, Zephyrus, far from the gentle soul he was supposed to be (a soft, warm breeze called a *zephyr* was named after him), caused a quoit tossed by Apollo to strike the lad's head. Hyacinthus died, and from his blood sprang the flower that bears his name. On the leaves appeared a legendary exclamation of grief: *AI, AI*.

Horticulturists reject this story on the ground that the original flower was a lily, gladiolus, or iris—not what is now called a *hyacinth*.

## HYGIENE

The English word *hygiene* can be traced to the name of the Greek goddess of health—*Hygeia*. As the daughter of Aesculapius, the god of medicine and healing, she was endowed with the power to ward off pestilence and to promote health. Symbolically, she is pictured holding a cup from which a serpent is drinking.

Another time-honored symbol bearing serpents is the *caduceus,* a herald's wand, which was carried by Hermes, the messenger of the gods, known to the Romans as Mercury. The caduceus was a staff made of an olive branch with two entwined serpents. When Mercury carried a caduceus, it had wings also, and with it Mercury could put to sleep anyone he chose.

The adoption of the snake as a medical emblem has been attributed to two beliefs: one, that snakes live eternally and are a sign of healing, as is evidenced by the shedding of their skin to renew themselves; the other, that snakes discover health-giving medicinal herbs. According to legend, a snake brought such herbs to Aesculapius, who, to show his gratitude, assumed the shape of a serpent. Perhaps the metaphor "He's a snake in the grass" is not so belittling after all, even though Vergil in *Ecologues* said: "Away from here, boys; a chill snake lurks in the grass."

## HYPOCRISY, HYPOCHONDRIA

There is a falseness in *hypocrisy* as there is in *hypochondria*. But each in a different way.

*Hypocrisy* means "insincerity." The word came from the Greek *hupocretes,* "one who plays a part." A hypocrite, the one guilty of hypocrisy, pretends either to feel what he does not feel or to be what he is not. In that falsity is a semblance of accuracy, for originally a hypocrite was an actor who assumed a role in a drama. Dr. Johnson said that, thespians aside, "a hypocrite puts on false character in order to conceal his weakness and to magnify his strength if any."

> The only vice that cannot be forgiven is hypocrisy. The repentance of a hypocrite is itself hypocrisy.
> —William Hazlitt, *Characteristics* No. 256

A hypochondriac is a person afflicted with a morbid depression of spirits because of a neurotic conviction that he is ill. His distress is genuine, and he is, in all likelihood, feeling real pain.

But what is not true is the seat of this malaise, as attributed by the Greeks who coined the word *hypochondria* (*hypo,* "under," and *chondros,* "the cartilage of the breastbone"). The ancient Greeks believed that melancholy arose from that part of the body because *melan,* a humor consisting of black bile, was secreted from that region. Science has proved that "melan khole" is a nonexistent substance, just as hypochondria is a nonexistent ailment.

## HYSTERICS

The male's ego in ancient Greece was as strong as contemporary man's. The Greek men, who prided themselves on their equanimity and self-control, decided that emotionalism was an affliction unique to women. They further decided that the source of female agitation must logically be caused by the malfunctioning of an organ possessed only by women—and that organ, they concluded, was the uterus, in Greek called *hustera*. From this notion was born the English word *hysterics*.

No longer, of course, are uncontrolled emotional states regarded as being within the sole province of women. Science has disproved the Greek thesis. Nowadays men who are wildly excited are said to be hysterical, even though there's not a womb among them. Which leaves no womb for argument.

# *J*

## IDIOT

Such derogatory remarks as "He's an idiot," "She acts like an imbecile," or "Peter looks like a moron" are far from uncommon. Although their intended meaning is the same (simply to downgrade someone), as technical terms they refer to people on different levels of intelligence.

The lowest on the measurable range of intelligence—the idiot—is completely nonfunctional. An idiot lacks ordinary powers and never develops beyond the mental age of three or four years. In ancient Greece, *idiotes,* from which the word *idiot* is a lineal descendant, meant "private people," referring to those who did not hold public office. Idiots were (and still are—in the eyes of some politicians) those not paid out of public coffers.

An *imbecile* has greater intelligence than an idiot, often attaining a mental age equivalent to that of a normal child of seven or eight years. Although of feeble mind, an imbecile can usually perform such personal functions as feeding and dressing himself. According to its literal meaning, an imbecile (Latin *in,* "without," and *bacillum,* "a small staff") is a person who needs support, for he is "without a walking stick." (The words *imbecile* and *bacterium* come from the same Latin source. A bacterium is shaped like a little rod; an imbecile uses one. Without a figurative cane for support, he is helpless.)

A *moron* (Greek, *moros,* "sluggish" or "foolish") is a dull or stupid person. The term was chosen by Dr. Henry H. Goddard in 1910 to designate the mildest form of mental deficiency. It was later adopted for use in this sense by the American Association for the Feeble-Minded. The mental age of morons is equivalent to that of a normal child of eight to twelve years, and their intelligence quotients are between 50 and 70. Many morons function well enough to perform simple tasks, and some are gainfully employed.

## IGNOMINIOUS

*Ignominious* means "disgraceful, dishonorable, contemptible." Its noun form, *ignominy,* is a combination of *i* (*in*) ("without") plus *nomen* ("name"), which signifies that one in disgrace is, literally, "without a name." He has lost his right to be recognized as "a somebody." But, according to Shakespeare's *Henry IV,* a person is not saddled with such dishonor after his death, as was said of Hotspur as he was lying in his grave: "Adieu, and take thy praise with thee to heaven! / Thy ignominy sleep with thee in the grave, / But not remember'd in thy epitaph." Hotspur's ignominy is not blazoned forth in his grave; only his fame is remembered.

## IGNORAMUS

*Ignoramus,* the first person plural of *ignorare* ("not to know"), was for many years an inscription used by a Grand Jury upon a bill of indictment meaning that no action can be taken. The return of the Grand Jury was, in other words, a "no bill" for lack of sufficient evidence to charge the defendant with a crime. An early seventeenth-century play titled *Ignoramus* popularized the term; the play's leading character, an incompetent lawyer, bore the same name. However, the word fell into disfavor when juries came to be called *ignoramus juries* (an *ignoramus* is a dunce). The term was so disparaging that a jury found sufficient evidence to indite a new phrase: "No true bill."

## IMMOLATE

The grinding teeth called *molars* are distantly related to grain, the word for which in Latin is *mola.* More closely related to grain is the English word *immolate,* which means "to sprinkle with ground meal in preparation for burning as a sacrifice."

In ancient days sacrifices to gods of fertility were common. The Romans paid homage to their grain-god by sprinkling meal on captives and then setting them ablaze, a ceremony they called *immolation.* Although such sacrificial rites have long been discontinued, the idea of self-sacrifice by immolation (setting oneself on fire) still persists, especially among some Asians. More often, the word *immolation* is now used in a figurative sense, as in the case of a pretty, young girl who abnegates worldly activities to enter God's service. She has immolated herself for the sake of her religion.

## IMPEDE

Two common English words that would not be recognized if employed literally are *impede* and *emancipate*. Yet their literal sense still makes sense, for it is what these words represent.

*Impede* means "to obstruct the way of" or "to block" (from Latin *impedire*, "to entangle," literally "to put the feet in shackles"). The verb consists of *-im* ("in") and *pes, pedis* ("foot"); hence an entanglement involving one's feet. The Roman police treated felons severely. To prevent escape, convicts were shackled with leg-irons. It may be said that running away certainly was "impeded." Incidentally, although both *impediment* and *impedimenta* were sired by the Latin singular noun *impedimentum* and both literally mean "that which impedes or encumbers progress," *impedimenta*, its plural form, refers to traveling equipment or baggage, the kind of supplies one fastens on the top of a station wagon before leaving for a vacation. Originally impedimenta were the supplies accompanying a Roman army.

To *emancipate* means "to free from restraint" or "to set free from servitude." In Roman times a purchaser of slaves laid his hand on them to symbolize possession. This act was called *mancipium* (Latin *manus*, "hand," plus *capio*, "take"), meaning "a taking by hand." Adding the prefix *e* ("away") gave English the word *emancipate*, meaning "to take away the hand." Once the "hand" was withdrawn, a slave became a freedman.

In sum, to *impede* is to entangle the feet; to *emancipate*, to withdraw the hand.

## INFANTRY

The poor foot-slogging soldier may well wonder why he is called an *infantryman*. Certainly the word *infantry* bears no relationship to feet, to walking, or to soldiering.

Although the several theories behind the evolution of this word differ, they are nevertheless somewhat related. The obvious English word within *infantry* is "infant." That word came from Latin *in* ("not") and *fans* ("speaking"), referring to a child not yet capable of speech. The Italians borrowed the word, spelled it *infante* and gave it the meaning "youngster." They then applied it to those who followed mounted knights on foot, those who were too inexperienced to become members of the cavalry. These unqualified soldiers came to be called, collectively, *infanteria;* whence the English *infantry*.

Another version, Spanish in origin, began with the word *Infante* (same spelling as the Italian spelling except it is capitalized), which, except for the Crown Prince, was the designation for a son of the sovereign of Spain. It is said that when a king of Spain was captured by the Moors, the Infante collected a group of patriots to rescue him. The men were successful; the Infante was extolled for his ingenuity; and his countrymen were honored by being named after the Infante—*infanteria*.

## INFARCTION

Everyone will agree that a heart ailment like a myocardial infarction (a disease of the muscle tissue of the heart caused by an obstruction that interferes with the circulation of the blood) is no laughing matter. And yet *infarction,* which means "obstruction," was sired by the same ancestor that bore the word *farce,* "a low comedy." Their common Latin forebear was the verb *farcire,* "to stuff."

The obstruction that *infarction* denotes is caused by "a stuffing" that prevents local circulation. A *farce* is also stuffed, but with jokes. Originally it was an interlude (a comical diversion to provide time to change scenery and to allow the performers to rest) that was crammed or stuffed in between the acts of a serious drama. Today a farce may still be something filled with broad humor, but its idiomatic sense has been extended to embrace a ridiculous situation or an empty show, like a party or ceremony that does not come off well.

Another kind of stuffing, but one from a different lineage, is *bombast,* from Old French *bombace,* which means "cotton padding." A *bombast* is inflated language (well padded) or a grandiloquent speech. A *bombastic* person, figuratively, is full of "hot air"—or, more precisely put, "filled with cotton padding."

## INFLUENCE, INFLUENZA

*Influence* is the intangible power of persons or things to affect other persons or things. It may be exercised properly or improperly, for the word contains no sense of goodness or badness. What it stands for is best exemplified by its synonyms—*power, control, sway, authority, supremacy.* From it has come the name of the disease *influenza,* and that is bad—not the name, of course, but the disease, which sometimes reached epidemic proportions. But to start at the beginning.

The Romans were governed, to a good extent, by astrological convictions. Astrologers, while predicting the course of human events through their study of celestial bodies, would consider the influence of the stars to determine their effect on the affairs of men. At that time *influence* meant "a flowing in," from Latin *in,* "in," and *fluere,* "to flow." Later the descendants of the Romans borrowed the word, continued its meaning, but gave it an Italian twist and called it *influenza.* However, when epidemics struck the Italian people, they blamed the disease on the *influenza* of heavenly bodies. Later the disease itself was given that name, which the English language adopted whole; and, from Medieval Latin *influentia* (that most important word meaning "to have the power to produce an effect without using force") came *influence.*

## INVESTIGATE

Behold Sherlock Holmes peering at the ground through a large, round magnifying glass. He has, of course, recently been commissioned to solve a heinous crime and has just now begun his investigation with a systematic examination of all available evidence. Peerless detective that he is, he knows where to begin—with footprints. (Today's detectives who first examine fingerprints may be starting at the wrong end.) *Vestigium,* from which the word *investigate* was derived, means "footprint" and *investigare,* "to track." Logically, therefore, an investigation should begin at the bottom of things, with footprints. Another

English word from the same source is *vestige,* "a visible trace," which may be only a part of a footprint, or even less.

Other *vest* words, like *vested, vestment,* and *vest-pocket,* come from the Latin *vestire,* "to dress." But not *vestal.* Vestal virgins were the caretakers of the sacred fire in the temple that honored Vesta, the Roman goddess of the hearth. They were not vested.

## JADE

Jade is a beautiful and costly gemstone. A person who looks jaded should therefore look attractive—and rich. But this is not so. The meaning of *jaded*, quite oppositely, is "worn out" or "dulled by excess." In its common-speech sense the adjective *jaded* was founded on an Icelandic noun, *jalda*, "a mare." English sailors who first visited this semifrozen country were appalled by the sight of the horses found there. The poor creatures were gaunt, underfed, and overworked. By the time the Icelandic word for horse, *jalda*, reached England, it was pronounced "jaded" and came to describe any broken-down or worthless horse, and, by extension, any person who looked worn out by fatigue or whose tastes had been exhausted by excess.

In the sixteenth century, Spanish explorers were introduced to a curious light green stone and told of its healing powers, especially its power to cure colic. The Spaniards called the stone *piedra de ijada*, "stone for curing pains in the side." From *ijada* ("flank") has come the term *jade*. Many Europeans sought it as a magical curative; others wore it merely as an ornament. The word is generic. The scientific name for Burmese jade, a rare mineral, is *jadeite*, a coinage by the French scientist Damour in 1863. Another, but a less precious, variety is *nephrite*. This stone, although found mostly in China, took on a Greek name, *nephros*, meaning "kidney," for it, too, was supposed to have curative powers—to remedy kidney ailments. The medical term for a kidney ailment is *nephritis*, a compound of *nephros* and *-itis*, "inflammation." Stones that form in a kidney are not nephrite or other gems, of course, even though the surgeon's bill for removing them is almost as costly as digging out the real thing.

149

# JAZZ

One surmise concerning the origin of the word *jazz* is that it came from *jaiza,* which was, among the natives of West Africa, a common term meaning "rumble of distant guns." Another, that it was a Creole word meaning "speed up" or "hurry." If so, it was nurtured in Louisiana. Some authorities, however, look to a different source. They ascribe its origin to a corruption of *Chas.,* an abbreviation for *Charles.* This last stemmed from the famous invitation to "come on an' hear, Alexander's Ragtime Band." Alexander's first name was Charles, but everyone called him Chazz. As the musical tempo of his band became more "up-beat," the audience would holler, "Come on, Chazz," pronounced *Jazz;* whence the name for this form of sophisticated, popular music. According to a third story, *jazz* entered American lingo as a hard-sounding *jass* from "jass house" ("a bawdy house"), its common name in New Orleans. At the beginning of this century black musicians played in these brothels, continuing until prostitution was outlawed during World War I. The slangy sexual sense of *jazz,* "to copulate," can find its roots in this source.

Just as *jazz* may be a verbal corruption of *Chazz* or *jass,* so it is thought that *zany* came from Italian *Giovanni,* "John." Its diminutive form was *Gianni,* which was expressed in dialect *Zanni,* and was a pet name for *Giovanni* among the Venetians. *Zany* came to be applied to a type of clown in an Italian farce who always served as a stooge, cutting into his partner's tumbles or interrupting his quips. From this practice of messing things up evolved the present sense of *zany*—"buffoon" or "awkward fool."

# JEANS

*See* DENIM

# JEEP

One who says the *veep* will arrive shortly is, of course, referring to the vice president—the V. P. Sounding those two letters as one syllable comes out *veep.*

The same shortening process has created the word *jeep,* a contraction of g-p. This came about through the military, which in 1937 sought a basic vehicle to serve the army's general needs. An all-purpose vehicle was built and designated "g.p." for "general purpose." Like the sound of the contracted v.p., g.p. became *geep,* or *jeep.* Possibly influenced by Elzie C. Segar's friendly character "Eugene the Jeep" in the comic strip "Popeye," the spelling for the car become *Jeep,* which is the sound the fanciful animal in the cartoon made: Jeep! Jeep!

## JINX

Since early times people have naturally tried to avoid anything that brings bad luck. The ancient Romans thought that the source of calamities lay in a bird, called *iynx,* which had occult powers. The *iynx,* which literally means "the shouting bird," was known for its strident noises and its twisted neck. It eventually came to be called the *wrynecked woodpecker,* but its older name spelled *jynx* and then *jinx* was assimilated into English to mean "a charm" or "a spell."

Many athletes and entertainers in America, fearful of being saddled with bad luck, have taken pains to outwit the demonic jinx. They do this by following self-imposed rituals and strategies, from touching second base on the way to the dugout, to opening doors only with the left hand (Christy Mathewson in *Pitching in a Pinch,* written in 1912, said: "A jinx is something which brings bad luck to a ballplayer"). They should be careful, however, not to confuse *jinx* with *jinks,* "wild ideas" or "frolics." Incidentally, the word *jinks,* which is always preceded by the adjective "high," is of unknown origin.

## JOHN BULL

The popular personification for England (and the English people) is *John Bull,* the counterpart of the American *Uncle Sam.* This sobriquet, from the pen of John Arbuthnot, a physician and man of letters, first appeared in 1712 in an allegorical satire on the bloody, foolish war over the succcession to the Spanish throne that began in 1701 and lasted until 1714 and involved, among others, Spain, France, England, and Austria. In 1727, the witty Scottish doctor's work was republished under the title

*History of John Bull,* in which John Bull was depicted as a blunt, hot-tempered farmer, somewhat pigheaded, but, with it all, honest and plain-dealing. Other countries were personified with similar names—the Frenchman, Lewis Baboon; the Dutchman, Nicholas Frog; and so forth.

The English have found the characterization of John Bull so much to their liking that they have adopted a drawing of it by Sir Francis Carruthers Gould as the prototype of the English people. It pictures an Englishman as sporting a vest that looks like a British flag peeping out from a cutaway coat over britches and boots. John Bull looks British, all right, and that's no bull.

## JUBILEE

A *jubilee,* strictly speaking, is a fiftieth anniversary. But the word *jubilee* has come to mean any special, happy anniversary. A married couple may celebrate a silver jubilee in the twenty-fifth year of their marraige, a golden jubilee in the fiftieth, and a diamond jubilee in the sixtieth.

The word *jubilee* originated in the Bible. Although the present and past meanings of *jubilee* are unrelated, they have an indirect connection. In Hebrew a ram's horn, called a *yōbhēl,* was used to trumpet the emancipation of all slaves, which under ancient Hebraic law occurred every fifty years: "And ye shall hallow the fiftieth year, and proclaim liberty throughout all the land unto all the inhabitants thereof: it shall be a jubilee unto you"—Leviticus 25:10. The name given the event—*jubilee*—was taken from the word for a ram's horn.

The term has been borrowed into many languages, beginning with the ancient Greeks and Romans, for no other language has a word with this precise signification. Hebrew *jubilee* and Latin *jubilare* ("to raise a joyful shout"), the parent of English *jubilant* (which means "joyful") and *jubilation* ("exultation" or "loud rejoicing"), were merely coincidentally related.

## JUNKET

It may not be easy to believe, but the junkets taken by politicians at public expense have something in common with cream cheese. In distant times Latin *juncus* referred to rushes, the kind that baskets were made from. Many years later the Italians prepared a cream cheese with spice that they called *giuncata* because it was marketed in baskets made of junk or bullrushes. The name of the product was taken directly from the name of the container. Then the name was applied to a dessert, a sweet, custardlike flavored milk curdled with rennet. (In Shakespeare's *Taming of the Shrew* Baptista says, "You know there wants no junkets at the feast.") Thereafter, it took on the meaning of the feast itself or a picnic. It also became a verb. Swift used it in "To feast secretly; to make entertainments by stealth. Whatever good bits you can pilfer in the day, save them to junket with your fellow servants at night." The noun *junket*, apart from its use for designating a dessert, today more often refers to a pleasure excursion, which may be a trip made by public officials—at public expense—perhaps the dessert that sweetens their salary.

## KALEIDOSCOPE

A *kaleidoscope* is a tubular instrument containing bits of colored glass that appear to change shape as the tube is rotated. The word is a beautiful combination of Greek forms; in fact, the Greek word for "beautiful" is incorporated within it. But that is getting ahead of the story.

In 1817 Dr. David Breuster invented a toy which he called *kaleidoscope*. He selected three Greek words that when combined had a literal meaning of "observer of beautiful forms." The words were *kalos* ("beautiful"), *eidos* ("form"), and *skopos* ("watcher").

The term has come into prominent use in its figurative sense; namely, a changing scene—that which subtly shifts color, shape, or mood. Lord Macaulay once wrote: "The mind of Petrarch was a kaleidoscope."

## KANGAROO

*See* MISTRANSLATIONS

## KIBITZER

Two words borrowed into English, *savvy* from Spanish and *kibitzer* from Yiddish, are well known and, in general, equally well accepted. Both are commonly used in colloquial speech, although *savvy* has not risen above the dictionary designation of slang, and *kibitzer* is at best listed as informal.

*Savvy* (sometimes spelled *savvey*) means "to understand," "to grasp the meaning of." It is a corruption of Spanish *sabe*— ¿*sabe (usted)?* "Do you know?"—from *saber*, "to know" (from Vulgar Latin *sapere*, "be wise," "be knowing"—or from French *savez (vous)?* "Do you know?"). The word is used today as in "Street kids have a lot of *savvy*."

A *kibitzer*, as every cardplayer can testify, is an onlooker who always knows what should be done. He's so sure he can do it better that he's quick with unwanted advice. Nowadays the meaning of *kibitzer* has been extended so far that it may be used of any person who meddles in someone else's affairs, a so-called back-seat driver.

If a kibitzer, asked how he knows so much, replied "a little bird told me," he would be jesting, of course, yet, by association, not entirely wrong, for the word *kibitzer* came from German *Kiebitz,* the name of a bird variously known as plover, lapwing, and peewit. Supposedly *Kiebitz* was imitative of the bird's shrill call. This means that someone annoyed by a kibitzer can tell him to shut up because his advice is "for the birds."

# KIDNAP

To *kidnap* is to seize and hold someone against his will, usually a child and usually for ransom. The word *kidnaping* (it may be spelled with two *p*'s) probably originated, according to the *OED,* among a class of people that followed the practice of kidnapping. It was not uncommon for thieves during the seventeenth century "to steal children and sell them as indentured servants for the American colonies." Bunyan wrote in 1684, "Thou practices the craft of a kidnapper, thou gatherest up Women, and Children, and carriest them into a strange Countrey." And, as printed in the *London Gazette* in 1688: "John Dykes . . . convicted of Kidnapping or Enticing away, His Majesty's Subjects, to go Servants into the Foreign Plantations."

A *kid* is a young goat. The resemblance of the German word for "child," which is *Kind,* may have led to the slang sense of *kid* as "a child." The second element in *kidnap* is cognate with Swedish *nappa,* and Danish *nappe,* "to seize," "to grasp." In the seventeenth century the Scandinavian terms were corrupted to *nab,* slang for "to grab hold of," "to snatch away." It is still used in that sense today, but with the added sense "to arrest," as a detective does who apprehends a criminal.

## L

## LACKADAISICAL

The word *lackadaisical* expresses a sense of listlessness.
Where it came from has never been established, but possibly
it stemmed from "lackaday," an old-time common interjection
of unhappiness or futility, which later became "alackaday."
(Shakespeare used the phrase "alack the day.") A person feeling
that the day was "alackaday" (it just as well had never come)
came to be regarded as indifferent to time; whence *lackadaisical*.
Another thought, that lackadaisical was a malformed combination of "alack and alas," an expression of sorrow, is justified,
it would seem, only if someone were complaining about the
lack of a lass.

## LACONIC

The Laconians were noted for their blunt brief speech.
They were people of few words, even when conveying important messages. A notable example of their parsimonious language is the answer they gave Philip of Macedon when he
threatened to invade their capital, Sparta. To the announcement
of the enemies' herald, "If we come to your city, we will raze
it to the ground," the reply of the Spartan leader was a single
word: "If."

And that is, in today's language, *laconic,* an adjective that
means "concise, succinct."

Laconia's capital, Sparta, has also contributed its name to
the English language as an adjective, Spartan, which reflects
the characteristics attributed to its inhabitants—self-discipline
and fortitude. Spartans lived with only bare necessities and
uncomplainingly endured severe hardships. Their bravery was
so respected and feared that they never found it necessary to
surround their city with walls.

## LADY, LORD

Traditionally, the man of the house brought home "the bacon"—that is, money to buy the household needs. The woman's duty was to make the bread that went with "the bacon." Long ago women were kneaders of bread—*hlaf* in Old English, "loaf," means "bread" and *dige* (prounced *dah*) means "kneader," from which combination emerged the term *ladah,* now pronounced *lady.* The breadmaker became the mistress of the house; the breadwinner, the master, the lord of the house (*lord* derives from Old English *hlafweard*—*hlaf,* "loaf," and *weard,* "keeper," literally "loaf keeper").

To buy bread or dough, one needs money. The word *money* arrived in English ultimately from Latin *monere,* "to warn." It can still be seen, in part, in the English word *admonition,* "a warning," and *monitor,* "one who admonishes." Its forebear was *Moneta,* an epithet of Juno, the goddess who gave warnings and guarded the finances. At her temple was established the first Roman mint where money was made, and through her name came the English words *money* and *monetary* and also their coining cousin, *mint.*

## LAMPOON

A *lampoon* is a satirical writing directed against a person, usually attacking or ridiculing him. It may be lighthearted or, quite oppositely, virulent or scurrilous. It may even combine humor and abuse. Prominent persons have been lampooned jocularly, but with serious overtones, at the famous Gridiron Dinners.

Teetotalers and lampoons do not go together, at least according to the latter word's original source, for a lampoon was a satirical, often scatalogical, drinking song popular during the seventeenth and eighteenth centuries. The word itself came from Old French *lampons* (an imperative form of *lamper,* "to guzzle"), and meaning "Let us drink," the closing refrain of these scandalous poems and songs.

## LEFT

*See* RIGHT

# LEGEND

> A myth is a pure and absolute imagination; a legend has a basis
> in fact, but amplifies, abridges, or modifies that basis at pleasure.
> —Rawlinson, *Historic Evidences*

*Legends* in today's English are stories which have come down from the past and which many people have believed, such as the tales of King Arthur and his knights of the Round Table. But that is not what a legend was centuries ago. At that time a legend was something to be read as part of the divine service, like the life of a saint or a narrative on the life of a martyr. More particularly, what was read was called *legenda.* In Latin, *legere* means "to read." Its gerundive form, literally "things to be read," is *legenda.* Since legends were intended to glorify, many of them were embellished with exaggerations and untruths. Hence they have come to be considered fanciful rather than factual.

In the seventeenth century the inscription on a coin was named a *legend.* On American coins one is "E pluribus unum"; another, "In God we trust." From this designation the sense of *legend* spread to encompass "an explanatory list of symbols appearing on a map or chart." It still refers to things to be read.

# LEOPARD

No one visiting a zoo will see a sign marked *pard,* for that is an archaic word for *panther.* (In Greek, the name for a male panther was *pardos.*) Allusions to pards were not infrequent in the literature of yesteryear. In the famous soliloquy in *As You Like It* that begins, "All the world's a stage," *pard* appears in one of the parts that men play—"Then a soldier, / Full of strange oaths and bearded like the pard."

*Leopards* were so named because at one time they were believed to be a hybrid between a lion and a pard. The Greeks called them *leopardos,* from *leon (leo),* "lion," and *pardos,* "pard." Although naturalists have determined that a leopard is a true species (not a cross-breeding between a lion and a tiger or a panther), it was thought wise to continue the mistaken name because it had become firmly fixed in science and literature.

Modern English adopted the name *leopard,* slightly altering its original spelling.

Today when one means to say it's impossible to change innate traits or long-acquired customs, the way he may put it, to be more graphic, is "a leopard doesn't change its spots." That is an ancient proverb referring to the rhetorical question posed in Jeremiah 13:23: "Can the blacke More change his skin, or the leopard his spottes?" The answer is no. The leopard can't even change its name.

## LEOTARD

*See* ACROBAT

## LESBIANISM

Those who maintain that there are two basic classifications for sexual deviation—homosexual and lesbian—are confusing the Latin *homo* ("man") with the Greek *homo* ("same"). *Homosexuality* is sexual relationship with another person of the same sex, since the *homo* part in that word comes from the Greek.

The story behind the word *lesbianism* began in the earlier half of the sixth century B.C. On an island in the Aegean Sea lived the Greek poetess Sappho, who became the leader of women whose behavior was characterized by strong homosexual feelings. The name given this manifestation, lesbianism (homosexuality between women), was taken from the name of the island, Lesbos.

According to another version, a poem written by Sappho pleaded with Aphrodite to help her arouse ardor in a certain woman—whence the belief in Sappho's homosexuality. Sappho's alleged lesbianism, it may be added, has never been satisfactorily established in the minds of many people. Unquestionably she was a Lesbian by birth, but not necessarily a lesbian by disposition.

## LETHARGY

The term *lethargy* was founded in Greek mythology. Hades, the land of the dead, was fed by five rivers, one of which was

*Lethe.* In this river the spirits immersed themselves to forget their former early life. In *Paradise Lost*, Milton described the river thus: "Far off from these, a slow and silent stream, / Lethe, the River of Oblivion, rolls / Her wat'ry labyrinth, whereof who drinks / Forthwith his former state and being forgets." The word for oblivion in Greek is *lethe;* for forgetfulness, *lethargos.* From the latter evolved the modern word *lethargy,* "a state of lassitude or apathy."

## LETTUCE

See **GALAXY**

## LIEUTENANT

See **MILITARY TITLES**

## LILLIPUTIAN

"The Lilliputian Shop" is probably a store that sells clothing for children. In other uses of *lilliputian* the reference is to a very small person or, disparagingly, to a person of little intelligence or importance.

Jonathan Swift, in 1726, coined the word *Lilliput* as the name of an imaginary country, which he described in his celebrated satire, *Gulliver's Travels.* The inhabitants of Lilliput were pygmies, no more than six inches tall (or is it "six inches short"?)—to whom Lemuel Gulliver looked like a giant.

The book contained a word that was the opposite number to *lilliputian*—*brobdingnag.* On another voyage, Gulliver was set ashore on the island of Brobdingnag, whose inhabitants were as tall as giants. They were "like steeple spires, and they covered 10 yards with every step." To those people, Gulliver looked lilliputian, as small as a pigmy. He seemed, in the words of the book, "nor half so big as a round little worm plucked from the lazy finger of a maid." However, *brobdingnag,* a synonym for colossal or huge, has had little acceptance, probably because no one can pronounce it.

## LITTER

It is hard to believe that any English word could have more disparate meanings than the word *litter*. A *litter* is a portable bed, a condition of disorder, a brood of young. Etymologically a "bed" is easily associated with *litter* because it comes from French *litière*, from Latin *lectus*, and both of these ancestors meant "bed." During ancient times elaborate litters were used to carry queens or to transport sick nobles. In Shakespeare's *King John*, the king said, "To my litter straight; / Weakness possesseth me."

Oftentimes persons found that the only bed available consisted of a pile of hay; hence *litter* came to mean "bedding of strewn straw" (*strewn*, past participle of *strew*, "to scatter," is of unknown ancestry but is probably related to *straw*). Because this bed was carelessly put together—thrown together, so to speak—a further sense evolved of "rubbish or objects so worthless as to be indifferently or negligently scattered about."

When *litter* means "brood," its root can be found in the Icelandic *lattr*, referring to a "breeding place" or meaning "born at the same time." Although commonly employed of kittens and puppies, the word is not exclusively in their domain. In *King Henry IV*, Shakespeare put these words in Falstaff's mouth: "I do here walk before thee like a sow that hath overwhelmed all her litter but one."

## LOVE

Everyone knows about love—it's what makes the world go round. *Round* and *love* are also associated in other ways.

In tennis, for example, *love* means "nothing." If the score in a game stands at 40–love, the player with love has no score. There *love* means "zero" (a round number) or, in the vernacular, "a goose-egg." And that's what "no score" originally meant— an egg, which in French is *l'oeuf*. When the English imported the game of tennis, the method of scoring came with it. *L'oeuf* to the English sounded like "love" and no one bothered to unscramble it. Except for one thing. Some word-followers believe that, although this derivation is an ingenious conjecture, it is nevertheless nothing more than folk etymology. (A theory without much support is that *love*, meaning "nothing," origi-

nated in the expression "play for money or play for love"—
that is, for money or for nothing, which makes love as much a
zero as it is in tennis.)

Another puzzling tennis term is "let ball," sometimes mistakenly but logically rendered "net ball." A let ball on its way
to the opponent's court strikes the net, and is therefore an
invalid serve. The ball has been hindered by touching the top
of the net. Old English *letten,* meaning "to hinder," is where
the tennis term started. The phrase in which this form of *let* is
used most commonly is "without let or hindrance," which really
says the same thing twice. And which is like the let ball, since
the server is given another shot.

## LUKEWARM

Saying the tea is "lukewarm" is like saying the temperature
is moderately temperate. *Temperate* (from the past participle of
Latin *temperare,* "to moderate") means, as to climate, "neither
hot nor cold," "mild." Hence the redundancy of "moderately
temperate."

On the other hand, *lukewarm,* despite its seeming redundancy, is an entrenched word in the English language and in
good standing with respected writers. The meaning of *warm* is
clear. *Luke,* from Middle English *louke,* meaning "tepid," was
adopted almost whole from Dutch *leuk. Tepid* is "barely warm,"
and therein lies the concern of some linguists that *lukewarm*
repeats itself in each syllable. Early writers did not agree on
the precise meaning of *lukewarm.* In Wyclif's 1388 translation
of *Revelation,* appeared the following: "Thou art lewk, neither
cold, neither hot," which defined *tepid.* But in 1398 Trevisa in
*Barth De P.R.* wrote, "The broth . . . comfortyth the teeth: yf it
be luke warm hote holde in the mouth." And that's warmer
than tepid.

The high school story of yesteryear that made the rounds
about *lukewarm* is that a bather came rushing onto the beach
early in the morning and asked the lone person at the water's
edge, "How's the water?" The reply was "lukewarm." The
bather dashed in, only to jump right back again, hollering, "It's
freezing. What's the idea saying it's lukewarm?" The beach
sitter, looking chastened, muttered, "By me it luke warm."

## LUNACY

Human beings have learned to fear many things. Fortunately, some fears have come to be disregarded as mere superstitions; others have been dissipated by enlightened disbelief.

One former serious concern was that exposure to the moon affects the mind. People were admonished not to sleep with the moon shining in their faces lest they become moonstruck and daft. The moon's phases, which determined states of madness (lunatics became more frenzied with the waxing of the moon), were controlled by Luna, the Roman moon goddess. (From her name have come the words *lunacy* and *lunatic.*)

Another example, but one that seems more sensible, centers on the word *malaria,* a combination of Italian *mala,* "bad," and *aria,* "air." The ancients believed that this dread disease could be contracted by breathing bad air from marshlands; they accordingly pitched their tents away from swamps. Although the reasoning happened not to be valid (malaria is transmitted by the anopheles mosquito), the advice was good, for fetid air arising from marshes could lead to other discomforts and ailments.

## LYNCH

The word lynching, which designates the practice of executing by hanging, and without a trial by a properly constituted court, has been attributed to several sources.

The most likely credit (if *credit* is the right word) is given to Charles Lynch, a wealthy Virginia planter and a justice of the peace, who decided, toward the end of the eighteenth century, to expedite due process of law by taking the law into his own hands, especially when it concerned the punishment of those loyal to the British throne during the American Revolution. His method dispatched them quickly.

A second theory is that another Virginian, Captain William Lynch, held a similar belief that corporal punishment—quick, clean, inexpensive—should be meted out upon the lawless, even those who were merely undesirable. They did not deserve the niceties of a legal trial but, according to a compact drawn up with his neighbors, should receive such punishment "as to us shall seem adequate to the crime committed."

Incidentally, Edgar Allen Poe, in an editorial on the law of lynching, published in an 1836 newspaper, attributed the origin of the word *lynch* to that same Captain William Lynch and cited in full Lynch's declaration that he and his neighbors would hereafter act as the sole judges and executioners. Any appeal the condemned cared to make would have to be made somewhere other than on Earth.

A third belief is that this method of putting to death originated in North Carolina at Lynch Creek, where supposedly a bizarre form of trial and execution was conducted on the corpse of a young man who had already been hanged, the thought being to justify the deed post facto. The executioners were really hanging this one on a dead man.

# M

## MACADAM

> LUCIFER: I should like to Macadamize the world
> The road to Hell wants mending!
> —Philip James Bailey, *Festus*

Americans can be thankful for the improved roads on which they travel to a man who was thrown out of this country because he supported the wrong side in the Revolution. Paved roads are known as *macadam* after their inventor, John L. MacAdam (1756–1836), whose name has a variant spelling, McAdam.

On his return to Scotland, his native land, MacAdam was appalled by the condition of its roads. They were of rubble granite so full of holes that the lives of the horses that trod on them were shortened; after a heavy rain the roads were a virtual morass and all but impassable. MacAdam conceived the idea of laying down a base of broken stones to be ground down by the pressure of traffic. He also recommended the drainage of roads by raising them above the adjacent grounds and making them convex instead of concave. Once MacAdam was entrusted with the reconstruction of some roads, his inventiveness was almost immediately established, and he was given authority to supervise the improvement of all the main British highways. Which is what MacAdam did for the rest of his life.

## MAGAZINE

*See* **BOOK**

## MAJOR

*See* **MILITARY TITLES**

# MALAPROPISM

*Malapropism* is the ludicrous confusion of words, especially those having similar sounds but different meanings.

Richard Sheridan, who in 1775 wrote *The Rivals,* coined the term *malapropism* from the French *mal à propos,* which means "unsuitable" or "out of place." An endearing character in this play, Mrs. Malaprop, enjoyed impressing her friends with elegant words, which, unfortunately for her, she was constantly misusing. She would warn, "Don't attempt to extirpate yourself from that matter. . . ." Or say, "I would by no means wish a daughter of mine to be a progeny of learning." She spoke of "supercilious knowledge" and "contagious countries." One of her most famous misapplications was "She's as headstrong as an allegory on the banks of the Nile." Today's Mr. Malaprop is Archie Bunker. He calls a specialist in female illness "a groin-ologist."

# MALARIA

*See* LUNACY

# MAMMOTH

The Barnum & Bailey spectacle is a mammoth production and the Dallas Cowboys have a mammoth stadium—that is, gigantic. *Mammoth* currently is used as an English adjective to mean "immense" or "of very great size." But that is not what the word meant initially, and English is not where the word originated.

The Russians contributed the term *mammoth* to the world. It referred to a large elephant, one with a hairy coat and very large upcurved tusks, a species now extinct. The forebear of *mammoth* is Tatar *mamma,* which means "earth." The evolution of this sense is attributed to the finding by Russian peasants of the remains of these Pliestocene elephants buried in the earth. The natives assumed that since the animals' remains were found in the ground, they must have been burrowing animals, like moles. Hence from *mamma,* meaning "earth" came *mammoth.*

Which makes one wonder whether the phrase "mother earth" is related to all this in any way. *Mamma,* the term used by children in many languages to signify *mother*, means "earth" as well as "mother" in Russian. Or is this merely a coincidence? No one knows. Etymologists have not made this connection. The word *earth* can be traced to Greek *eraze*, meaning "to the ground," and then to Old English *eorthe* and Medieval English *erthe*.

## MANURE

Etymologically there's no reason to isolate a refined word like *manure* in the backyard. According to its original sense, it should be a proud part of everyone's life, for its genesis can be found in the Latin *manu operari*, "to work by hand." Farmers spent much time tilling the soil, and this was, during these earlier days, constant handwork (manual labor), especially the fertilizing, which required a mixing by hand. The genteelists who objected to the word *dung*, the excrement of animals, were responsible for its euphemistic displacement with the more refined *manure*.

Later even *manure* became objectionable to the squeamish. They preferred *fertilizer*. One may wonder when all this will stop. According to a famous story about Harry S Truman, the President was explaining that farming meant manure, manure, manure, and more manure. At which point a prim-looking lady said to the President's wife: "You should teach Harry to say 'fertilizer,' not 'manure'." Bess shook her head and sighed, "You don't know how long it took me to get him to say 'manure.'"

## MARATHON

In everyday usage a *marathon* is either any physical activity that goes on at great length or any test of endurance. In fact, the American language, under the misconception that *-thon* means "endurance" or "long duration," has acquired many words simply by attaching that ending. Now there are *talkathons*, *telethons*, *danceathons*, and *walkathons*. No one has as yet come up with *workathon*.

Primarily a marathon is a footrace that, to be exact, covers 26 miles 385 yards (about 42.2 kilometers). The word *marathon* originally did not signify a race; rather, it was the name of the town from which the Greek messenger Phidippides ran to Athens in 490 B.C. to announce to his countrymen their great victory over the Persians. It is reported that upon his arrival, he gasped: "Rejoice! We conquered!" then fell dead from exhaustion.

The Olympic Games conducted in ancient Greece did not include a distance race. That outstanding feature was adopted in 1896 to commemorate the famous run from Marathon to Athens. Appropriately, the victor of the first marathon was a Greek, Spyros Louis.

## MARMALADE

Many words and phrases can credit their acceptance to the foibles of folk etymology, as apocryphal as Aladdin's lamp.

One such is *marmalade*. It was said that when Mary Queen of Scots was out of sorts, she would refuse to eat. The only food that could tempt her was a conserve of oranges, for which she had an inordinate fondness. Hence the name of this jam after the Queen's indisposition: *Marie malade* ("sick Mary"), which (omitting the second syllable) became *marmalade*. (The true story behind the word *marmalade* is that its original ancestor, the Latin *melimelum*, meaning "sweet apple," traveled through various tongues, landing in Portugal, where it became *marmelada*. English borrowed it and switched the final *a* with the middle *e*.)

## MAROON

The verb *maroon*, meaning "to put ashore on a desolate island" (a practice common among pirates and buccaneers), evolved strangely from the word applied to fugitive slaves who hid in the woods or roamed the desert islands. A runaway slave was called a *maroon* (a person left to fend for himself with the maroons was therefore said to be *marooned*). *Maroon* is a shortened form of *cimarron*, which in Spanish means "wild." The basis for that word is the Spanish *cima*, meaning "top" (from Latin *cyma*, "young cabbage sprout"), since young sprouts are always on top. Spaniards considered dwellers on mountaintops wild people; whence *cimarron*.

The color *maroon* (same spelling), a brownish crimson, came from the French *marron*, "a chestnut," which is a dark and shiny reddish brown. Perhaps it, in turn, originated in the Hebrew word for "chestnut," *armon*, which would make it an old chestnut.

## MARSHAL

*See* CONSTABLE

## MARTINET

Jean Martinet gave his name, although unwittingly, to the English language as a synonym for a strict disciplinarian.

During the reign of the Sun King, Louis XIV, the Marquis of Martinet was an inspector general of infantry. He was a punctilious drillmaster who instituted such a rigid set of standards that his soldiers became a model unit in battle. Although he was thoroughly disliked by his men because of his demanding system of drill, it is said that he helped make the French army the best in Europe. During the siege of Duisberg in 1672 Martinet was killed by a shot from his own artillery. Whether the shot was fired at him accidentally or intentionally has not been established. But certainly his name has been retained intentionally, for it can be found in any English dictionary today as an eponym for taskmaster, a person who demands uncompromising obedience, an absolute adherence to the rules.

## MASOCHISM

*See* SADISM

## MAUDLIN

*Maudlin* means "sickly sentimental" or "overemotional." A person who whines or cries easily and too much is said to be maudlin. If he drinks too much and goes on a crying jag, he's also maudlin.

The word *maudlin* derives from the last name of Mary Magdalene, a prostitute believed to have wept while repenting before Jesus. Early artists conventionally painted her as a weeping penitent with red eyes and sometimes with a red nose, too. Her name traveled through the centuries and through several countries, arriving finally with its present meaning and spelling—*maudlin*.

Both Oxford and Cambridge have a college named after Magdalene, but the former spells it with no final *e* (Magdalen College). Regardless, both institutions are pronounced alike— Maudlin.

## MAUSOLEUM

*Mausolus*, a satrap of Caria, was the independent ruler of a part of the Persian kingdom. He had illusions of controlling larger territories, especially certain Greek islands which he coveted. To this end he engineered a successful coup, after first inducing the Greek allies to turn against Greece.

In 353 B.C. Mausolus died. His grief-stricken widow, Artemisia, erected at Halicarnassus a sepulchral monument in which to bury his ashes. His tomb was so vast and splendid that it came to be accounted one of the *Seven Wonders of the Ancient World.* The memorial reached over a hundred feet high and contained statuary of Mausolus and his wife, who followed him in death a few years later. Parts of this structure were brought to England by Sir Charles Newton in 1859 and are now on display in the British Museum.

The Romans adopted the word *mausoleum* from the Greek *mausoleion,* which referred only to the tomb of Mausolus. The word passed from Latin into English and came to mean "any large and stately tomb, or the building in which it is housed." In everyday speech a dark and gloomy structure is called a *mausoleum.*

In contradistinction to a *mausoleum,* an imposing monument enshrining the dead body itself, a *cenotaph,* according to Brewer, is an empty tomb, a monument or tablet to the memory of a person whose body is buried elsewhere. The most noteworthy cenotaph is in Whitehall in London. Erected in 1920 in memory of soldiers killed in World War I, it has become a memorial for peace celebrations. From Greek *kenotaphion,* "empty tomb" (*kenos,* "empty," plus *taphos,* "tomb") came, in order, Latin *cenotaphium,* French *cenotaphe,* and the present English derivative.

## MAVERICK

A maverick, in general usage, is a person independent of party labels. He is affiliated with no group, never having joined one or else having left it to pursue his own unorthodox ways.

The word *maverick* came from the name of a man who had no reason to expect that his name would be immortalized. Samuel A. Maverick, a Texas banker, who lived in the mid-nineteenth century, acquired a herd of cattle that he felt no need to brand, since they were pastured on an island. Some of his cattle, however, would wander off across the water into neighbors' ranches. The custom was that anyone could put his brand on unbranded cattle and claim them as his own. Which is what the cattlemen did when they found unbranded cattle on their ranch, even though they suspected that Maverick was their owner. The term *maverick*—to designate unbranded cattle—became widely accepted by cattlemen.

In the area of politics a person who wanders from his party and takes an independent stance is a *maverick*. Outside of politics, the term may apply to anyone who refuses to conform to established rules and sets his own course. A maverick is, in other words, a free-lancer who resists being branded.

## MEANDER

The ancient Greek river *Maeanderes* (in Asia Minor) followed a winding, crooked course, curving from side to side. Concerning it, Ovid wrote: "The limpid *Meander* sports in the Phrygian fields; it flows backwards and forwards in its varying course, and meeting itself, beholds its waters that are to follow, until it fatigues its wandering current, now pointing to its source, and now to the open sea." The English word *meander* was taken directly from the name of the river and given the meaning "to follow a winding course." It developed a figurative sense of wandering aimlessly, twisting and turning rather than heading directly toward a goal.

A word that seems completely unrelated to the name of any river is *agate*. The gemstone was named after the Greek word *Achates,* a river in Sicily.

The Greek word for "river" was *potamos*. From it, together with another Greek word, *hippos,* "horse," came the interesting name of the herbivorous mammal *hippopotamus* or "river horse" (some words in Greek are not written sequentially). The name of the river that flows into the Chesapeake Bay—the Potomac River—is not of Greek origin. It comes from an unknown source, probably Indian.

## MELBA TOAST

Mme. Melba (1861–1931), whose real name was Helen Porter Mitchell, was an opera singer who took her stage name from the first syllable of Melbourne, Australia, the city of her birth. The famous soprano was inordinately fond of certain foods prepared in a special way. For example, she liked the bread used to make her toast somewhat stale and cut paper thin. Because she ordered it so very often, the chef named it after her—and *Melba toast* is still very much in current usage. She also had a favorite dessert—a combination of ice cream and peach halves, topped with a sauce of currants and raspberries. *Peach Melba,* as it came to be called, has become a popular dessert in many fine dining rooms.

Luisa Tetrazzini was another vocalist whose name now enriches our culinary heritage. A coloratura soprano whose voice had a remarkable range, her role in "Lucia di Lammermoor" made this opera a favorite during the early twentieth century. A certain chef was so enraptured by her singing that he named a dish after her, one not meant for the calorie-conscious but for the carefree gourmet. Consisting of chicken, blanketed in pasta and immersed in a rich creamy sauce of cheese and mushrooms, and served as a casserole, this concoction has been immortalized under the name chicken Tetrazzini.

## MESMERISM

Dr. Franz Mesmer, an Austrian physician in the mid-eighteenth century, became convinced that his hands had curative power (which he called *animal magnetism*) and that this power permeated the universe and could profoundly influence the human body. He was alluding to the phenomenon of hypnotism, a word not yet invented, but later coined by Dr. James Braid, an English physician.

Dr. Mesmer achieved remarkable curative success, especially with patients who were hysterical. He received the support of the medical profession, but his insistence that his cures were natural phenomena eroded this support. Eventually he was branded an impostor and a charlatan. Nevertheless, his experiments marked the beginning of scientific study of this strange force, even though his belief in "animal magnetism" (an occult force that flowed through the hypnotist) has not been substantiated nor given credence by later physicians. The name Mesmer lives on. From it came the verb *mesmerize,* a synonym for *hypnotize.* A person enthalled, hypnotized, or held spellbound is, in a word, mesmerized.

## MIDSHIPMAN

*See* CADET

## MILESTONE

Rome, as many people know, was conceived of as the center of the world. Thus the ancient saying, "all roads lead to Rome." Obviously Augustus believed it, for he set up a system of markers to reckon distances along the highways, and quite naturally, the base-stone or central marker was placed in the Forum. The Latin name given this keystone was *milliarium,* which meant "a milestone," a derivative of *mille,* "a thousand." All distances were measured from this marker by stones placed every mile, incised with the number of miles from Rome. The Romans were surprisingly accurate, considering the statute (or land) mile as the standard, which measures 5,280 feet. The Roman mile was 5,000 feet long, for it was made up of a thousand paces (*mille passus*). A Roman pace was a measure of distance from where one foot touched the ground to where the same foot touched again. This in effect is two paces or about five feet.

Nowadays a *milestone* may still be a highway marker of distance, but more often it is used figuratively to mean an important event in someone's life, perhaps a turning point in his or her career.

## MILITARY TITLES

A colonel, being only one rank below a general, is a particularly important officer. The title *colonel* evolved naturally, since he was in charge of a column of soldiers. The Latin word for "column" is *columna,* which the Italians changed to *colonello,* and the French, to *coronel.* In time the word for "column" was transferred to the commander of the column. He became the *colonello* or the *coronel.* The English adpted the French spelling, but later changed it to colonel, a two-syllable word with the *r* sound retained—*kurnel.* Incidentally, the French have since adopted the English spelling: *colonel.*

A *major* (the word means "greater") is so called because his rank, but for the general's or colonel's, is more important than the other officers'. One grade below him is the *captain* (from Latin *caput,* "head"). A captain is the commander, the leader of others and therefore their "head." When a lieutenant salutes his "head," his captain, he raises his hand to his cap, another word stemming from *caput.* A *cap,* of course, sits on one's head.

The officer directly under the captain, and the one in charge in the captain's absence, is the *lieutenant,* a place-holder. And that is what that military title means in Old French—*lieu,* "place" and *tenant,* "holding," which came from Latin *locum tenens,* "holding a place."

## MINIATURE

A *miniature* may be a small painting to the people of today, but it meant something entirely different when Latin was a commonly spoken language. Then it meant, from *miniatus* (past participle of *miniare*), "painted with red lead or vermilion." This came about because Latin *minium* (English "cinnabar") was the substance from which the pigment was made.

During those times, before the advent of printing, books were manuscripts because they were written *(scriptus)* by hand *(manu).* The headings were done in red to distinguish them from the black text. Then the sense of *miniare* shifted to refer to a colored initial, necessarily small, in an illuminated manuscript. The Italians labeled it *miniatura,* a word that passed into

English as *miniature,* referring to any small-scale representation, even though no *minium* had been used in the work.

## MINUTE

> Are you in earnest? Seize this very minute.
> —Goethe, *Faust*

When one says "He'll return in a minute," he's really not suggesting a sixty-second wait nor, on the other hand, does he mean instantly, as though in a flash. He means in a short time, a moment, a small, almost unmeasurable, period of time.

The ancestry of *minute* meaning the sixtieth part of an hour can be traced, according to Klein, to *minuta,* Medieval Latin for *pars minuta prima,* literally "the first small part," an expression originated by mathematician Ptolemy to denote the sixtieth part of the unit. From *minuta,* English adopted the noun *minute.* The genesis of adjective *minute,* which means "exceptionally small" or "tiny," can be found in *minutus,* "made small," past participle of *minuere,* "to lessen" (other derivatives are *diminish* and *minimize*). These two forms of *minute,* the noun and the adjective, are not only spelled alike but originally were pronounced alike. Today, of course, the adjective is accented on the second syllable and its first syllable has a long ī.

Although minutes may tick away, the term *minutes,* also borrowed from Latin *minuta,* does not refer to a record of proceedings minute by minute, but to the written summary of a meeting. That word emphasizes the fact that in former times proceedings were normally taken down in small handwriting *(minuta scriptura?)* and later transcribed into larger, more distinct writing. Nowadays, more often than not, minutes are taken in shorthand and then put into typescript. That's the modern long and short of it.

## MISTRANSLATIONS

A *kangaroo* is a herbivorous marsupial found in Australia. How this animal got its name is obscure. One theory is that the word *kangaroo* is an Aboriginal Australian word meaning "the jumper." If so, it is apt. Another theory is that Captain

James Cook in 1770 asked the natives in Australia for the name of this strange-looking animal. Their reply was *kangaroo,* which is what he noted on the ship's log. What the Captain did not know is that *kangaroo* is Australian for "I don't know."

Possibly the mistranslated word that has had the widest dissemination is *glass*—in "Cinderella's glass slipper." Charles Perrault's *Cendrillon,* from which the English version of *Cinderella* was adapted, used the expression *pantoufle de vair,* meaning "fur slipper." But early English translators of this charming French tale mistook the *vair* for *verre,* which means "glass." Thus Cinderella's fur slipper was transmuted into a glass slipper. And so it has remained.

## MNEMONIC

One of Zeus's wives was Mnemosyne, the goddess of memory. The English language is indebted to her for the word *mnemonic,* "a memory aid" or "the art of improving one's memory." (In Greek, *mnemonikos* means "mindful.")

A *monicker* is sometimes easier to remember than a person's name. Originally spelled *moniker* (the *c* was added just to aid pronunciation), it is not a legal name, but one that a person (usually entertainers and hobos) makes up and prefers to be known by. An unsubstantiated theory is that the term is a corruption of *monogram,* which initially referred to the markings of gypsies on walls and towngates to announce that they had been there.

## MOB

To find out what's new with the old group, a crony might facetiously ask, "What d'ya hear from the mob?" The word *mob,* meaning "a large disorderly crowd," has been accepted on all levels of writing ever since its inclusion in Dr. Johnson's lexicon, where it was defined as "the crowd, a tumultuous rout." But *mob* has not always been welcomed into literary circles. Purists howled when it first appeared as an abbreviated form of *mobile vulgus* (Latin for "the excited or fickle crowd"). They vigorously attacked it as being nothing more than a slangy word. Jonathan Swift, the author of *Gulliver's Travels,* in condemning it said that only the full Latin term was acceptable. Richard Steele in his *Tatler* wrote: "I have done my utmost for some years past to stop the progress of *mob* . . . but have been borne down by numbers. . . ." However, the British apparently preferred a shortened version. They contracted it to *mob. vulg.* and then further to *mob.* Ever since that time the word *mob* has been accepted on all levels of English, not only in Britain but also in the United States.

## MOMENT

*A moment* is a short time, possibly longer than an *instant*, but yet unmeasurable. If one says "Give me a moment" or "I'll see you soon," or "Wait a minute," the ideas are synonymous.

Interestingly, *moment* came from a Latin word that did not denote time, but motion—*momentum*, meaning "movement" or "that which causes motion," a derivative of *movere*, "to move." After it acquired its sense of "time," *momentum* also came to mean "an important factor" or "consequence," as would be an event of great moment in someone's life. Shakespeare, as Dr. Johnson pointed out, used *moment* in both ways—in *Antony and Cleopatra*, "I have seen her die twenty times upon far poorer moment" (importance), and in *Merry Wives of Windsor*, "If I could go to hell for an eternal moment, or so, I could be knighted" (a particle of time).

A person negotiating a transaction looks for the *psychological moment*, the critical moment to say "Sign here." But this phraseology, according to Fowler, is inaccurate, a misinterpretation by the French of the original German phrase, *das Momentum*, which corresponds to English *momentum*, not *moment*, and it is therefore not a moment of time. The psychological moment, he observes, is the influence exerted by a state of mind, time when all psychological factors indicate success. Nevertheless, the expression has degenerated and its special sense has disappeared. The *psychological moment* now means nothing more than *the nick of time*, which, incidentally, unless *psychological* is appropriate, is a better expression to bear in mind at "the psychological moment."

# MONICKER

*See* MNEMONIC

## MONTHS

Julius Caesar reformed the ancient Roman calendar (which in many respects followed the movement of the moon) and named it the Julian calendar (English *calendar* came directly from Latin *Kalendae,* the first day of each month in the Roman calendar and the day on which accounts were to be settled). Except for minor changes made by Pope Gregory in 1582 (the length of the calendar and the tropical years were made to approximate each other), the Julian calendar is still in use today. Before Caesar, the calendar consisted of ten lunations, beginning with March (named for Mars, the Roman god of war) and ending with *decem,* the tenth month. With the addition of January (named for *Janus,* the god of beginnings), the first month of the year, and February (named for *februa,* a Roman ceremony of purification), the second month, the calendar of twelve months was now complete. The name April was derived from the Latin *aperio,* "to open," which is what flowers and plants do in the spring, and May from *Maia,* the daughter of Atlas. From *Iunius,* a Roman Family name, came June, and in honor of Caesar, Mark Antony coined *Julius* (originally Quintilis), now July. *August* (originally Sextilis) was named after Augustus, Caesar's grandnephew and heir. The change in the name of the eighth month was rooted in the envy of Augustus toward the accomplishments and fame of his granduncle Julius Caesar. Augustus thought that he, too, should have a month named in his honor. He selected the month following Julius's, first, because it was next in line, and second, because he had had many successful ventures and appointments during that period. Septem (7), Octo (8), Novem (9), and Decem (10)—all Latin numbers—have been anglicized simply by the addition of *-ber.*

## MORGANATIC

When a man and woman marry, the usual expectation is that when one of them dies, the survivor and their children will inherit the property of the deceased spouse. There is one kind of marriage, however, in which this expectation cannot be fulfilled: the *morganatic* marriage. This, of course, does not refer to a marriage of J. Pierpont Morgan or of his descendants.

The morganatic marriage (which originated in Germany during feudal times) enabled a nobleman to marry someone below his rank—that is, someone not of the nobility. At the wedding ceremony, the bridegroom would offer his left rather than his right hand to the bride as a sign that neither she nor his children by her would be elevated to his position nor share in his estate. On the followng morning, he would present her with the traditional morning gift (from the German *Morgengeba* "morning gift"), which was the only share of her husband's wealth she would ever receive.

Morganatic marriages are rare today, but they have a modern counterpart. When entering into an antenuptial contract, the parties agree on the dispositon of their assets in case of divorce or death. Which may prove that love is not blind—nor binding—after all.

## MORON

*See* **IDIOT**

## MORPHINE

Both morphine and heroin are addictive narcotics. The drug *morphine* (an alkaloid narcotic principle of opium), taken to deaden pain, quite clearly was named after the Greek mythological god Morpheus. (Morpheus was the god of dreams; his father, Hypnos (whence *hypnosis* and *hypnotism*), was the god of sleep. Therefore, a person asleep can be "in the arms of Morpheus" only if he's dreaming.)

*Heroin* is a derivative of morphine. But instead of becoming somnolent (Latin *somnus,* "sleep") from absorbing this poisonous drug, one has his ego inflated. In fact, he feels like a conquering hero. And that may well be, etymologically speaking. The word *heroin* was taken from a Greek word, *heros,* meaning "hero," "protector," "defender"; it was left almost unchanged in English. The reason for dropping the *s* was that *heros* sounded like a plural (although the English language has several nouns ending in *s* that are singular—*kudos,* for example). In any event, the word *Heroin* was coined by a German narcotic manufacturer, H. Dresser, as his trademark. Today, *heroin,* unless medically controlled, is a mark of another trade—one with no heroes.

## MUSE

In Old French, *muse* meant to sniff about, like a dog that has lost the scent and seems in doubt. From that sense of holding the snout in the air, from "staring stupidly," came the present meaning of *muse,* "to ponder, meditate, or reflect," perhaps because a person engaged in such thought holds his head in a fixed position, as did the ancient French dog. Rooted in that same source are *amuse* ("to entertain") and *bemuse* ("to confuse or stupefy").

Before returning to *muse,* it may be noted that originally the meaning of *amuse* was to put into a stupid state. It then came to mean "to delude." In Middle English a woman might say that she never amuses her husband. Today that statement (meaning "never deludes") would not be considered amusing, at least not by the husband. With time, the delusion, or better stated, the sense of diversion that evolved from the word *amuse* was of a pleasanter type.

The capitalized term *Muse* is often associated with the Greek mythological Nine Muses, the children of Zeus (the king of the gods) and Mnemosyne (the goddess of memory)—whence *mnemonics,* "the art of improving or developing the memory." Stories concerning their names, attributes, and functions differed among classical authors, but each Muse was said to rule over a certain art or science.

From ancient paintings and statuary, it is gathered that the Muses are Clio (history); Erato (love poetry—English *erotic*); Urania (astronomy); Euterpe (lyric poetry); Melpomene (tragedy); Polymnia (sacred song); Terpischore (dance—English *terpsichorean*); Thalia (comedy); Calliope, Chief Muse (epic poetry and science).

## NADIR

*See* ZENITH

## NAUGHT, NAUGHTY

For a long time *naught* and *naughty* had similar meanings. *Naughty* meant "worthless," something that was "worth naught," or, as is said today, something that is good for nothing. *Naughty* was a more vigorous form of *naught* (from Old English *nowiht*, literally "no whit"—*no*, "no," plus *whit*, "creature" or "thing"). The modern equivalent of *naughty* is "nothing," which is also what *naught* means. Shakespeare wrote, "to ask naught for oneself. Away! All will be naught else." *Naughty* experienced many diverse sense changes, finally arriving at its current meaning of "mischievous," especially in reference to a child, and "risqué," of a woman who is sexually suggestive. *Naught* and *naughty*, like the branches of many family trees, are far apart now, but their common root remains.

Although in any context *naught* may be spelled *nought*, some writers prefer *nought* to mean "cipher" and *naught* in all other senses, as in "She gave all her devotion for naught." Incidentally, the word *aught*, which has the same meaning as *naught*, derived directly from it. This came about because the *n* of *naught* was frequently fused with the preceding article *a* to form *an*. One spoke of *an aught* instead of a *naught*, and "an aught" it became.

## NAUSEA

People suffering from *nausea* are probably more interested in relief than in the word's etymology. But those who desire to avoid a ludicrous mistake ought to know where *nausea* came from and what it and its various forms mean.

The Greeks originated the word. It refers to "a stomach distress, often accompanied by an urge to vomit." But its initial specific sense applied only to seasickness, an ailment that induced those symptoms. The first syllable of *nausia*, which was its original spelling, is *naus*, Greek for "ship," which makes the signification of *nausia* easy to see. In English, the spelling of the word became *nausea* and its meaning was extended to cover any "stomach disturbance characterized by a feeling or need to vomit," whether suffered on land or at sea.

Misusing the adjective form of *nausea*, which is *nauseous*, to describe a sickness at the stomach is common. The sufferer is not *nauseous* but *nauseated*. It is a mistake, therefore, if Johnnie is sick, to say, "Johnnie is nauseous," for that means that Johnnie is *causing* nausea (he is making other people sick), whereas it is the noxious substance, like smoke or gas fumes, or the illness itself that is nauseous. The thing to remember is that just as a person is scandalized by something scandalous, so he is nauseated by something nauseous.

# NECTAR

*See* AMBROSIA

# NEMESIS

When it is said that Notre Dame is the nemesis of Southern Cal what is meant is that Notre Dame is a formidable and usually victorious rival. Strictly speaking, however, that is not what a *nemesis* is. The word comes straight from Greek mythology and means "an avenger" or "an act of retribution."

According to the Greek classics, Nemesis (her name comes from *nemein*, "to dispense," "to give what is due") was the goddess of retributive justice. Her divinely appointed task was to maintain the equilibrium between good and evil in the universe. Armed with a sword and scourge, she would ceaselessly seek transgressors of the law and pursue them in her chariot, ready to flay the offenders and to mete out further divine punishment. Although closely associated with vengeance, Nemesis was also responsible for rewarding the just for their good deeds. Nowadays, however, a nemesis is thought of only as a person who punishes another for evil deeds, like "J. Edgar Hoover during World War II was the saboteurs' nemesis."

## NEPOTISM

The bestowing of jobs on relatives, with no consideration given for talent, is a practice called *nepotism*. That word comes from the Latin *nepos*, which at one time meant "descendant," referring to a grandson. Later its meaning was changed to "nephew" (a son of one's sister or brother) because early popes conferred special favors and ecclesiastical offices upon their natural children, euphemistically referred to as "nephews." Nowadays *nepotism* is no longer confined to the rulers of a church, and it is no longer applied only to nephews. It is preference shown to any family member or close friend by reason of the relationship and can often be found, especially in the political arena, lurking behind a padded payroll.

## NEWS

The belief that the word *news* was coined from the initial letters of the four points of the compass—North, East, West, South—has no foundation in fact. It may be that the news reported in newspapers comes from all directions, but the word *news* is simply the plural of *new*, as in the case of French *nouvelles*. The "news," therefore, consists of what is new, even if it all came from only one area, say, the South. During the fourteenth and fifteenth centuries, the word was spelled *newes* or *newys*, and pronounced with two syllables. The Latin equivalent for "new things" was *nova;* the Anglo-Saxon, *niwi;* and the Greek, *neos*. Although plural in form, *news* is used with a singular verb ("Good evening, folks. The news *is* good tonight"). But, of course, that's not news.

## NICE

*See* **SILLY**

## NICKEL

The word *nickel* is a popular name of a United States coin worth five cents. The name took hold, so it is said, when miners were disenchanted by their find of a shiny metal that contained no copper. They blamed their ill-luck on a busy goblin, Nicholas, who originated in the German *Kupfernickel* (*Kupfer*, "copper," and *Nickel*, "demon"), on whom the Germans vented their anger when the metal they had mined failed to yield any copper. These miners would probably have agreed with an adage compounded by Franklin P. Adams: "What the United States needs is a good five cent nickel."

## NICOTINE

*Nicotine* is a substance in tobacco that medical authorities have determined is injurious to health. Yet a man who led an academic life—a writer on philology and the author of the first French lexicon—unwittingly lent his name to this poisonous drug.

In 1560, while Jean Nicot was serving as the French ambassador in Lisbon, he acquired some seeds of a strange plant that had recently been brought over from America. The seedlings were later introduced into the soil of France, and the growth of the tobacco plant began. The smoking of tobacco, or, as was said at that time, ". . . the taking in of the smoke of the Indian herbe called Tobaco. . .," became immediately popular. Imported into England, it was well received. But some persons frowned on it, King James for one. He said that smoking was "a custom loathesome to the eye, hatefull to the nose, harmfull to the ear, dangerous to the lungs, and in the black stinking fumes thereof, nearest resembling the horrible Stygian smoke of the pit that is bottomless." (King James clearly was a forerunner of the surgeon-general.)

Monsieur Nicot has been immortalized by the name of the toxic substance found in tobacco, *nicotine,* of which he knew nothing and which, quite naturally, he did not mention in his French dictionary, printed in 1600, six years after his death.

It may be noted that the derivation of *tobacco,* the leaf that is processed for smoking, can be traced to Carib *tobaco,* the name of the pipe in which the natives smoked the plant. The Spaniards confused the Carib word for reed pipe with the leaves that were burned in it, and that meaning for *tobacco*—cultivated American leaves for smoking, chewing, or sniffing—has taken universal hold.

# NIGHTMARE

A person living through a nightmare ("a dream causing fear or anxiety") may wake up screaming, drenched in perspiration. Which is not to say that this experience refers to a ride on a neighing, sweaty female horse. The -*mare* in *nightmare* is not a filly but an Old English word meaning "incubus," which, in the Middle Ages, was a legendary evil spirit that sometimes oppressed people during sleep. (The Scandinavian demon *Mara*—the original mare?—was also supposed to descend and lie on a sleeper.) With time, this conviction was dispelled. Now it is no longer thought that frightening dreams are induced by an evil spirit. But the use of the word *mare* has continued, prefixed by *night (nightmare)* because most people have their dreams during the night while sleeping.

# NOON

*Noon* is recognized as the time of day when the sun is directly overhead. But this has not always been so. According to the Romans, midday was the sixth hour, since hours were counted only from sunrise to sunset, beginning at 6 a.m. The term *noon* (lineally descended from Latin *nonus,* meaning "ninth") represented the *nona hora* (about 3 p.m.), when the monks recited the nones, or prayers. The midday, when the sun is at zenith, came to be called *noon* in the fourteenth century for the convenience of those who felt obligated to attend church services at "noon" before eating, since the world, according to the King James version of the Bible, was in darkness until the ninth hour.

In the meantime the original midday hour, the *sexta hora,* developed a new, and leisurely, life. The Spanish language, in which the word for "six" is *seis,* molded *sexta* into *siesta,* an afternoon nap or a break in the day's routine. The *siesta* began at noon, but eventually the word lost its time-related significance. Today a rest period at any hour is a siesta.

# NOSTRUM

*See* **PANACEA**

## NYMPHOMANIA

The word *nymphomania,* which means an abnormally strong sex drive in women, is not uncommon. Much less common is the term for the equivalent affliction in a male: *satyriasis.* The root of the former word, *nymphe,* from classical Greek, means "a bride." (A belief persisted that a bride on her honeymoon had a madness for sexual satisfaction, but more likely that belief was nurtured in the mind of the satyrical groom.) In mythology the term *nymph* designated several classes of female divinities of lower ranks—those who peopled the seas and oceans, those who lived in mountains, and those who inhabited trees and glens. The *satyr,* from which the latter word came, was a sylvan demigod with the pointed ears, the legs, and the short horns of a goat. He was represented as being wanton and lascivious, thriving on sensual pleasures, and was usually pictured drinking wine, playing musical instruments, or dancing with nymphs. What is odd is that the mental disturbance called *nymphomania* (a well-known term) is a rarity, whereas *satyriasis* (a little-known term) can probably be found lurking on every street corner. Today a synonym for *satyr* is *lecher*—or, as the kids would put it, "a dirty old man."

## ODD

The spelling of *odd* has changed little through the centuries. In Old English, it was spelled *odde* and in Old Norse, *oddi*. Originally the word meant "point"—the apex of a triangle (which is the odd-numbered angle in addition to the two angles paired at the triangle's base). Of course, today *odd* is viewed in the same light. An arrowhead is a triangle, but its apex, the point of the arrow, seems to be the odd angle. Likewise with a pennant. The free-flowing angle (the one away from the holder) looks like a point; it is the odd angle of the three. Although originally applied only to a group of three, in which two were paired and one was an unpaired unit, eventually the term *odd* was extended to any number between even ones. Which, as a wit once said, was an odd place to put it.

## ODOR

Everyone agrees that an aromatic flower has a pleasant odor. But whether the word *odor* by itself implies a fragrant or a disagreeable scent is a matter of dispute.

The fact is that the noun *odor* (a word that has not changed in meaning or spelling since the days of the Romans) suggests neither pleasantness nor unpleasantness. It merely denotes "a quality of something that affects the sense of smell." But over the years a connotation of unpleasantness has evolved, perhaps because such adjectives as spicy, fragrant, or sweet usually qualify *odor* when the smell is agreeable; unqualified, *odor* seems to signify something disagreeable: "What an odor!" The contention on the other side is that offensive odors are also described by adjectives (like rank or foul) or referred to by less euphonious words (like *stench* or *stink*). Which brings up a perhaps apocryphal story attributed to Dr. Johnson concerning the word *stink*. It seems that Johnson rarely bathed. A tablemate, after

**187**

staring and sniffing at him for a while, said: "Doctor, you smell." Dr. Johnson stared back and then calmly replied, "No, Madam, you smell. I *stink*."

## OEDIPUS COMPLEX

Psychiatrists of the Freudian school have popularized the term *Oedipus complex*, a libidinal attraction of a male toward his mother, usually accompanied by manifestations of hostility toward his father.

Oedipus was the subject of many Greek tragedies, but his pathetic fate was best dramatized by Sophocles in *Oedipus Rex* and *Oedipus at Colonus*. Oedipus was the son of Laius, king of Thebes, and of his queen, Jocasta. The parents were told by the oracle to beget no children, for the king would perish at the hands of his own son, who would then marry his mother. To circumvent this prophecy of doom, the king exposed the infant Oedipus on a mountain top, his feet bound and pierced. He was found by a shepherd and presented to the king of Corinth, who then reared him as his son, giving him the name Oedipus because of his swollen feet (*oedipus* in Greek means "swollen feet").

When Oedipus was grown, he was informed by the oracle of the future tragedy of his life. Believing that the Corinthian king was his father, Oedipus left, resolved never to return to Corinth. On his way to Thebes, his chariot and another man's coming in an opposite direction, could not pass at the same time because the road was too narrow. An argument erupted, a scuffle ensued, and Oedipus killed the stranger who turned out to be Laius, his natural father.

Oedipus went on to Thebes, where the celebrated Sphinx, sitting majestically on a rock, kept posing what seemed to be an unanswerable riddle to the Thebans. Whoever failed to solve her riddle, she would murder at once. In desperation, the Thebans offered their kingdom and the hand of Jocasta to anyone who would rid the country of this monster. Oedipus solved the riddle; in innocence married the widowed queen; and became, by her, the father of four children. When Oedipus and his mother discovered that their relationship was incestuous, Jocasta hanged herself and Oedipus put out his eyes. And thus the prophecy came to pass.

## OK

The term *OK* is an expression of assent or approval used worldwide. Its origin, however, has been a subject of controversy among etymologists ever since it entered the English language during the early part of the nineteenth century. According to one theory, which has a thin following, *OK* is an anglicized version of the Choctaw Indian *okeh,* meaning "it is so." Another theory holds that it represents the initials of an early railroad clerk, Obadiah Kelly, who stamped *OK* on parcels for shipment. A third theory is that bananas without flaws were designated "au quai"—that is, ready to go to the quay for loading on the ship; hence *okay.*

And then there are those who ascribe its beginning, and probably with better reason, to the O.K. Democratic Club. This group, during the presidential campaign of 1840, used the symbol *OK* (which stood for Old Kinderhook, the New York birthplace of Martin Van Buren) as its rallying slogan. Although Van Buren's bid for reelection was unsuccessful, the symbol survived. In fact, it has attained such universal acceptance that, except perhaps for Coca Cola, it is the best known term on earth.

## OMELET

An *omelet* (more fancily spelled *omelette*) is an egg pancake, a dish of whipped eggs cooked in a thin layer. Its name came from a Latin word whose meaning bore it no relationship—*lamina* ("layer"), which sired *lamella,* a word used by Romans to mean "a thin metal plate or blade." That word then traveled, in French, through various stages (in French *amelette* meant "thin plate"). Its orthographic changes culminated in the present-day spelling *omelet* and influenced its meaning, since battered eggs resembled "a thin layer" or, in French a *crêpe,* a very thin pancake.

One who asks for a poached egg gets it in the bag—not quite, but almost. In Old French *pocher* meant "to enclose in a bag." The bag itself was called *poche.* When an egg is poached, the chef cooks the yolk in a "bag" or "pocket" of white. From this *poche* also comes the English word "poke," as in to "buy a pig in a poke." But when the chef poaches, what one gets is an egg in a poke.


## ONE

In the beginning there had to be one. The number *one*, of Anglo-Saxon origin, is a word of importance and great significance. To Pythagoras, who thought numbers represented all elements of all things, *one* was a point. And that, too, may be the beginning of all things. Religionists have invested it with a sacred quality, for there can be, according to Judeo-Christianity, only one God. When His forgiveness is sought, a person promises to atone for his wrongs—that is, he will "atone" (or, with the word separated into its two elements—"at one"), meaning a oneness between God and man. (Incidentally, the word *only*, like the fusing of *at one* into *atone*, is a merger of "one" plus "ly," literally *one-ly.*)

The Latin forebear for "one," *unus*, has sprouted many English words; *unit, unity, union, unison.* On one thing Americans are *unanimous* ("of one mind"); namely, that their mottoes sound better in Latin; for example, *E pluribus unum* (meaning "One out of many"). And just as *one* came from *unus*, so too through the same process of vowel transference, *onion* came from *union.* Everyone might agree that switching the vowels has made both these words strong. As Aesop said in *The Bundle of Sticks*, *"Union gives strength"* (and onions aren't weak either).


## OPEN SESAME

A sesame is an edible seed, a food used for seasoning or, if squeezed, a source of oil. It must have been a familiar plant in the region of the Forty Thieves, since it was a key word in one of the tales in *The Arabian Nights.*

In this story, Ali Baba, the principal character, having overheard the thieves' magical password, "Open Sesame," opened the stone door to the cave where the robbers stored their loot and helped himself. His brother Kassim later extorted the password from him, entered the dungeon to rifle it, but was trapped when he forgot the magical words that would open the door again. He kept crying out "Open Wheat!" "Open Barley!" but those sounds would not budge the door. The thieves returned, found Kassim, and killed him.

The phrase "open sesame" signifies the magical charm that makes certain persons always welcome. It naturally represents a trait cherished by salesmen and others seeking to influence the public. It may also be said of cultural endeavors. In Harvey Cushing's Pulitzer prize-winning book, *The Life of Sir William Osler,* appears this statement, "The master work [of Sir William] . . . is the open sesame to every portal." Indeed, Dr. Osler's *Principles and Practice of Medicine,* published in 1891, did open the doors to the pursuit of medical advancement.

## ORDEAL

In earlier times the purpose of an "ordeal," then spelled *"ordal,"* was to determine truth. "Ordal" meant "judgment." The word was a combination of Old English *or* ("out") and *dael* ("a deal"), meaning "that which is dealt out to one." It was not meant to punish, although the consequences of some "trials by ordeal" were fatal. According to Hindu codes, for example, only a faithless wife would be burned while walking through fire. The early courts in Britain were no more sensible. An accused was made to carry a red-hot iron or burning coals; if he did not flinch or was not burned, he was accounted innocent. Or if, after thrusting his hand into a vat of boiling water he showed no ill effects, he was adjudged not guilty. In medieval Europe, a suspected murderer was made to touch the corpse of the victim, since the murderer's touch, it was believed, would make the victim's blood flow again. The prevailing theory, of course, was that supernatural powers exonerate the innocent and convict the guilty. Today's *ordeals*, fortunately, are not so trying.

## OSCAR

Each spring millions of television viewers watch the Academy of Motion Pictures Arts and Sciences' elaborate ceremony where Oscars (golden film trophies) are bestowed on the best performers and other professionals involved in movie production during the previous year. The ten-inch statuette had never had an official name. When, in 1927, the Academy decided to present a statuette, it was merely designed, but not named. For several years the golden figure remained nameless. It was not until 1931 that the statuette received its present monicker. And then by mere chance. A minor official of the Academy, upon being introduced to the statuette, which was sitting on an executive's desk, noted its resemblance to her uncle. A newspaper reporter sitting nearby overheard her comment, liked it, published it, and thus initiated a permanent name for this prized trophy. Her remark was, "He reminds me of my uncle Oscar."

## OSTRACIZE

*See* BLACKMAIL

## OUNCE

Several things may be said about the word *ounce,* a unit of weight. It derived from French *once,* which came from Latin *unica,* meaning "a twelfth part," and thus one-twelfth of a pound in troy weight. (Incidentally, the word *inch,* "one-twelfth of a foot," also comes from *unica.*) Both the avoirdupois system, which has sixteen ounces per pound, and the troy system originally used the same ounce, but each system eventually adopted its own ounce—the troy ounce of 480 grains and the avoirdupois of 437.5 grains.

The abbreviation for *ounce* is *oz.,* although the word contains no *z.* Clearly *oz.* is a symbol, but where it came from is not certain. One thought is that it is an abbreviation of *ouza,* Italian for *ounce*; a second, that *z* was a terminal mark used by early printers. Another such instance is in *viz,* an abbreviation of Latin *videlicet,* "it is permitted to see." Originally *videlicet* was abbreviated *vi.* but then was followed by the termination symbol *z.* With time, the *z* in both *oz.* and *viz* became frozen tailpieces.

# PALACE

The erection of a residence for Augustus Caesar in Rome on the Palatine Hill—the *mons Palatinus*—has given English the word for this kind of large and stately building: *palace*. The hill had been named after a pastoral deity, Pales, who was regularly honored on April 21, the day that Romulus drew the first furrow at the base of the hill. The Latin name for this palatial structure, *Palatium*, was absorbed into Italian as *palazzo* and then into French as *palais*.

The well-known London music hall, the *Palladium*, derived its name from *Pallas Athene*, whose statue brandished a spear in defense of Athens (*Pallas* was an epithet of the Greek goddess). During the days of Grecian splendor the statue commanded the most prominent place in the Parthenon, a building named for this virgin goddess (*parthenos* in Greek means "virgin").

According to legend, Troy was secure from Greek conquest as long as the *Palladium*, a wooden image of Pallas, remained within its city walls. From this notion has come a general meaning of *palladium*—a safeguard on which anyone or anything can depend for his or its safety. Perhaps the Trojans were right. After carrying the wooden statue away, the Greeks burned Troy to the ground.

# PALETTE

An artist works with a palette and an easel. The word *palette* (the slab on which the artist mixes colors) originated in Latin (*pala*) as a culinary term. It was the spade used to put bread into an oven. Later the word came to designate a spatula and still later the present artist's piece of equipment.

*Easel* (a frame for holding a canvas), from Dutch *ezel*, means "ass" (German *Esel*, Latin *asinus*). Who dubbed it so, and why, is not known. Perhaps it reminded someone of a clotheshorse, another rack named for a beast of burden (the French call an "easel" a *chevalet*, "little horse"). Nonetheless, both racks serve a similar purpose—to hold things patiently and silently for long periods.

Another wooden frame named after an animal is the *sawhorse* (carpenters saw wood on it). This contraption resembles a horse so much that if it had reins a child could ride it as a cockhorse. A *sawbuck* is a sawhorse, especially one whose X-shaped legs project above the crossbar (*X* is the figure of Roman number 10; thus the slang name for a ten dollar bill—*sawbuck*).

## PALL MALL

*Pall Mall* is pronounced pell mell, just the way *pell mell* is pronounced, but the words are unrelated. The first one is a noun, the name of a game; the second is an adverb, meaning "in a reckless or confused manner," "in disorderly haste," or "headlong."

During the reign of Charles II, the sports-minded Englishmen imported a game from Italy and played it first on a croquet court located near Buckingham Palace and later on adjoining alleys. The purpose of the game was to bat a ball (Italian *palla*) with a mallet or maul (Italian *maglio*, from Latin *malleus*, "hammer") through an iron hoop. As in golf or croquet, the player with the fewest strokes was the winner. The game was so exceedingly popular that the prominent players converted an alley into a fashionable walkway on which eventually they erected exclusive clubs. They then named the area after the game and made Pall Mall a symbol of elegance. Today it is the name of a well-known street in London's West End.

The adverb *pell-mell*, meaning "confusedly," emerged from the name of the game to describe the helter-skelter behavior of the players, who often rushed thoughtlessly to strike the nearest ball. This adverb was apparently needed, for, with its sense of "headlong," it has survived, but not the noun—the name of the game—nor the game itself.

## PALLIATE

The sense of *palliate* is "to moderate the intensity of," "to lessen." Its noun form, *palliative*, refers to something that acts to soothe pain or distress. In early times, the Latin *pallium* meant "cloak," a garment frequently used either as a disguise or as a cover for something not to be seen. Figuratively, therefore, *palliate* has come to mean "to cloak an error or an offense" (to put a cloak over an offense and thus hide it) or, at the least, to make it seem less serious or violent. William Pitt in 1741 in a speech before Parliament used *palliate* in just this way: "The atrocious crime of being a young man . . . I shall neither attempt to palliate nor deny."

Another common English word that derives from the name of a Latin garment, but seems to have no connection with it, is *escape*. It comes from the prefix *ex* ("out of") and *cappa* ("cape"). The cape was an ordinary article of clothing. When a person was attacked and the cape grasped, he would squirm out of it, leaving the attacker holding the bag—or, in this case, the cape. Breaking loose and fleeing was an escape—a leaving "out of the cape," an *ex cappa*.

## PAMPHLET

*See* BOOKLET

## PANACEA

Since the beginning of time, man has been seeking remedies to cure his illnesses. Three words have emerged to represent the most effective cure-alls, although their beneficial properties have never been scientifically proven.

Possibly the oldest term, and certainly the most inclusive, is *panacea*. A *panacea* is a universal remedy; it will solve all problems. Although the word is of uncertain origin, one theory is that it comes from *Panakeia,* the daughter of Aesculapius, the Greek god of the medicinal art. Her name meant "all-healing."

The second oldest is *elixir*. This, too, was a remedy that had the power to cure all human disorders. It is in effect a panacea. But an elixir also maintained vitality; hence the expression "elixir of life." The word came from the Arabic *al* ("the") and *iksir* ("dry powder"). Alchemists used it to transmute base metals into gold. Of course, they were no more successful than those who sought the *elixir vitae*. Ponce de Leon may have lived longer had he remained in sunny Florida and continued his search for that mythical fountain, but he would not have regained his youth. And Goethe's Faust also wasted his time searching for the imaginary cordial. Milton's *Paradise Lost* contains a healthier view of an elixir, as something more akin to an invigorating substance—figuratively: "What wonder then, if fields and regions here / Breathe forth elixir pure!"

A *nostrum* is a medicinal remedy whose formula is kept secret by its maker or seller. The word for this quack curative came from the Latin *nostrum,* the neuter form of the adjective *noster,* meaning "ours" or, as extended, "of our own make." *Nostrum* is a good old Latin word, but the medicine men have worked it to death.


# PANACHE

A *panache* is an ornamental plume, especially one worn on a helmet, which is its literal meaning in French. Nowadays *panache* is a "heroic gesture, flamboyance, or swagger" or "skill displayed with a dramatic flourish." The association of feathers and verve came about because such attributes seemed the natural characteristics of someone daring enough to wear a tuft of feathers, particularly in battle.

The play titled *Cyrano de Bergerac,* written by Edmond Rostand in 1897, has made *panache* a good, workable literary word. Cyrano, of the prodigious nose, was a colorful figure who had to fight many duels to vindicate it. At the end of the play, as he lay dying, he said that only one thing could he call his own: "Et c'est . . . mon panache" ("And that is . . . my panache")—a white plume, his symbol of uncompromising integrity and incorruptible honor. (For those who wonder whether Cyrano really fought many duels or was merely a fiction, the answer is that Cyrano did live during the seventeenth century and was victorious in over 1,000 duels. He was an atheist philosopher and a satirical poet.)

At a meeting of the French Academy, Rostand explained the significance of *panache:* "A little frivolous perhaps; a little melodramatic certainly, the *panache* is no more than a charming gesture. But this charming gesture is so difficult to make in the face of death and supposes so much strength (for isn't wit that soars the most graceful triumph over the body that trembles?) that it is a charming gesture I would wish for us all."

## PANDEMONIUM

*See* BEDLAM

## PANDER

A *pander* or *panderer* (both spellings appear in the dictionary) is a pimp, one paid for arranging illicit sexual affairs. In a wider sense a pander ministers to the baser needs or passions of others.

The semantic development of *pander* began with a mythical Greek soldier known not for deviousness or for procuring women to engage in sexual intrigues but, according to Homer's *Iliad,* for leading the Lycians in the Trojan War. His name was *Pandarus.* Later poets and playwrights took a different tack, representing him (sometimes with a slight change in spelling) as a procurer. This was so in Boccaccio's *Filostrata* with Pandaro and in Chaucer's *Troilus and Criseyde* with Pandare, who in each instance obtained the love and good graces of Cressida for the pleasures of Troilus, son of the king of Troy. (Cressida got even with Troilus, however. She deserted him for a Greek.)

Shakespeare through Pandarus in *Troilus and Cressida* intoned: "Since I have taken such pains to bring you together, let all pitiful goers-between be call'd to the world's end after my name; call them all Pandars."

## PANDORA'S BOX

According to classical mythology, *Pandora* was the name of the first woman on Earth. She was fashioned by Vulcan at the behest of Zeus, the greatest of the Olympian gods, who was seeking revenge for Prometheus's theft of fire from heaven. Zeus intended to use this woman to bring misery upon the human race. For this purpose the gods endowed her with all the necessary tools—beauty, charm, boldness, cunning—and then named her *Pandora* (meaning "all gifted," from *pan,* "all," and *dora,* from *doron,* "gift"). Thus equipped, she was conveyed to earth and presented to Epimetheus as his bride. In her hands she bore a casket that Zeus had forbidden her to open. One day, overcome by curiosity, she unlocked the box and looked in. Forthwith there flew out a multitude of afflictions for mankind: diseases to wither the body; envy, spite, and revenge to weaken the mind. According to one account, Pandora slammed the lid closed before the last ingredient could escape—hope.

Although the phrase *Pandora's box* is a classical allusion, in general usage it refers to a situation which spawns a tangle of extensive but unforeseen troubles—"gifts" no one wants. To open this box, graphically speaking, is to open "a can of worms."

## PANIC

The Greek god *Pan* was the god of nature—the flocks, the fields, and the forests. He is pictured as having a human torso and the legs, horns, and ears of a goat. Since he dwelt in the woodlands, any eerie sound emanating from a forest, particularly at night, was believed caused by him purposely to frighten people. From this fear instilled by *Pan* has come an alarming word, *panic*, meaning "a sudden, overpowering terror."

Not only may weird sounds cause a panic. A panic may be triggered by rumors of an impending disaster, like a bank failure. Informally the sense of panic is very much the opposite, "to create a high degree of amusement." In theatrical circles, an excellent comedy is said to "panic" the audience.

*Pan* is often shown playing on his pipes. This musical instrument was fashioned by him from reeds that grew alongside a river. According to legend, *Pan* was much enamored of a nymph named *Syrinx,* who did not return his affections. Since she was unable to escape him, she had herself turned into a reed. This plan failed her, however, for Pan cut the reed into seven pieces, from which he fashioned his *panpipe*. Nevertheless, the anglicized name of this lovely nymph continues to this day, but inappropriately in the form of an ordinary household appliance—a syringe.

## PANTS

The lineage of the word *pants,* the kind commonly worn today, began in the fourth century when a physician was made the patron saint of Venice—San Pantaleone. (The literal meaning of *Pantaleone* is "all lion." *Pan* means "all" and *leone* is "lion"). The passing years transmogrified him into a lovable but simple-minded character in Italian comedy (called Pantaleone) who wore a combination of stockings and tight-fitting trousers, slippers, and spectacles. With a slight orthographic change to *pantaloon*, his name then was equated with "clown." (The sense connection between the saint, with his leonine name, and a comical figure has not been established.) The word in plural form (*pantaloons*) subsequently entered the English language to describe a particular type of trousers. *Pants*, of course, is merely a clipped version of *pantaloons*. Shakespeare, in outlining the ages of man in *As You Like It*, noted:

> The sixth age shifts
> Into the lean and slipper'd pantaloon,
> With spectacles on nose and pouch on side. . . .

## PARADISE

Everyone knows what *paradise* is. It's where you think you are when you're in love. But *Paradise* (capitalized) is another kind of place—the Garden of Eden from which the first humans were expelled. If the Garden was, in reality, a paradise, then leaving it was somewhat difficult because it would have been, according to the word's origin, a walled garden.

The word *paradise* can be traced from the Old Persian *pairidaege* (*pairi*, "around," and *dix*, "mold"), an enclosed area, especially a royal park or hunting ground. The word traveled to Greece, where, as *paradeisos*, it meant "a walled-in pleasure park." (The Greek writer Xenophon used the term to describe the gardens of Oriental potentates.) As a figure of speech for "heaven," *Paradise* does not appear in the Hebrew of the Old Testament.

## PARASOL

A *parasol* and an *umbrella* may serve the same purpose: to shield a person from the rays of the sun.

A *parasol* is a light umbrella, used mostly by women as a sunshade. Some persons consider *parasol* a French word, but it is not, although the French have adopted it. The word filtered into the English language through the Italian *parare*, "to ward off," and *sole*, "the sun." (The French, concerned as much about rain as about sun, have distinctive words for their safeguards against those elements—*parasol* when it's sunny, *parapluie* when it's rainy (*pluie* means "rain").)

The word *umbrella* (its Latin root *umbra* means "shade") also migrated to English—from Italian *ombrella*. In America, umbrellas, although commonly used as shades at swimming pools, are more often used to protect against rain. In England, where rainy days are common, umbrellas are regularly carried as part of a person's accouterments. But there they are called *bumbershoots* (a humorous alteration of *umbrella*—(b(*umbra*) plus "shoot" from chute of "parachute"). The English are unlike Americans, according to Alfred E. Smith. He said, "The American people never carry an umbrella. They prepare to walk in eternal sunshine."

## PAREGORIC

Almost all mothers have occasionally given an ailing child a dose of paregoric to relieve pain, especially stress from diarrhea. *Paregoric* is a camphorated opium tincture, which basically is made from the same formula used in the early 1700's. The name of the medicine was taken from a Greek word that means "speak soothingly."

In ancient Greece the citizens of a city-state met regularly in the *agora*, the meetingplace of the people's assembly, where speeches designed to placate the people or raise morale were delivered. The word that evolved to describe these activities was *paregorikos*. It meant "comforting" and was a combination of *pare* (variant spelling of *para*, "outside") and *agora* ("marketplace," "assembly"), and referred to the soothing effects of these exhortations (words of cheer and encouragement) spoken to the Athenian citizens in the "marketplace." Today the method of delivering *paregoric* is different—no longer aural, now oral.

## PARLOR

Although today's general room for family activities is called a den, a study, a family room, or a living room, in yesteryear it was usually called a *parlor*. The room was appropriately named from the French *parler*, "to speak," since originally a parlor was a reception room in a monastery or nunnery where people could converse. The term was later used of a room in private dwellings in which family and guests gathered to sit and talk with one another.

In more formal times women excused themselves after an evening meal to allow the men to smoke cigars and discuss matters regarded as unsuitable for feminine ears. The room to which the women retired was called the *drawing room*, but it had nothing to do with the art of drawing. Its full, though seldom used, name was *withdrawing room* because it was the room to which the women would withdraw.

Those women who wished to relax for a moment by themselves or to powder their nose were shown to a boudoir, which today is an elegant designation for a bedroom. Originally, however, a boudoir was not designed as sleeping quarters but as a room where a young lady would be sent to get over her indisposition, her sulks. The French *bouder*, which means "to pout," was the ancestor of *boudoir*, a room for "pouting." In former times a girl did not powder in her boudoir; she pouted.

## PAWNBROKER SIGN

At one time the sign of the pawnbroker, three golden balls, was a common sight. But why this particular symbol was chosen has never been fully established by word sleuths. School kids agree that the three balls simply mean "two to one you'll get gyped."

The coat of arms of the first great pawnbrokers (*pawn* from Old Frisian *pand*, "pledge"; *broker* from Old North French *brokier*, "to open a cask of wine," hence a wine retailer, and then an agent) was displayed by the celebrated Medici family. It consisted of three gilded balls. Later moneylenders, according to one theory, appropriated the Medici sign as a symbol of their trade. Another belief that persists is that the Medici coat of arms did not consist of balls but of pills because the Medicis, great Florentine merchants though they were, were also men of medicine (which may have merely been a pun on their name).

A story that has given substance to the "ball" theory comes from the exploit of Averado de Medici, a commander under

Charlemagne. He was attacked by the giant Mugello, who swung a club from which dangled three iron balls. Averado slew the giant, took his weapon, and brought it home as a trophy, which later became a symbol on the Medicis' coat of arms. Mugello apparently didn't know that the three balls on his club meant "two to one you'll get killed."

## PAY

Although workers receive "pay" for their labor, it is given merely to keep them from being discontented, not as a reward for service rendered. *Pay*, etymologically, is simply a device to keep the peace, as its forebear makes clear—Old French *payer*, "to pay," "to appease," which ultimately came from Latin *pacare* ("to pacify") and which, in turn, was derived from *pax* ("peace").

The ejaculation "There'll be the devil to pay" means that someone's going to be chewed out; he can expect a hard time. However, not only is the word *pay* there unrelated to "wages," but also the notion expressed is completely foreign to the meaning of the original proverb, which, fully stated, is "the devil to pay and no pitch hot." In nautical language a *devil* is a seam in a ship's hull, below the waterline, and *pay*, in the sense used here (from Latin *picare*), is "to make waterproof with pitch." Hence to pay the devil is to apply pitch to a keel seam.

Also in seamen's lingo is *payed*, meaning "to let out a line or cable." The past tense of *pay*, "to discharge a debt," is *paid*, and that of *pay*, "to waterproof with pitch," is *payed*.

## PEACH MELBA

*See* MELBA TOAST

## PECULIAR

Talk about oddities. Nothing is odder than the story concerning the word *peculiar*. The ancestry of *peculiar* can be traced to Roman times, to Latin *pecus*, meaning "cattle." Before the Romans learned how to mint coins, cattle were used in their place as a common medium of exchange, and, since property was evaluated in terms of cattle, another Latin word, *peculium*, came to express the sense of "one's own property," from its literal meaning "property in cattle." From *peculium* came Latin *peculiaris,* meaning "exclusively one's own" or "distinctive." Hence the present meaning of *peculiar,* "distinctively, that is, peculiarly a particular individual's." And, since what is true of only one person may seem odd or strange, *peculiar* gradually assumed that sense, which is now predominant.

The Romans finally came up with a word for "money"— *pecunia.* From it have come such English words as *pecuniary* and *impecunious.*

Just as *peculiar* has come far afield from its root sense, so has its synonym, *eccentric,* defined as "out of the ordinary," "not usual," "odd." Its Greek elements are *ex,* "out," and *kentron,* "center," which refers to someone or something away from the center of things. And since being off center is regarded as unusual, if not outright strange, *eccentric* developed its present sense of "peculiar."

## PEDIGREE

A person who extols the importance of his pedigree, his family tree, may not realize that, although it may be as solid as an old oak, the word has no dignified or prestigious forebear. True, tables of descent and ancestry resemble trees: the person whose genealogy is being traced, the trunk; his descendants, the branches; and his ancestors, the roots. But in the minds of some people, those genealogical lines resemble the imprint of the foot of a bird, especially a crane. Because of that resemblance the French called one's lineage *pied de grue* ("foot of a crane"), which came to be similarly pronounced in English but spelled *pedigree.*

## PEEPING TOM

A "Peeping Tom" is a man beneath contempt, for he sneakily looks at what he has no license to see. He is a voyeur, a pruriently prying person who peeps at night through other people's windows.

The term has appeared frequently in literature, an allusion to the story of Lady Godiva's celebrated ride in 1040 through

Coventry. In this story Godiva's husband, Leofric, Lord of Coventry, imposed exorbitant taxes upon the people, arousing his wife's vehement objections, for she sympathized with his subjects. Leofric ignored her persistent pleas to reduce the taxes. In a sporting mood, he then said he would cut the taxes if she would ride naked through the streets of the city. Lady Godiva, much to his amazement, accepted the challenge. Astride a white horse, and completely unclothed, she did indeed keep her promise. Everyone, it has been said, honored her request to stay indoors behind drawn blinds or shuttered windows—everyone except one man, Tom the tailor, who peeped at her as she rode by and was instantly struck blind. Legend has it that Leofric, after lowering his wife from her horse, then lowered the taxes.

## PELL MELL

*See* **PALL MALL**

## PENIS

According to the *Oxford English Dictionary,* the word *penis* first appeared in print in 1693. A translation of *Blancard's Physiological Dictionary* had this notation: "Penis, the Yard, made up of two nervous Bodies, The Channel, Nut, Skin, and Fore-skin, etc." Dictionaries nowadays define *penis* simply as the male organ of generation.

The ancestor of *penis* is the same word in Latin, *penis,* meaning "a tail." Originally the Latin term applied to a small artist's brush (made of a cow's tail) that resembled a little tail. The word *pencil* was also sired by *penis,* but more directly from its diminutive form, *penicillum.* Its immediate forebear was Old French *pincel* (whence French *pinceau,* "paintbrush," "pencil"). Klein points out that it should be borne in mind, when considering the sense development of *pencil,* that formerly small brushes were used for writing.

*Penicillin* is an antibiotic drug discovered in 1929 by Scottish bacteriologist Sir Alexander Fleming. He coined the name for this wonder drug from *penicillium,* a fungus with branches that resemble little pencils.

A *phallus* is a "penis." The Romans borrowed the word from Greek *phallos.* Modern dictionaries define it as "the penis or clitoris." But the latter term is excluded in most people's minds. The term *phallus*, has been known for centuries as the image of the male organ of copulation, an organ venerated in Dionysiac ceremonies. Symbols of this organ were commonly worn as an amulet to protect against evil or injury and were worn even by actors in Old Comedy as part of their costume. Among the Egyptians a phallus was the emblem of fecundity. Worship of the phallus is now called *phallicism.*

## PENNY

*See* CENT

## PEST, PESTER

Whether a person who pesters someone may rightly be called a pest depends on what the words *pest* and *pester* are assumed to mean. Etymologically, they are not related, not even distant cousins. But because *pester* seems to have been an outgrowth of the noun *pest* (many verbs are derived from nouns), it has acquired as a verb the sense conveyed by *pest.*

The English language borrowed the word *pest* directly from French *peste* (from Latin *pestis,* "plague") during a bubonic epidemic in the sixteenth century. The term came to be employed only with reference to a pestilential disease, an epidemic with extremely high mortality. Persons thus stricken were carted away in a *pestcoach* to the *pesthouse.* That the pest was exceedingly annoying, to put it mildly, is quite clear. This sense of annoyance later came to be applied to any annoying person or thing; in short, a nuisance. (Charles Dickens said, "I was a nuisance, an incumbrance, and a pest.") And since insects, particularly the ubiquitous mosquitoes, are most pestiferous, they have come to be known by that very word—pests.

To *pester* originally meant "to tether a grazing horse." The Romans made certain that their horses did not wander too far by shackling their feet with what they called in Latin a *pastorium*: "a foot shackle." Middle French adopted the word *empestrer,* meaning "to hobble" as applied to animals—that is, to tie up an animal for grazing. English borrowed that word, but aphesis reduced it to *pester.* The sense of "annoyance," now associated with *pester,* had no parental root similar to *pest's.* This meaning of "to bother," "to vex," "to annoy" came about simply because the words *pest* and *pester* seemed, semantically, as though they belonged together, even though they came, as previously mentioned, from entirely different families and were not even on speaking terms.

## PETREL

In Britain, gasoline is called *petrol,* from petroleum, which in turn came from the Latin *petra* ("rock") and *oleum* ("oil"). *Petrol* should not be confused with *petrel,* a small gull which flies so low that it seems to be walking on the sea. This bird was named after Peter, who "walked on the water," in the Gospel narrative. Sailors who observed these birds skimming the waves thought they were a sign of an imminent storm; hence the expression *stormy petrel.*

From *petra* and *facere,* "to make," came *petrify,* "to make into rock" or "turn into stone." A person confounded with fear, figuratively speaking, is petrified. But this does not apply to a person called a "stormy petrel," for (analogized to the seamen's omen) he is warning of trouble or, and this is entirely unrelated, he may be a person fond of fighting (stirring up strife) or just a vehement haranguer. In the one sense he is warning of a storm brewing; in the other, he is kicking one up.

## PETTICOAT

*See* CHAPERON

## PHALLUS

*See* PENIS

## PHILADELPHIA LAWYER

A Philadelphia lawyer is an awesome legal adversary. He is shrewd and able—at least that was the popular belief during the 1700's.

The phrase "a Philadelphia lawyer" was coined in 1743 when Peter Zenger, the publisher of the New York *Weekly Journal,* printed a series of articles attacking the provincial government for abuses committed against the people and charging the governor with personal corruption. Zenger was arrested and tried for criminal libel (at that time "truth" was no defense; in fact, a defense of "truth" would work against the defendant, since it was believed that the greater the truth, the greater the libel). Zenger asked Andrew Hamilton, a distinguished Philadelphia lawyer, then retired, to come to his defense. Hamilton traveled to New York, brilliantly defended the beleaguered publisher, and obtained a "not guilty" verdict. More important than the birth of a phrase, the trial, according to one authority, "was instrumental in establishing a precedent for freedom of the press in American law."

Several things should be remembered about this sensational case. First, the phrase "Philadelphia lawyer" does not imply a devious attorney (despite the adage "If you are innocent, trust in God; if you are guilty, get a Philadelphia lawyer"). Second, the name of the defending lawyer was Andrew Hamilton, and not Alexander Hamilton, the first Secretary of the Treasury.

# PHILANDER

A person may flirt with an idea—that is, toy with it. But if a man acts in the same way toward a young woman, he is playing at love, trifling with the lass's affections. He might then be called a coquet (obsolete) or, more likely, a philanderer.

The root of *philander* ("to engage in love affairs frivolously") may be found in the Greek word *philandros* (*philos,* "loving," and *andros,* "man"). In medieval romances and in English plays, *Philander* was a common name for an ardent male hero who coquetted with a woman. He was a prominent character in the *Way of the Word* by William Congreve, the most brilliant of the writers of Restoration comedy.

In *Orlando Furioso,* a leading opus by Ariosto, *Philander* was a Dutch knight beloved by Gabrina, wife of Argeo, Baron of Servia. Gabrina tried to seduce Philander, but she was unsuccessful. She thereupon accused him of adultery to Argeo, who forthwith had Philander imprisoned. Gabrina then implored the captive to defend her honor against the designs of a wicked knight. Philander agreed and was concealed to await the knight's arrival. Upon a signal from Gabrina, Philander rushed out and killed the would-be adulterer, only to discover that it was Argeo. Gabrina then insisted that Philander face punishment for his misdeed or marry her, which left Philander not much of a choice. Philander married her; but she soon tired of him and poisoned him. Gabrina, the seducer, did not make out much better. She wandered about until she became an old hag and eventually was hanged on an old elm, where she was fit to be tied.

## PHILIPPIC

A *philippic* (Greek *Philippos,* "Philip") is a vehement and denunciatory speech—a synonym of *tirade* (from Italian *tirato,* "a discharge of firearms"; hence a volley of words).

About 350 B.C. Philip of Macedon was named the guardian of the throne for his infant nephew. After a few months as the regent, he decided to ignore his nephew's rights and to assume for himself the title of king. He then planned to increase his power by enlarging his kingdom. With this in mind, he set out to conquer all of Greece. In an effort to rouse the Athenians to defend themselves against the troops of Macedonia, Demosthenes in a series of stunning speeches (later called Philippics) exhorted his people to resist Philip. They tried, but they failed. The Greeks were simply not strong enough to overcome their powerful foe, and thus their independence was wrested from them.

The name *philippics* (with the initial letter in lower case) was also given to a set of orations delivered by Cicero, not against someone named *Philip,* but against Mark Antony. Hence such a diatribe, although termed a *philippic,* can now be aimed at anyone. No longer must a "Philip" be the target. But before deciding to hurl a philippic, one ought to bear in mind the possible consequences—Demosthenes was forced to commit suicide, and Cicero could not escape execution.

## PHOENIX

Phoenix is such a well-recognized term in the United States that it has become the name of a large city and the symbol of a prominent insurance company. Yet, while this country is only a little more than two centuries old, the word *phoenix* has a history of more than thirty centuries behind it.

In ancient Egypt, where men devoted their entire lives in preparation for death, the phoenix was a symbol of resurrection and immortality. This fabulously scarlet-and-gold-plumaged bird reputedly lived for over 1,000 years. As death approached, it would prepare to immolate itself by building a nest of aromatic boughs and spices. Then it would sing a melodious dirge and, by flapping its wings, set the nest afire and be consumed. From the ashes the phoenix would emerge newly born!

The many legends associated with the phoenix have varied, but through all of them runs the thread of man's immortality as represented by the rebirth of the phoenix immediately upon its death. The Egyptian priests also analogized the bird, and its miraculous renewal through fire, with the sun which, when setting, always promised another dawn. Figuratively a *phoenix* is a person or institution that rises from the ashes of its own destruction vigorous enough to start anew.

## PIANO

An Italian whose name is not well known, but to whom the generations should be indebted, is Bartolomeo Cristofori. In 1709 he invented the piano. His contraption was crude by modern standards, but his basic idea—a mechanism whereby the strings of the instruments are struck by felt-covered hammers—still prevails. The importance of this innovation was that it allowed the player a measure of control over the volume of his playing.

The word *piano* is a shortened form of *pianoforte,* an Italian combination of *piano e forte,* which literally means "soft and smooth" and "loud and strong." The ability of a pianist to attain smoothness and to control loudness, distinguished this versatile instrument from its predecessor, the spinet, invented by Giovanni Spinetti in 1664. (The spinet was identical in principle with the harpsichord.)

The violin is an even more ancient musical instrument. It was played during Roman times (remember Nero?), and its Latin name was *vitula.* Although somewhat different from the present-day violin, it was a stringed instrument caressed by a bow. The Italians called it a *violino,* the precursor of the English word *violin.*

## PLACES AS NAMES

Milliners, who design and make women's hats, originally were natives of Milan and were known as *Milaners.* Milan was a fashion center for women's headgear, and from the name of the city evolved the words *millinery* and *milliner,* both spelled with a double *l.*

Many people know, or can readily guess, that the word *cordovan,* a durable leather used in the manufacture of men's shoes, is associated with the name of a city in Spain, Cordoba, where the leather was first tanned. In Spanish, the *b* is sounded like a *v.*

With no change in spelling or pronunciation have come the anglicized terms *madras,* "a cotton cloth used in the manufacture of shirtings and draperies" (Madras is a seaport in South India), and *karakul,* a sheep from *Kara Kul,* a Russian lake region (the name literally means "black lake"). A *jersey* is a slip-on shirt made of wool and worsted, the chief products of the English Channel island of Jersey.

*Paisley* refers to a popular print named after the city where it was designed and woven, Paisley, Scotland. In a valley of that country, a clan created a pattern now used throughout the world—*glen plaid.* It got its name from the name of the valley: Glen Urquhart. And, incidentally, the well-known pattern called *argyle* also has a Scottish name. It came from the name of the county where it originated—Argyll. *Cashmere,* an English spelling version of Kashmir, is a costly product made of wool from goats living on the Himalaya Mountains. *Poplin* has a religious woof. It came from the Italian *papolino* because it was first manufactured in Avignon, ₐ papal seat.

## PLEONASM

*See* REDUNDANCY

## PLUTO

Pluto is a common name for a dog, at least in Disney's world. It also is the name for the mythological Greek god of the underworld. Pluto's domain was Hades, the temporary abode of the dead before their transfer to Elysium or Tartarus.

One of Pluto's dastardly deeds was the rape of Proserpine (called Persephone by the Greeks), who was then destined to live with her rapist for one third of each year. According to this myth, her time spent in Hades represented the bleakness of winter. The rest of the year spent in the upper world symbolized the remaining seasons.

Pluto, despite the foregoing, is not necessarily a name to be held in contempt. Perhaps, instead, the name should be treated with respect, for Pluto (Greek *ploutos*, "wealth") was the giver of wealth. He is etymologically responsible for the words *plutocracy*, "rule by the wealthy," and *plutocrat*, "a member of that society," a person who rules by his wealth. One who calls "Here, Pluto" should use a polite and pleasant tone of voice—for who knows?

## POLITICAL TERMS

The words *radical, extremist, moderate,* and *conservative* are often employed as nouns in political terminology. Their roots, however, were not nurtured in the soil of politics.

A *radical* is a person who seeks to get to the root of the matter, for the origin of the word *radical* lies in the Latin *radix,* which means "root." One seeking fundamental changes in government (something that affects its very root) may be regarded as a radical. Some radicals, however, prefer to be called *liberals* (Latin *liberalis, liber,* "free"), people who are not bound by tradition, whereas others consider themselves, and prefer the label, *progressive* ("one who walks forward," Latin *pro,* "forward," and *gradior, gressus* "walk"), meaning those who favor social improvements. What one person considers radical—"affecting vital principles"—another may consider moderate. Points of view are tagged differently by different people.

*Moderates* oppose political philosophies that seem to be outside reasonable bounds. They disapprove of measures that are extreme or excessive; they lean toward preserving the status quo, welcoming only those changes that are not substantial. In the opinion of those who seek uncompromising changes, a moderate is a conservative.

The word *conservative* comes from the Latin *cum*, "with," and *servare*, "to keep." Conservatives are preservers; they are disposed to maintain existing conditions, accepting the least change possible. In the opinion of some people in public affairs, conservatism is an extreme position, on one end of the political spectrum, and so may be radicalism. However, neither a conservative nor a radical is an extremist. An *extremist* is one who "goes to extremes—in anything." Politics aside, these terms, employed as adjectives, have ordinary usage: "The architect is making a *radical* change in the design of the portico"—fundamental. "As predicted, the rain was *moderate*"—not intense. "He is considered a *conservative* spender"—neither prodigal nor stingy. "Carl was known for his *extremist* belief in strenuous exercise"—inordinate.

## POMP AND CIRCUMSTANCE

The word *pomp* (from Greek *pompe*, "a pagan procession") is often used derisively to mean "an ostentatious display," like the flaunting of wealth or power. But it is a word of solemn splendor (that is, "a dignified showing of magnificence") when it refers to a stately ceremony, especially one involving religious rituals. The inclusion of this term by Sir Edward Elgar in the title of his five "Pomp and Circumstance" marches, one of which is a common musical prelude to graduation exercises, reflected the extended meaning of *pomp* by the Romans—"a triumphal procession," which is what a parade of graduates is. The word *circumstance*, meaning "ceremony," in Elgar's title is archaic. Shakespeare used it in this sense in *Othello*, "pride, pomp, and circumstance of glorious war." The literal meaning of *circumstance* from Latin—*circum*, "around," and *stare*, "to stand," referring to a large number of people standing around, is entirely different from its current definition.

## PORTEND

Everyone has a tendency to look at the dark side rather than the sunny side, an ingrained human failing. The downgrading of English words follows a similar pattern. Neutral words, those that portend neither good nor bad, usually end up as words of concern, trouble, or even doom.

The word *portend* in the last sentence is a case in point. Certainly advance notice need not always be bad. But customarily things portend disaster or doom—never the good, the fortunate. Although an *omen* is merely a prophetic sign that betokens neither good nor ill, its adjective form, *ominous* ("portending evil," "threatening," "sinister"), connotes an unappealing predicament, with no foreboding. In that sentence, even without "unappealing" the sense of *predicament* would be unpleasant—something perplexing or in a sad plight. And here again not because of the word's origin. The parental verb of *predicament* is Late Latin *praedicamentum,* from *praedicare,* "to proclaim"—which may be a joyous announcement of a new holiday. The word *foreboding* always casts a pall of gloom, even though its root, *bode,* simply means "to tell" (a *boda* was a herald). The prefix *fore,* while adding the dimension of futurity, also changed the sense of the word to suggest dread, the dark side of things only. Which harks back to the very first sentence.

## PORTMANTEAU WORDS

The blending of words or their parts has spawned many new English words. These children now have a life of their own. Although the offspring enjoy meanings entirely different from those of their parents, they show traces of their lineage. Some blends were created to fill a void in the language; others were onomatopoeic telescopings of two words—that is, words that imitate natural sounds, like *squish* from "squirt" and "swish."

Although many blend words evaporate quickly from the language, others find a home for themselves. Lewis Carroll in *Through the Looking-Glass* dubbed these amalgams *portmanteau words.* Humpty Dumpty said, in explaining to Alice his use of *slithy* (a combining of *lithe* and *slimy*): "You see, it's like a portmanteau . . . there are two meanings packed up into one word."

Although the history of some of these blend words is questionable, no one disputes their expressive effects on the English language. *Blurt,* for example (a combination of "blow" and "spurt") has no synonym with its precise meaning. And what can substitute for *splutter,* from "splash" and "sputter," or replace *grumble*, from "growling" and "rumbling," or *flaunt* from "flout" and "vaunt," or *flare* from "flame" and "glare." And, reverting to Lewis Carroll, *chortle* from "chuckle" and "snort" and *squawk* from "squall" and "squeak." No one can live in today's world without these mergers. But for them there would be no *brunch*.

## POSH

So many surmises have surfaced on the origin of the word *posh* that it would take a page and a half to enumerate and explore them all—and then to no avail because its origin is unattested. In today's language *posh* means "swanky."

The charming story that *posh* is an acronym for "port out, starboard home," referring to the desirable cabins from England to India and return, is an intriguing bit of folk etymology, but just a tale. The Peninsular and Oriental Steam Navigation Company that serviced this route, beginning in 1842, said they had never heard of *posh* used in this acronymic sense. The clincher is that the word's first appearance in print was not until October 1935 in the London *Times Literary Supplement*. Finally, we all may agree that this *posh* case may be stamped "closed," since in 1962 the librarian of the P.&O. declared that investigation has come up with no evidence that P.O.S.H. had ever been stamped on anything.

## POUND

A pound, almost everyone will agree, is the equivalent of sixteen ounces. Although that statement is correct, it is not the complete truth. In *troy weight* (the weight used by jewelers and pharmacists) the pound consists of twelve ounces. This measure of weight, which preceded the *avoirdupois weight*, the one in general use, was named after Troyes, France, a center for merchant activity in the twelfth century. (The English dispute the French claim, saying that they have been using Troy weight since the time of Edward the Confessor.)

The system of the avoirdupois weight is based on "a pound containing 16 ounces or 7000 grains and equal to 453.59 grams." The term *avoirdupois* came from the Old French *aveir de peis*, which means "goods (such as silk or feathers) sold by weight." (The trick question "Which is heavier, a pound of feathers or a pound of gold?" is correctly answered, at least technically, with a pound of feathers. Gold is weighed by troy weight, and its pound consists of 5,760 grains. Of course, if feathers and gold are weighed by the same system of weights, their weights will be the same.)

The legal and standard money of Great Britain is the *pound* (from Latin *pondus*, a unit of weight for solid substances). Originally it was the weight of one pound of silver sterling. Nevertheless, the pound is symbolized by a slashed capital L (£), which does not stand for "pound" but for *libra* (another Latin term meaning "pound," referring to money). The abbreviation for "pound," *lb.*, comes from the initial letter of each syllable of *libra*.

The full name of the English pound is "pound sterling." The origin of the word *sterling* is obscure. Dr. Johnson thought that it probably came from "Esterlings" (the stress is on the second syllable), who were employed as coiners during the reign of King John. Others believe that *sterling* stands for "star" or "starling" ("little star"), since that design was always embossed on sterling.

## PRECARIOUS

Anything precarious is characterized by the dangers of instability and insecurity. The implication is that for safety's sake, a person whose position is precarious had better start praying (*precarious* comes from the Latin genitive form *precis*, "prayer"). But since the effectiveness of prayer is uncertain (no one knows whether it will be answered), *precarious* came to mean "something that could not be depended on," "unreliable," "dubious." A related word is *imprecate*, "to pray against" (*im* means "against"), which is more often seen in its noun form, *imprecations:* "He heaped imprecations upon his enemy." In this usage the word is a synonym for *curse*.

*Precocious*, unlike *precarious*, begins with a prefix, *pre* from the Latin *prae* ("before"). Appended to *cox* from *coquere* ("to cook"), *precocious* literally means "to cook beforehand." It adopted the sense of premature ripening, which, as applied to children who evidence early mental, physical, or artistic development, signified superior abilities before one's normal time. It was, so to speak, a cooking up of something ahead of schedule.

## PREPOSTEROUS

The most preposterous word in the English language is *preposterous*. It is a combination of *pre* ("before") and *post* ("after"), which is, as the Germans say, "putting the horse behind the wagon." That, of course, is absurd; but that is what *preposterous* means: "absurd."

If somebody were told that *bosh* is not a British expression, he might say, "You must be bloody wrong; that's preposterous" or "That's nonsense" (which is what *bosh* stands for). But, although the British have arrogated the word to themselves, it is of Turkish origin coming from *bos,* which means "empty" or "useless." *Bosh* first appeared in English in the novel *Adventures of Hajji Baba of Ispahan,* written by James Morier in 1824.

## PRIMROSE

Roses are red, violets are blue, and primroses are yellow. Perhaps, but a *primrose* is not a rose, and it is not the "prim" (the prime) or first flower in spring. The appended word *rose* was an etymological blunder—the original name of the flower was *primerols,* a curious corruption of the French *primeverole* and the Italian *primeverola,* which were compounded from the Latin *prima vera* ("the first spring 'flower'"), in which no rose is implied. Also, despite the sense of "first" in the initial syllable, many flowers bud before the primrose. A primrose, therefore, is neither a rose nor the first bloomer. Poetically, nevertheless, it is so regarded: "Primrose, first-born child of Ver, / Merry springtime's harbinger"—Beaumont and Fletcher, *The Two Noble Kinsmen.*

"A primrose path" is not found in any garden; to walk along or to follow "a primrose path" is to adopt a life of ease and pleasure, especially sexual pleasure. The expression, therefore, is condemnatory—a euphemism, in a strict sense, for "following a road of sin." Thanks for this phrase goes to Shakespeare who, in *Hamlet,* has Ophelia say in contradiction to her brother's advice: "Do not, as some ungracious pastors do, / Show me the steep and thorny way to heaven; / Whiles, like a puff'd and reckless libertine, / Himself the primrose path of dalliance treads, . . ."

## PROCRASTINATE

A word whose sense is putting off until later is *procrastinate,* from Latin *pro* ("for") and *cras* ("tomorrow"). A procrastinator puts off his duty or obligation to some undetermined tomorrow because he's either lazy or indifferent toward his responsibilities. Certainly he does not agree with Benjamin Franklin's aphorism: "Never leave that till tomorrow which you can do today" or with Edward Young: "Procrastination is the thief of time."

## PROCRUSTEAN

The adjective *procrustean* denotes the use of violence to gain uniformity. According to a Greek legend, Procustes was a brigand who lived near Attica. He placed his victims on an iron bed. If they were too short, he stretched them to fit; if too long, he hacked off the part of their limbs which hung over the end of the bed. Clearly Procrustes was a firm believer in the fitness of things. Today people required to act in a specified way are said to be lying on Procrustes's bed; they have no choice but to conform.

## PROFANE

The dictionary defines *profane* as "characterized by irreverence or contempt of God or sacred things." The source of this word is the Latin *pro fanum,* which literally means "that which is situated *before* (that is, outside) the temple." According to the Romans, the uninitiated who came to the temple were profane. They were unholy, not sacred. Later the word came to mean "irreligious or blasphemous" and then, with its religious overtones dwindling, "common or vulgar." It has also assumed the meaning "to put to unworthy use." Shakespeare used it in this sense when he had Prince Henry say, "I feel much to blame, / So idly to profane the precious time."

*Profane* has become a useful word to represent the secular, the worldly, when a comparison is made with the religious, the spiritual. The great Santayana used *profane* in just this way: "The profane poet is by instinct a naturalist. He loves landscape, he loves love, he loves the humor and pathos of earthly existence. But the religious prophet loves none of these things."

## PROMETHEAN

Prometheus was a Titan who, according to Greek mythology, created man out of clay. But he is best known for having stolen fire from heaven. For this offense Zeus had him chained to a rock where during the daytime an eagle ate his liver, which renewed itself each succeeding night, only to be eaten again the next day. Anything "life-giving" or "boldly original" is said to be *promethean.*

## PROTAGONIST

*See* TRAGEDY

## PROTEAN

Proteus, the prophetic old man of the sea, lived in a cave and went to sleep each noon. He prophesied only if seized, but no one could catch him unless he was asleep. If not captured, he would, like the sea that keeps changing, assume a different shape and elude anyone who came to consult him. A person who is "exceedingly variable, able to change an attitude at will" or is "shifty and fickle," is *protean.* In a complimentary sense, it may refer to someone blessed with versatile talents or a flexible nature.

## PROTOCOL

*Protocol* is a common word in polite society and in the diplomatic corps. By and large, it is a code of etiquette (custom and regulations) dealing with diplomats and others at a court or capital. But it applies as well to more everyday activities, for example, who goes first in a school procession and who sits next to whom at a family dinner.

In its initial Greek form, the word *protocol* was *protokollon*, and its meaning was completely unrelated to what has just been said. The Greek word combined *proto* ("first") and *kolla* ("glue") and was used to designate the first sheet of a roll of papyrus which consisted of sheets glued together. The *protocol*, the top sheet, listed the contents of the manuscript and its purport. A meaning of *protocol* to this very day is "an original draft, minute, or record from which a document, especially a treaty, is prepared," a first gluing, in effect. Dr. Johnson defined *protocol* as "an original copy of any writing" and quoted Ayliffe: "An original is stiled the *protocol*, or scriptura matrix; and if the protocol, which is the root and foundation of the instrument, does not appear, the instrument is not valid."

*Protocol* still is, in one sense, the glue that makes people stick to orderly procedure.

## PUMPERNICKEL

According to the *OED*, the earliest instance of *pumpernickel* appearing in print was in 1756. In that year a traveler in Germany, named Nugent, reported in *A Grand Tour of Germany* "Their bread is of the very coarsest kind, ill baked, and as black as a coal, for they never sift their flour. The people of the country call it Pompernickel."

The etymology of this Westphalian hard rye bread is so obscure that one can only conjecture as to its origin. One notion is that *pumpernickel* was compounded of *pumpern*, "to break wind," and *Nickel*, "bumpkin." The first part, the state of flatulence it generates, was due to the coarseness of the bread that made it so hard to digest as to induce "wind breaking." The second has several versions. Since peasants who regularly ate this bread had generally been considered stupid people by urban sophisticates, they called the bread after the term they applied to the so-called rural blockheads, *pompernickel*, now spelled *pumpernickel*. Another idea is that *Nickel*, meaning "devil," was appended to the word's first element because such unbolted bread would give even the devil indigestion. Then there is the story about Napoleon, who, after tasting a slice, made a wry face and then gave the bread to his horse Nicole, saying "Bon pour Nicole," the sense of which is it's only good enough for horses.

# PUNCH

The word *punch* has several unrelated meanings. It may signify a tool, a drink, or a sock in the jaw.

The first, a tool for making holes, apparently is a shortening of *puncheon,* from an Old French word similarly formed and meaning "a stamp or die." Etymologists, however, have been unable to substantiate this notion.

The second, a drink usually made of sweetened fruit juices, is from Sanskrit *panca* or Hindustani *panch,* which means "five," the theory being that there were five ingredients—alcohol, water, lemon, sugar, and spice. According to legend, from the native word for *five* has come the name for this popular drink. The first use of *punch* in England noted in the *Oxford English Dictionary* came from the quill of R. Addams, who, in 1632, wrote to a T. Colley, a merchant: "I hop you will keep a good house together and drincke punch by no allowanc."

A strike with a quick blow of the fist is a *punch.* This term, too, has an uncertain origin—possibly a contraction of *puncheon* or an emanation from Middle English *punchen,* a collateral form of *pounsen,* "pounce," meaning "to swoop down on," "to attack." Dr. Klein favors the latter idea. Figuratively *punch* refers to "a vigorously telling force or effect."

Those who wonder why Dickens, in *Pickwick Papers,* used quotation marks around "punch" (especially since that word had appeared in print previously under the name of some respected writers, such as Byron and Scott) might well consider the possibility that he viewed *punch* as a slang term. Now, of course, *punch* is accepted on all literary levels, although its figurative sense is still listed as informal.

# PUNY

This is not a story, just a matter of opposites—the weak and the strong, the puny and the robust.

The sense of *puny* has changed through the years. The word's ancestor was the Middle French *puisné* (a combination of *puis,* "next," and *né,* "born"), and it referred to someone younger or in an inferior position to someone else. The theory behind the word was that children born afterwards (born later) possess less strength and vigor than the children born before them.

English adopted the term (in fact, the English and French words sound almost alike). Its sense of inferior in power, weakness, or lack of importance became established through Shakespeare's *King Richard II,* who exhorts himself, "Am I not King? . . . / Is not the King's name twenty thousand names? / Arm, arm, my name! a puny subject strikes / At thy great glory." Nowadays *puny* means "small and feeble." It is used of anyone or anything less than normal size or strength.

*Robust* implies healthiness and strength. A robust person is vigorous and sturdy. He is expected to be powerfully built, for the word *robust* comes from the Latin *robustus,* "oaken," which means "as strong and sturdy as an oak."

## PYRRHIC VICTORY

A *Pyrrhic victory* is one gained at too great a cost; it is a hollow triumph. No one is victorious when both victor and vanquished suffer devastating losses. In the year 279 B.C. King Pyrrhus of Epirus fought the Romans in a long drawn-out bloody battle. Pyrrhus won, but he lost so large a part of his army, and his surviving soldiers were so exhausted that he exclaimed, according to Plutarch, "One more such victory over the Romans and we are utterly undone."

From Greek mythology comes another instance of a ruinous victory. Cadmus, whose father was king of Phoenicia, was sent to find his sister Europa who had been carried off by Zeus, but his search was interrupted by a dragon who overcame his companions. Cadmus killed the monster and then, on the advice of Athena, sowed its teeth into the earth, out of which immediately sprouted armed men. By throwing a stone among them, Cadmus caused the warriors to turn on one another and fight till all but five had perished. (The surviving five, called Sparti, "the sown men," became the ancestors of the Thebans). Cadmus was punished, however, because of the bloodshed he had caused. For eight years he had to do penance. Like a Pyrrhic victory, a *Cadmean victory* was bought at too high a price.

# Q

## QUARANTINE

*See* **FORTY**

## QUICK

The Biblical phrase that refers to "the quick and the dead" ("Ordained of God to be the Judge of quick and dead"—*Acts*) is not a part of common speech but is occasionally seen in print. No one wonders about the word *dead,* but there can be a question concerning *quick.* In its ordinary sense, *quick* means "speedy, rapid, fast," but in contrast to *dead* it means "alive," referring to people who are among the living. In simple terms, "the quick and the dead" means "the living and the dead."

As the first element in such words as *quicksand* and *quicksilver, quick* suggests an attribute of life—the ability to move or shift. Originally *quick* was spelled *cwic,* which looks like a phoneticism.

Those who use the phrase "you cut me to the quick," meaning you have hurt my feelings, are, metaphorically but perhaps unwittingly, referring to live tissue. A person cut to the quick has had his skin penetrated to the living flesh, as might happen if fingernails are pared too closely.

## QUINTESSENCE

*Quintessence* is the force or spirit at the highest essence of a substance. (*Essence,* from Latin *esse,* "to be," refers to that which is fundamental to the very existence of a thing.) Today *quintessence* represents the best, the exemplar: "Nureyev—the quintessence of grace." It also is used to mean an essential part of a theory, speech, or condition.

The ancient Greeks used *quintessence* quite differently. Originally, according to their belief, four elements constituted all existing matter—earth, air, fire, and water. Later the Pythagorean philosophers thought that above the four basic elements existed a fifth or higher essence which permeated nature and formed the substance of the planets and stars, an essence even purer than fire. It became (from the Latin *quinta essentia,* "the fifth essence") the telescoped *quintessence*—the finest extract, the rarest of all.

Milton in *Paradise Lost* speaks of *quintessence* in the story of the creation:

> Swift to their several quarters hasted then
> The cumbrous elements—Earth, Flood, Air, Fire;
> And this ethereal quintessence of Heaven
> Flew upward, spirited with various forms,
> That rolled orbicular, and turned to stars. . . .

## QUIXOTIC

*Quixotic* is not an everyday word. But it is not a bookish word either. It means "impractically chivalrous, extravagantly romantic, visionary." A person who is idealistic but unrealistic is said to be *quixotic.* The word comes directly from the title of the famous satire *Don Quixote* by Miguel de Cervantes.

The hero of the novel, Don Quixote, deeply affected by the silly books of romantic chivalry popular at the time, fancies himself a knight and sallies forth to reform the world and to aid the downtrodden and the distressed. He and his squire, Sancho Panza, imitate the heroes in books of chivalry and become involved in embarrassing and absurd situations. Perhaps the most ridiculous episodes involved tilting at windmills and turning lovely inns into castles.

The practical result of this devastating satire was to put an end to knight-errantry and to put a distinctive word, with the sense of "impractical," into English dictionaries: *quixotic.*

## QUIZ

*Quiz* is an unusual word in that it owes its being to a practical joke. It seems that a James Daly, the manager of a Dublin theater, offered to bet that he could coin a word which overnight would become the talk of the town, even though the word had no meaning. Daly's boast seemed so preposterous that he had many takers, but (with the luck of the Irish?) he won his bet. What Daly did was hire small boys to chalk a single word on all the downtown walls and billboards. The next morning the Dubliners were amazed to see this strange word everywhere they looked. Tongues started to wag, especially since it was imagined that the word was indecent. The word, of course, was *quiz*.

The Daly story has not been authenticated; lexicographers note that the origin of *quiz* is unknown. School kids fear a *quiz*, an informal test that, because it will be graded, has to be taken seriously—even though the word's meaning is "a practical joke."

## RAGLAN SLEEVE

A raglan sleeve has the shoulders slanted and extended in one piece to the neckline. The sleeve was named after Lord Raglan (1788–1885), who was the first to wear a loose-fitting overcoat with sleeves that continue to the collar.

Lord Fitzroy Somerset, the baptismal name of the first Lord Raglan, served as an aide-de-camp to the Duke of Wellington, the victor at Waterloo. During the celebrated battle Raglan lost an arm (it is said that he called for his severed arm in order to retrieve from one of its fingers a ring his wife had given him). In 1852 England joined its ally France in the Crimean War against Russia, and Raglan was named the commander-in-chief of the British forces.

Historians have criticized Raglan for his military ineptness. In all fairness, however, it should be pointed out that he had had no active experience in leading troops in the field. Although Raglan was a sympathetic general and well-liked by his troops, his leadership was nothing short of disastrous. His ambiguous order at Balaklava led to the senseless destruction of the brave Six Hundred during the historic charge of the Light Brigade. Raglan has been immortalized, however, not because of any daring or strategic military feats but because of the sleeve of his coat that bore his distinctive identification—the *raglan sleeve*, which perhaps he affected to hide his missing arm.

The officer who led the charge of the doomed Six Hundred at the battle of Balaklava on October 25, 1854, was James Thomas Brudenell, the seventh Earl of Cardigan, who popularized a worsted over-waistcoat that buttoned down the front and that came to be called after him—a *cardigan*. Military historians agree that Cardigan was bumble-headed and not militarily equipped to be a commander. Furthermore, Cardigan never bothered to unscramble Raglan's ambiguous communiqués. This combination, of military incompetence and faulty communication, resulted in Cardigan's tragic assignment to his troops, immortalized by Tennyson in his famous poem *The Charge of the Light Brigade.*

> Forward, the Light Brigade!
> Was there a man dismayed? . . . Someone had blundered.
> Theirs not to make reply,
> Theirs not to reason why,
> Theirs but to do and die. . .
> Into the jaws of death,
> Into the mouth of hell,
> Rode the Six Hundred.

## RAVEL

*See* CONTRADICTIONS

## THE REAL McCOY

*The real McCoy* may be as fictional as the real Simon Pure. But it, like Simon Pure, has come to mean "bona fide," "the genuine article," or "the real thing." So many theories concerning the origin of this phrase have been advanced, each unrelated to the others, that one may feel free to take his pick. Mencken, who included at least a half-dozen in his writings, observes wryly that "the origin of this term has been much debated and is still unsettled."

According to *The World Book Dictionary,* the American English expression *the real McCoy* came from the Scottish phrase "the real MacKay." MacKay was a Scotch whisky exported to the United States and Canada by A. and M. MacKay of Glasgow. The story concerning the origin of *the real McCoy* that makes the most sense, however, and also has the widest following, is that Norman Selby, a celebrated boxer of the 1880's, fighting under the name Kid McCoy, became the welterweight champion in 1896. During a barroom brawl, someone disputed the genuineness of the Kid, claiming he was not the popular pugilist but a fake. Whereupon the angered Kid slugged the doubter on the jaw, who, after picking himself up from the floor, muttered, as he rubbed his aching jaw, "He's the real McCoy, all right." Perhaps this is all folk etmyology. But until a story with more sock comes along, at least here's one with a punch.

## RED-LETTER DAY, RED TAPE

*See* **RUBRIC**

## REDUNDANCY

*Wordiness* is a serious, tiring fault, judging by its many available synonyms. For example, there are *verbiage, prolixity, verbosity,* and plain *long-windedness.* Then *loquacity, garrulity, talkativeness,* and *glibness.* Further, *profuseness, padding, bombast,* and *gassiness.* And so on to *big mouth* and *hot air.*

In addition, several rhetorical terms denote the use of more words than are needed to convey clear meaning. The commonest is *redundancy*—Latin *redundare*, "to overflow," as waves rise back (*unda*, "a wave"). Aristotle called it "the accumulation of words that add nothing to the sense and cloud up what clarity there is." Examples of redundancy are almost limitless: *fellow* colleague; doctorate *degree*; blend, congregate, connect, gather, or mix *together*; skirt *around*, electrician by *trade*; and *old* proverb or a *new* recruit.

*Tautology* (from Greek *tautos*, "the same," and *logos*, "the word") is a needless repetition of the same thought in different words, as are "necessary essentials" and "true facts"—or "a beginner who has just started" and "a modern architect of today." *Pleonasm* (derived from Greek *pleonasmos*, "superabundance") is the name for that which expresses "more than enough" to convey a thought. It is a repetition, especially of two words used for the same grammatical function ("two twins") or superfluous wording ("most perfect"). This fault is not an offense against grammar but a matter of style. Simply stated, it is an unnecessary fullness of expression.

Concerned writers avoid unnecessary words, for their inclusion would violate a basic principle of good writing. Needless words, like deadwood, should be lopped off.

> A sentence should contain no unnecessary words, a paragraph no unnecessary sentences, for the same reason that a drawing should have no unnecessary lines and a machine no unnecessary parts.
> —William Strunk, Jr., *The Elements of Style*

## REMORSE

*See* **COMPUNCTION**

# REPUBLIC

If a republic is not a democracy and a democracy is not a republic, can the United States be both? Yes, in a broad sense; in a narrow one, no.

The term *republic* derives from the Latin phrase *res publica,* which means "public affairs" or "the state." A *republic* is "a state in which the supreme power rests in the body of citizens entitled to vote and is exercised by representatives chosen directly by them." That the United States is a republic is proclaimed in the pledge of allegiance to the American flag: "I pledge allegiance to the flag of the United States of America and to the *republic* for which it stands."

A *democracy* (from Greek *demokratia—demos,* "people," and *kratos,* "power," "rule") is a "state" in which the supreme power is vested in the people and exercised directly by them rather than by elected representatives. Typical of such states were the ancient Greek city-states, called *demos,* and the New England town meetings. Although the power of government in the United States remains in the people, it is not exercised directly by them but by the representatives they choose. The United States may therefore properly be called a *representative democracy.* President James Madison, in distinguishing between a republic and a democracy, said: "In a democracy the people meet and exercise their power of government in person; in a republic, they assemble and administer it by their representatives and agents."

# RESTAURANT

*See* CAFETERIA

# RIGHT

It is better to be right than wrong. Or even left. At least one may conclude that from the study of language. Words associated with the right side are generally complimentary or signify something desirable, but those pointing to the left are quite the opposite. For example, everyone tries to get up on the "right" side of the bed and hopes to stay on the "right" side of the boss—at least if he's in his "right" mind.

Other languages reflect the same kind of bias in favor of the right and against the left. In Latin, the word for "right" is *dexter,* from which has come the English *dexterous* (or, alternatively, *dextrous*), meaning "skillful." Which is what a person who uses the "right" hand is expected to be. (An *ambidextrous* person should be even more skillful, since he has two right hands—*ambi,* "both," and *dexter,* "right hand"). On the other hand, the Latin *sinister* is the left hand, that is, the wrong hand. Further, left-handers are thought to be unlucky. In augury, birds that appear on the left side portend ill luck, but not those on the right side; they presage good luck. Today *sinister* means evil or ominous.

"Lefties" fared no better in French. The French word for "left" is *gauche* (pronounced "gohsh"), which suggests awkwardness or lack of social grace. A guest who drinks from the finger bowl, no matter how dexterously he handles it, is still gauche.

English also favors the right over the left. The word *right* developed from Old English *riht,* which means "to lead straight; to guide; to rule." *Left* evolved from Old English *lyft,* which means "weak." Our prejudice against the left can be seen in such terms as "two left feet," meaning "awkward," and "left-handed compliment," which is no compliment at all.

Even in marriages, a left-handed one is not so good as a right-handed one. Left-handed marriages (called *morganatic*) are consummated by male members of royal families with women below their rank. By giving the bride his left hand, the bridegroom signifies that he is not elevating her to his level nor is he endowing her with royal privileges. That needs the right hand.

## RIVALS

Rivals are people at odds with each other, competitors. In Rome *rivalis* meant "relating to a stream," and the *rivali* were those who lived on opposite sides of a river, using (and often competing for) the same source of water. That disagreements should develop was expectable, not only because water was essential to their survival but also because rivers were natural boundaries. In any event, disputes concerning water rights were common among these people, and they came to be known as rivals. According to Trench in *The Study of Words,* "'Rivals', in the primary sense of the word, are those who dwell on the banks of the same river. . . . There is no such fruitful source of contention as a water-right."

The legal rights of people living alongside a river are called riparian rights. The origin of the adjective *riparian,* which means "pertaining to the bank of a river," was founded in Latin *ripa,* "riverbank."

## ROBOT

Robots are mechanical workers that perform human tasks. They have become a somewhat common sight in Japan and are gradually showing up in American factories.

The word *robot* first appeared in 1922 in a terrifying play called *R.U.R.* (which stands for *Rossum's Universal Robots*). Karl Čapek, the Czech playwright, borrowed the word from the Slav *robota,* meaning a "servile laborer." This play, so popular that it made the term *robot* familiar to almost everyone, was set in a degenerate society where automated machines were made to do the work of human beings. Eventually the robots became monsters, turned on their human masters, and overpowered them.

Science fictionists believe that since human brains function through electrical impulses, an electronic brain capable of original thought can be invented and installed in a robot. Impossible! one might say. Which is exactly what people at the turn of the century would have said about sending a man to the moon.

## ROGER

*See* SOS

## ROMAN NUMERAL IV

*See* CLOCK

## ROMANCE LANGUAGES

Romance languages are not languages of love. They are cognate languages descended from the Roman tongue—Latin. People in distant lands (French, Spanish, Portuguese, Romanians, Italians) all spoke a dialect derived from Latin, but because of their geographical separateness, their speech habits differed, each in individual ways. The various dialects, which turned into languages, were designated *romans* to distinguish them from classical Latin. Although almost all serious works continued to be written in Latin, tales of love were written in *romans,* the popular tongue, or, as it came to be called, the *Romance* languages. Hence the saying "in Romance we read," which eventually came to refer to the tale itself rather than to the language. From this word, and because of the nature of these early writings, the term *romance* evolved in the sense used today, "a love affair." Who would have dreamed that high romance was originally couched in low language?

## ROSTRUM

A *rostrum* is a platform on which speakers stand to address an audience. But that is not what it was during Roman times. Then, a rostrum was a "beak," a word derived from the Latin *rodere*, "to gnaw," a logical evolution, since beaks usually gnaw. These beaks, or rostra, were the prows of captured Carthaginian ships whose forepieces were shaped liked a bird's beak. The Romans used these souvenirs of victorious battles to decorate the speaker's platform in the Forum. Eventually, the platform itself came to be called a rostrum, as is so in English today.

A *podium* (Greek *podion* means "a small foot") is a raised platform that sits on a rostrum so that a speaker or conductor who stands on it can command a view of the audience or the musicians. A larger podium, one that can accommodate many people, perhaps a dozen, is called a *dais* (Old French *deis,* from Latin *discus,* "a quoit," which in Late Latin became "a table").

Usually found on a podium is a *lectern,* a stand with a small slanted table top on which speakers assemble their notes or small exhibits. Lectern comes from Latin *lectus,* the past participle of *legere,* "to read," so named because priests in medieval England read the Scriptures from this "reading desk."

# RUBBER

Christopher Columbus was responsible for many things in addition to his discovery of the New World. For example, thanks to Columbus, one can erase a mistake by rubbing it out.

To start at the beginning, Columbus' explorers found natives playing with bouncing balls—something unheard of in Europe. The balls were made from a milky substance that oozed from certain trees. The name the natives gave this stuff (which was natural India rubber) was *cahchu*, called by the French *caoutchouc*. This, essentially, is the substance of an art eraser, the present-day latex. The Caribbean word might have stuck if not for the English chemist Joseph Priestley. About 1770 he noticed that the South American gum would "rub out" pencil marks; whence the word *rubber*. Today, of course, rubber has a hundred and one uses unrelated to "rubbing," and many far more important than "erasing." Incidentally, *to erase*, literally, is not to "rub out" but to "scratch out," which is what the Romans who erred did on their wax tablets. The Latin past participle *erasus* (from *eradere*, "to scratch out") gave English *erase*. Another derivative from this same verb is *eradicate*.

# RUBRIC

The name of the red-colored gem, the *ruby*, comes from Latin *ruber*, which means "red." *Rubric* has passed directly into English from Latin *rubrica*, "red earth for coloring." Although rubric now means "an authoritative rule," "an explanatory commentary," or even "a motto, pet phrase, or settled custom," it originally referred to the ecclesiastical practice of writing headings in red ink and later to the directions in the margins of church books also written in red ink to distinguish these notes from the black ink of the text. Today *rubric* has lost its redness.

*Red-letter days* are festive, memorable days. The expression evolved from the practice of marking feast days in red on church calendars. By extension, any particularly happy or important day has come to be called a red-letter day—or a banner day, a day to hang out a banner, which need not be red. However, in the opinion of Lamb, as quoted in his *Essays of Elia*, "The red letter days now become, for all intents and purposes, dead-letter days."

The phrase most often used to stigmatize bureaucratic procrastination (and introduced by Charles Dickens) is *red tape*. Before the invention of modern filing systems, government employees customarily tied up official documents with red ribbon, or tape, and then placed them in bundles in cubbyholes. The exasperating delays encountered by citizens from officials when seeking information from those documents took on the name of the tape that first had to be removed—*red tape*.

## SADISM

A sadist delights in cruelty. His pleasure is to inflict mental or physical pain on others. Loosely speaking, his satisfaction comes simply from watching someone worry or appear apprehensive, or from twisting the tail of a puppy to hear it yelp. However, the form of mental aberration from which sadists suffer is founded on sexual gratification, the obtaining of sexual release by inflicting pain upon a love object.

A Frenchman, Count Donatien Alphonse François de Sade (1740–1814), who practiced perversion (he was sentenced to death for crimes of poisoning and sodomy but escaped, only to end his days at the Charenton lunatic asylum), was the first to write on this sexual aberration. Although it had probably existed for centuries, this type of sexual perversion finally received public attention through his writings. Today the name *sadism* (actually coined much later by Kraft-Ebbing) refers to this form of psychic deviation.

An even odder form of sexual gratification is the very opposite of sadism—abnormal sex pleasure derived from being abused by another person. In 1893 Leopold von Sacher-Masoch, an Austrian, brought this kind of perversion into the open by attributing it to the central character in one of his novels. The sexual satisfaction he pictured was obtained by submitting to physical abuse, even in the form of flagellation, which became one of the more popular forms of masochism. Today *masochism* as a general word refers to any kind of emotional pleasure that stems from abuse or domination by another person.

A wit, who prefers to remain anonymous, once observed that the difference between a masochist and a sadist is that a masochist screams "Hurt me! Hurt me!" The sadist grins back meanly and says, "No, I won't!"

## SALAD DAYS

*See* DOG DAYS

## SALARY

A salary, during the great days of the Romans, was called a *salarium,* "salt-money." The ancients regarded salt as such an essential to good diet (and before refrigeration it was the only chemical that preserved meat) that they made a special allowance in the wages of soldiers to buy *sal* (Latin for "salt"). With time any stipend came to be called a *salarium,* from which English acquired the word *salary.* (Clearly a person who salts his salary away is carefully preserving it.)

The expression "worth his salt" refers to a person whose work merits support, salary, or the like. As put by Robert Louis Stevenson: "It was plain from every line of his body that our new hand was worth his salt."

Another ancient saying that has continued more or less to this day is "to be below the salt," which signifies an inferior position. This phrase evolved as a matter of seating arrangements. The table at which the king and his dignitaries sat was graced with large, decorative saltcellars. The less important courtiers sat at a table lower than the king's. That they were less favored was made clear, since they were seated "below the salt." But some word sleuths say that this is all folk etymology. Perhaps it should be taken *cum grano salis,* "with a grain of salt."

## SANCTION

*See* CONTRADICTIONS

## SANDWICH

Casinos during the eighteenth century were not serviced by girls in bunny garb carrying trays of delicacies so that hungry players could remain at their post without leaving to take time out to eat. Regardless, one inveterate gambler, a noble attached to the Court of George III, was such a devoted attendant at the gaming-table and became so engrossed in his cards that he would not quit to eat. On one occasion, during a twenty-four hour session, he ordered his servant to bring him cuts of roast beef placed between slices of bread which he could munch while he played. From this gastronomic quickie has come the most ubiquitous item on the menus of American restaurants—the sandwich, named for John Montagu, the First Lord of the Admiralty during the American Revolution and the fourth Earl of Sandwich.

(The sandwich man, not the one behind the counter, but the one parading as a sandwich, with advertising signs front and back, is an expression from the pen of Charles Dickens. He dubbed this man "an animated sandwich.")


## SARCASM

> The arrows of sarcasm are barbed with contempt.
> —Washington Gladden, *Taming the Tongue*

*Sarcasm* has a somewhat milder sense today than it had in the original Greek. From its root, *sarx,* meaning "flesh," came its progenitor *sarkazein,* which, in translation, is "to tear flesh." *Sarcasm* no longer suggests a plucking off of the skin, but its motive nevertheless is to inflict pain with a taunting remark— caustic and sometimes ironical. It is always bitter. A classic example of sarcasm is Byron's depiction of Southey in *The Vision of Judgment.* Southey has slipped and fallen into his lake—

> He first sank to the bottom—like his works,
> But soon rose to the surface—like himself;
> For all corrupted things are buoy'd like corks,
> By their own rottenness, light as an elf,
> Or wisp that flits o'er a morass.

A more modern example was written in a review by Robert Benchley: "It was one of those plays in which all of the actors unfortunately enunciated very clearly."

*Excoriation* was just as brutal in ancient times. To *excoriate,* in today's language, is to "denounce" or "censure." But to the Romans, it meant (from *excoriare,* "to strip off the skin") to remove a piece of skin (Latin *corium,* "skin"). The word is now used only figuratively, "to rip a person's hide off" or, in a more practical sense, "to bawl him out so that he'll never forget it."

Today no matter how bitter the sarcasm or how severe the excoriation, physically no harm has been done—at least none that is apparent.

A synonym of *excoriate* that can be a fooler is *scarify* (from Latin *scarifare,* "to scratch"). It does not mean to scare or frighten. To *scarify* is to scar, to make punctures on the skin; hence, figuratively, "to lacerate by cutting criticism," "to excoriate."

## SATYRIASIS

See **NYMPHOMANIA**

## SAVVY

See **KIBITZER**

## SAXOPHONE

> Drum on your drums, batter on your banjos,
> sob on the long cool-winding saxophones.
> Go to it, O jazzen.
> —Carl Sandburg, *Jazz Fantasia*

A musical instrument that has added to the happiness of many people was invented by a man whose life ended unhappily.

Adolphe Sax, born in the early nineteenth century, was the son of a wind instrument maker in Brussels. His first love was the bass clarinet. After working to improve its tonal qualities, he had an idea for a sister instrument. And that was the humble beginning of the saxophone.

It is said that Sax experienced many accidents during his youth, from swallowing a needle to swallowing sulphuric acid. But he survived and his passion to market his instrument drove him to Paris to try his luck. Sax endured all kinds of disappointment in the French capital. Suppliers of musical instruments refused to display his new invention. Musicians showed no interest. Finally a show was held in 1844 at which various instruments were featured, among them Sax's yet unnamed musical device. The audience was delighted by the performance, and Sax was on his way to financial success. He became the musical instrument supplier to the French army, and soon was recognized throughout the world as an outstanding craftsman in his field.

Although he knew how to handle musical instruments, Sax did not have the talent, unfortunately, to handle money. He slipped into bankruptcy and spent his remaining years in total obscurity.

## SCAPEGOAT

A *scapegoat* is a person blamed for the mistakes of others. The word began as two words, *escape goat.* The Bible (Leviticus XVI, 10) describes the Hebrew ceremony of sacrificing one goat to the Lord and then allowing a second one, bearing the sins of the people, to escape into the desert. William Tyndale, the great sixteenth-century translator of the Old Testament, offered the following as the literal meaning of that passage: "And Aaron cast lottes over .ii. gootes; one lotte for the Lorde, and another for a scape-goat." Like confession and other similar religious practices that absolve one of sin, the sins of the Hebrews were thus transferred to the "escape goat." Today the connotation is somewhat different: a scapegoat is a whipping boy, often a victim of hatred and prejudice. He is the repository of other people's inadequacies.

*Scape* is aphetic (the loss of an unaccented initial vowel) for *escape*, like *squire* for *esquire*.

## SCARLET PIMPERNEL

The romantic novel *The Scarlet Pimpernel,* written by Baroness Emmuska Orczy in 1905, deals with the rescue of aristocrats by the brilliantly elusive Pimpernel during the French Revolution. *Scarlet,* as everyone knows, is a color. What is not so well known is the meaning of *pimpernel.* It is a plant of the primrose family with bright scarlet flowers which close at the approach of rain.

The term *scarlet* was borrowed from the name of a magnificent fabric brought back to Europe by early Crusaders. The cloth was so exotic, so rich in color—and even threaded in gold—that it was more elaborate than any other previously seen.

The Persians, who called it *escarlet,* made it in varied colors—blue, green, brown, black—but a vivid red inclining toward orange predominated. The most coveted pieces were those dyed bright red. And since the fabric with that particular color was so highly valued, with time the fabric lent its name to the color *scarlet.*

## SCHEDULE

*See* BIBLE

## SCOTCH

A native of Scotland does not like to be called a Scotchman; he favors Scot or Scotsman (a woman may be called a Scotswoman). The usual adjective to describe the people or anything pertaining to Scotland is Scottish. But there are exceptions—for example, Scotch plaid and Scotch terrier. Strangely, some words bearing a form of the word Scotch have no association with Scotland. The lowercase *scotch* in Old English is an example. Shakespeare's famous "I have yet room for six scotches more" was not uttered by a toper but by Scarus, a devoted friend of Antony in *Antony and Cleopatra.* What he meant was that although wounded, he could withstand six more whacks. The word originated in the Old French *escocher,* "to cut a notch" or "to nick." Its current figurative meaning is "to put an abrupt end to" or "to stifle," as in "to *scotch* a rumor." The *scotch* in *hopscotch,* a children's game, refers to an incision—lines or scotches in the ground over which the players leap (hop), and the phrase *scot-free* comes not from Scotland but from Elizabethan scofflaws who ignored their tax responsibilities. A *scot* at the time of Shakespeare was a municipal tax. Those who dodged the tax were said to be scot-free.

The Welsh, like the Scots, have a word they object to—the lowercase *welsh* which means "to go back on a promise." When capitalized (Welsh), it becomes either an adjective, meaning "pertaining to Wales," or a noun, referring to the inhabitants of Wales: the Welsh (*the* always precedes *Welsh* in this usage). Although those using "welsh" in the sense of reneging on a bet are probably not thinking of Welshmen, the easy solution to this entire matter, when referring to such a misdeed, is to use its variant spelling—*welch.*

## SHIBBOLETH

A *shibboleth* is a password, a catchword, or a saying distinctive to a group. Nowadays it is more often used to signify something that is repeated so often as to be stale and no longer useful.

During the war between the Gileadites and Ephraimites, the latter group tried to infiltrate the enemy lines. The test word to detect friend from foe, since the Ephraimites were unable to make an *sh* sound, was *shibboleth*, which in Hebrew meant both "a stream" and "an ear of corn." They would, by saying *sibboleth*, disclose their true identity. In the *Old Testament*, "Judges," this strategy is explained: "Let me go over; that the men of Gilead said unto him, Art thou an Ephraimite? If he said, Nay; Then said they unto him, Say now Shibboleth; and he said Sibboleth: for he could not frame to pronounce it right." Hence today's English word meaning "password" or, as now extended, "platitude" or "slogan," has come from a stream or an ear of corn.

This test is still used in modern-day intelligence to distinguish members of an opposing army. In World War II, Americans sifted the Chinese from the Japanese by having the latter say such words as *unintelligible* and *canceling*. The Japanese have difficulty in sounding an *l.* They pronounce it with an *r* sound. But sounding an *l* is no problem for the Chinese. In fact, they love *l*'s so much that they pronounce everything *velly, velly* good.

The Dutch detected German infiltrators by using as a password the name of a seacoast town with a tricky pronunciation, *Scheveningen.* It is said that only a Dutch tongue can manage this word. Others are bound to get themselves in Dutch.


## SIDEBURNS

*See* BEARD


## SIESTA

*See* NOON

# SILHOUETTE

A *silhouette* is a profile portrait cut out of black paper, a shadow outline. Children make them and so do shadowgraphists at a resort or a fair.

The word *silhouette* came directly from the name of Etienne de Silhouette, an author and statesman who had reputed skill as a financier. In 1759, after becoming controller-general of France, he took immediate steps to meet the country's financial crisis and was warmly praised for his ingenuity and astuteness. But then he proposed reforms to restrict royal household expenditures and to cut government pensions—a proposal that touched a sensitive spot in the pocketbooks of those in power. Strong opposition to these policies developed, and he was greeted with ridicule. Soon outline drawings appeared mocking him, and the name *silhouette* was applied to them as being the cheapest and simplest form of art. People even compared them to his parsimonious fiscal policies, and his name came to stand for anything plain and cheap. However, some writers attribute the term to the brevity of his career, which was like a shadow; others, to his hobby of making portrait profiles, the least expensive way of making likenesses (his chateau at Bry-sur-Marve was decorated with them).

In any event, in terms of black profiles, his name has been immortalized.

# SILLY

It may be difficult to believe that the meaning of the word *silly* has been so changed since its origin that it has made a 360-degree turnaround. In Old English, *saelig* (the forebear of *silly*) meant "blessed" or "saintly," as in a reference to Jesus, "the harmless silly babe." It then came to refer to holy men in the sense "unworldly," since such men could be easily duped. It also came to mean, according to Shakespeare's usage, "rustic" or "plain." And later, "weak" or "harmless" (sheep were called silly, harmless animals, as were people—"this silly aged king"), from which the present meaning of *silly* evolved—"inane" or "foolish." The idea behind the word's ultimate transition was that a weak person was bound to be dumb and therefore say or do absurd things, which, in a word, is "silly." Also a silly person may be regarded as stupid or lacking common sense. Saying "I'll knock him silly," therefore means that I'll beat his sense out of him, which, of course, is the very opposite to "beating sense into him." It's amazing what a good beating can do.

Another word whose meaning has made an about-face is *nice*. Unlike *silly*, however, *nice* went the other way. It began where *silly* wound up; its meaning during the fourteenth century was "foolish." But since *nice* came from Latin *nescius*, "not knowing," a combining of *ne*, "not," and *scire*, "to know," its root sense was "ignorant." Ignorant people were considered stupid; hence "foolish" or "silly." The meaning of *nice* changed many times (from "foolish" to "petty" to "fastidious" to "coy" to "shy" to "reserved") as it marched through the generations en route to its current sense of "attractive," "well-mannered," "pleasing to the senses." In only one instance can the idea of "foolish" still be detected, and that is when it shows a sensitive critical discernment, as in the expression "a nice distinction," which means that the distinction is not wholly valid, but very fine, subtle, or, quite oppositely, nit-picking, and therefore somewhat foolish.

## SIMON-PURE

*Simon-pure* means "the genuine article or the real man." When the unqualified authenticity of a thing is beyond dispute, it may be said to be simon-pure.

The phrase "the real simon-pure," which originally alluded to a character impersonated by another, derived from a 1718 play by Susanna Centlivre titled *A Bold Stroke for a Wife*. Mrs. Centlivre, whose reputation was far from simon-pure (she lived for a while disguised as a boy and then became a strolling actress; her third husband was the cook to Queen Anne), was a prominent writer of farcical comedies.

In the play, Simon Pure is a Pennsylvania Quaker of impeccable reputation. A certain Colonel Feignwell steals from him a letter of introduction to a man of means who has a beautiful daughter, Miss Lovely. The impostor, pretending to be Simon Pure, fools everyone and wins the hand of the wealthy man's daughter. Fortunately, the true Simon Pure appears in the nick of time and establishes his identity, despite the extreme difficulty in doing so. The only thing about all this that is not a farce is the genuineness of the hero—he was simon-pure.

## SIMONY

*See* ABACADABRA

## SINCERE

Several theories have been advanced to explain the derivation of the word *sincere,* but none has been substantiated. The most logical attributes the genesis of the word to the Latin *sincerus,* meaning "pure" or "clean." But many etymologists hold that *sincere* is a compounding of *sine cera,* which means "without wax." In the time of the ancient Romans, devious dealers in marble and pottery would conceal defects in their products by filling the cracks and holes with wax. Honest merchants, who did not doctor their products, proudly displayed their wares as being without wax—that is, they were *sine cera.* Perhaps, but a buyer had best not forget another Latin phrase— *caveat emptor.*

## SINECURE

"A sinecure is a benefice without cure of souls"—Ayliffe. The word *sinecure* comes straight from the Latin *sine,* "without," and *cura,* "care," which makes its literal meaning "without care." It represents what some people might consider the ideal job— pay with no work. Originally a sinecure was a paid ecclesiastical position which did not require the jobholder to concern himself with the cure or condition of the parishioners. Nowadays it may be any office with emoluments but no duties, especially one obtained as a reward for political services.

The French version of *sine cura* is *sans souci.* It translates into "free and easy," "devoid of care." Which is just how a person with a sinecure in his pocket feels.

## SIREN

Although a *siren* (a whistle that produces a penetrating warning sound) may save a life, a *siren* (a temptress) could ruin it.

When *Siren* is capitalized, it refers to a figure in Greek mythology. The *Sirens* (from Greek *sirenes,* meaning "entanglers") were half-women and half-bird sea nymphs who, by their sweet singing, lured mariners to destruction on the rocks surrounding their island. To understand the story of the *Sirens,* one must begin with the Argonauts and Orpheus, since they brought about the sad end of the Sirens.

The Argonauts, heroic sailors of the Argo, the ship Jason ordered built to help him fetch the Golden Fleece, sailed the ship dangerously near the beach on which the Sirens were singing. Aboard was the celebrated poet Orpheus whose golden lyre enchanted everyone who heard his music. He played his lyre, thus preventing the crew from hearing the Sirens' deadly songs. The Argonauts sailed safely by the Sirens' habitat. Since it was decreed that the life of the Sirens should endure only until someone should be unmoved by their song, they leaped into the sea and were transformed into rocks. In another version, Ulysses, sailing home from Troy, skirted the island where the Sirens lived. He stuffed the sailors' ears with wax and tied himself to the mast. With the crew thus secured, the vessel sailed on until Ulysses could no longer hear the Sirens' song.

Today a woman regarded as a siren is one who is insidiously seductive or, as is said in a literary style, a woman of dangerous blandishments.

## SIRLOIN

The *sirloin* is a choice cut of beef from the part of the hindquarters just in front of the round. The word evolved from the French *surlonge,* a combination of *sur,* "over," and *longe,* "loin." But some romanticists insist that this succulent part of the loin of beef was dubbed "Sir Loin" by King Henry VIII. Apocryphal though the story may be, one can readily imagine the gluttonous king, dripping at the mouth, knighting this meat to make it a royal dish.

Another strip of tender meat is called the *tenderloin.* That word also refers to a district of a city that teems with violence and lawbreaking. A precinct in New York was given this name, so it is said, by a police captain who, upon transfer to this crime-ridden area known especially for its corruption and graft, remarked, "I've had nothing but chuck for a long time, but now I'm going to get me some *tenderloin!*"

## SLEUTH

A common but informal name for a detective or a keen investigator is *sleuth*. When this word originated in Middle English, however, it did not have this sense. Then *sleuth* (from Old Norse *sloth*) meant "the track or trail of an animal or a person." It was the front end of a compound, *sleuth-hound*, "a dog used for trailing," a word eventually shortened to *sleuth*. The sleuth-hound, or sleuth, was a Scottish beast, but since it was widely known for its tenacious pursuit of an object, writers outside Scotland liked its metaphoric sense, as in Gaskell's *Life of Charlotte Brönte*, ". . . the West Riding men are sleuth-hounds in pursuit of money." This means, of course, that nowadays when a sleuth dogs someone, he is doing his job.

## SNOB

Everyone knows that a snob is a person who affects social importance and exclusiveness while disdaining those people he considers inferior. Charles Lever in *One of Them* put it this way: "Ain't a snob a fellow as wants to be taken for better bred, or richer, or cleverer, or more influential than he really is?" No one knows for certain the history of this word, nor why centuries ago it was applied to cobblers' apprentices. What is known, however, is that these lads began to imitate the refinement and good manners of the gentlemen they served. In time they became overbearing toward younger apprentices who had not yet acquired such elevated tastes. They were, so to speak, snobby snobs.

Another conjecture, which enjoys some authoritative support, is that the word *snob* evolved from a combination of *s* for "sine" and *nob* for "nobility." During the seventeenth century, Cambridge University admitted commoners who, when registering, had to distinguish themselves from the titled students by adding after their name *sine nobilitate*, "without nobility." This was later abbreviated *sine nob*, then *s. nob.*, which coalesced into *snob* and became (according to its current meaning) an apt description, since many of them, upon admittance into the inner academic sanctuary, acted as though they were of aristocratic birth. They were, so to speak, the forebears of all the snobs that followed.

## SOLON, SOLECISM

A *solon* is a wise and skillful lawmaker or, as a member of a legislative body, one who merits distinctive recognition.

During the great days of classical Greece, about 500 B.C., Solon (whose motto was "Know thyself") was a great Athenian statesman. Regarded as one of the Seven Sages, he was the only one of them sagacious enough to make his name survive through the years and become a part of the English language. The current meaning of *solon* is "wise man."

The Cypress town Soli, named for Solon, should not be confused with another town on the coast of Cilicia, in Asia Minor, which had a similar name—Soloi. This town had been colonized by Greeks, but was located so far away from Greece that its inhabitants forgot the purity of their native language and acquired a dialect of their own. Greeks who occasionally visited this area were appalled by the colonists' errors in speech, a substandard form of Attic dialect. The Greeks coined a word to describe this corrupt speech—*soloikismos.* From it came the English word that means a mistake in the idiom of the language or a grammatical error or blunder: *solecism.*

## SOMNAMBULIST

Is a sleepwalker dreaming? Not etymologically speaking. A person who is dreaming is in the arms of *Morpheus,* the god of dreams, and therefore, at least theoretically, would be unable to walk. (From Morpheus came the name of the drug that puts one to sleep, but not necessarily to dream—morphine.)

Morpheus' father, *Somnus,* was the god of sleep. He lent his name to the front end of that ornamental synonym for a sleepwalker—*somnambulist.* Its back end comes from a Latin verb, *ambulare,* which means "to walk." One who walks in his sleep is somnambulating. And one who talks in his sleep is a *somniloquist* (from Latin *somnus,* "sleep," plus *loqui,* "to speak"). A less esoteric word, *insomnia,* is unfortunately well known to many who can't get a good night's sleep.

In Greek mythology the god of sleep was *Hypnos.* From his name came the word *hypnosis* (an artificially induced sleeplike condition, a trance-sleep) and all the other *hypno* words. The noun *hypnotism* was coined in the nineteenth century by James

Braid of Manchester, the first investigator of this strange condition to use this term. But the phenomenon of hypnotism itself was first brought to public light through the studies and experiments of a Viennese physician, Franz A. Mesmer (1734–1815). From his name has come the word *mesmerize,* which is synonymous with *hypnotize.*

## SON OF A GUN

The expression "son of a gun" is used daily in conversation as an exclamation of surprise, as in "I'll be a son of a gun if that's not my old roommate." The fact is that "a son of a gun," in sea slang, referred to a child actually born under a gun. And from that cant phrase has come the one so many people use unwittingly today.

Years ago, when the British Navy was a mighty force to be reckoned with, wives of sailors were permitted to accompany them to sea. Naturally, births on shipboard were not infrequent. The convenient place for the ship's surgeon to deliver a child was on the gun deck (which was screened off), and the birth, therefore, took place "under the gun"; whence "son of a gun." The noted lexicographer Frank Vizetelly mentioned the phrase as "applied for boys born afloat, when wives accompanied their husbands to sea." Which leaves one wondering what the girls were called—"pistol-packing mammas"?

## SOS

The distress signal SOS is not an abbreviation of "Save Our Ship" or "Save Our Souls." In fact, it is not an abbreviation at all. Therefore, the punctilious do not punctuate it (not S.O.S.). The international agreement making SOS the distress signal was adopted because the combination of three dots, three dashes, and three dots is distinctive and easily transmitted.

Another common expression taken from the Morse code is *Roger.* The *R* in the code—dot, dash, dot—represents "received," meaning "Your message is understood," a formula that developed during the early days of wireless communication. The voice code *Roger* for *R* evolved logically with the advent of radio. Now, almost as common as *O.K.* in daily speech, *Roger* stands for "I understand" or "Affirmative."

There's no doubt that the happiest response someone flashing an SOS can get is *Roger*.

## SPANIEL

A spaniel is a dog of Spanish descent, but its name arrived in English in steps. In Old French, the dog was known as *chien-espagneul;* in Spanish as *español.* The English language borrowed it, but, through aphesis and a slight orthographic change, made it *spaniel.* In all these languages the dog's name simply meant "Spanish dog."

The family of spaniels consists of ten breeds of which the cocker is perhaps the most popular. This friendly dog, with its silky, wavy coat, got its name because of the way it cocks its pendulous ears.

## SPARTAN

*See* LACONIC

## SPHINX

A *sphinx* is a mysterious, enigmatic person. In Greek mythology the Sphinx was a she-monster. She had the winged body of a lion and the head and breasts of a woman. (The Egyptian Sphinx is the figure of a reclining lion without wings, the upper part being that of a human being.) The Greek Sphinx was a propounder of riddles. She was also cruel and heartless. It is said that she proposed riddles to the Thebans and killed all who failed to solve them. In one popular version, the Sphinx asked passersby this riddle: "What walks on four legs in the morning, on two at noon, and on three in the evening?" Those unable to answer it were strangled by her and flung over a cliff. (*Sphinx* in Latin means "the strangler.") The carnage finally came to an end when Oedipus, lately returned to Thebes, solved the riddle. The answer he gave was "Man, for he crawls in the morning of his life, walks erect in the noon of his power, and uses a crutch in the evening of his age." The Sphinx was astonished. In fact, she was so frustrated and angered upon hearing the right answer that she threw herself off the cliff.

## SPINSTER

The word *spinster* is an old word. It first appeared in print in 1362, but its meaning was different from what it is today. A spinster was one who spins (from Middle English *spinnen,* "to spin"), in former times a common occupation of an unmarried woman. In fact, it was then believed that no woman was fit to become a wife until she had spun a set of linens for her body, her table, and her bed. Shakespeare used the term *spinster* in several plays—"The spinsters and the knitters in the sun" *(Twelfth Night);* "The spinsters, carders, fillers, weavers" *(Henry VIII).* Beginning with the seventeenth century, the term *spinster* came to be appended to a woman's name to designate a state of celibacy. An unmarried woman's name would appear in official documents thus: "Johanna Hunt, spinster."

The meaning of *spinster* today is "an unmarried woman, especially one beyond the usual age for marriage." She is euphemistically called *a maiden lady* or derisively *an old maid.* J. Roberts in 1719 first wrote about spinsters in this sense: "As for us poor Spinsters, we must certainly go away to France also." Charles Dickens in *Pickwick Papers* spoke of "Tupwan and the spinster aunt."

## SPOONERISM

Almost everyone is occasionally guilty of getting "his mix all talked up." This fault (sometimes done purposely for humorous effect) is called *spoonerism* after the Rev. W. A. Spooner, an Oxford professor and cleric (1844–1930). He was addicted to the accidental transposition of sounds and letters in words, frequently with ludicrous results—"well-boiled icicle" for "well-oiled bicycle," for example. His students enjoyed his twisted tongue so much that they decided, after one hilarious mix up ("The kingkering congs their titles take" instead of "The conquering kings . . ."), to name this type of error after him, thereby immortalizing him.

When Spooner preached, his facility of speech did not improve. He said to one person who had come to pray, "Aren't you occupewing the wrong pie?" When he received no answer, he pursued the subject and asked, "Were you sewn into this sheet?" On another occasion, at the close of a wedding ceremony, when the bashful groom seemed not to know what to do next, he intoned, "It is kisstomary to cuss the bride."

The technical word for the error involved in transposing letters, which interchanges consonant sounds, is *metathesis*, meaning "a change of place," from Greek *metatihenai*—a tongue-twister in its own right.

## SQUIRREL

*See* FERRET

## STAMINA, STAMEN

*Stamina* is the staying power a person needs to see an arduous task through. It is the essence of endurance. A *stamen* is a botanical term applying to the pollen-producing reproductive organ of a flower. Both *stamen* and *stamina* come from the same Latin source: *stamen.* (*Stamina* is simply its plural form.)

Originally the Latin *stamen* was the warp (the lengthwise thread) in cloth. The sense of "thread" had a divine beginning but a mortal ending. According to Roman legend, the three goddesses of Fate (the spinners of the thread of life) were in control of a person's destiny. *Clotho* held the spindle; *Lachesis* drew the thread; *Atropos* snipped it off. These threads as well as those used by human beings were called *stamina*. In time *stamina* entered the English language with a signification like that of warp's (that is, a foundation on which a textile is woven or the essential or fundamental part or nature of something). Its sense then reflected the physical or moral vigor required to resist disease or withstand fatigue or hardship. In sum, the word *stamina* has come to combine the qualities of perseverance and durability.

The botanical *stamen* was a term used in the first century by Pliny. That was the name he applied to the male organ of a flower, since it resembled a thread.

## STRAIT

A strait-laced woman may follow a straight and narrow path, but her bodice, even if worn straight, has been laced strait. The phrase "strait-laced" now signifies prudery or moral rigidity. This figurative notion devolved from the practice of lacing a corset as tight as possible. The tighter the strings were drawn, the narrower became the opening at the sides of the corset and the more narrow the body. A lady would tell her maid, "Make it tight and narrow." This sense of physical narrowness became likened to the conduct of prudes, those who were "strait-laced" even if they wore no corset.

As used here, strait (from Latin strictus, past participle of stringere, "to draw together," "to bind"), meaning "narrow," is the proper word, not straight. A strait is a narrow sea passage (Strait of Gibraltar, Strait of Magellan) and also a position or condition of distress, as is one "in poor, in sad, or in financial straits." Straight, on the other hand, means "that which is stretched," having derived from the Middle English past participle of strechen, "to stretch."

Incidentally, returning to the opening sentence, the phrase "the straight/strait and narrow path," attributable to Matthew (VII:13) in the King James Version, reads: "Because strait is the gate and narrow is the way, which leadeth unto life." If nowadays, instead of "straight and narrow," one were to read "strait and narrow" (a more faithful rendering), he might wonder about its correctness because the adjective straight has long since supplanted strait, and everyone is accustomed to getting it straight.

## STRAWBERRY

Just as there is no *apple* in a *pineapple* and no grape in a *grapefruit,* so there is no *straw* in a *strawberry.* This last curious fact has raised a puzzling question for etymologists, especially since in no other language does the additive "straw" accompany these berries.

Several theories have been advanced to explain where the "straw" came from. The one most widely accepted is that the runners of the strawberry plant stray haphazardly. In Anglo-Saxon, *strawberry* was called *streow berie* (*streowan* means "to stray"). Hence one idea was that the original name was *strayberry,* from which, by corruption, came the present name. Another opinion holds that the long runners resembled straw, and still another, that strawberries were strung on straw for display and sale at marketplaces. Some authorities suggest that the word was derived from the practice of covering strawberry beds with straw, so as to prevent the earth from soiling the berries. But no one really knows—everyone seems to be clutching at straws.

## SUB ROSA

It is easy to see that a *sub poena* (usually spelled *subpoena*), which in Latin means "under penalty," is a writ commanding a witness to appear in court. And also easy to understand is *sub nomine*, which means "under the name," applying to what is under the main caption or title. But one may have cause to wonder how *sub rosa* (literally "under the rose") has come to mean "confidentially" or "secretly."

The genesis of this phrase lies in Greek mythology. Cupid, the son of Aphrodite (the goddess of love), learning that Harpocrates (the god of silence) had observed Aphrodite's amorous adventures, bribed him not to reveal what he had seen. The bribe was a rose. And so the rose came to be recognized as an emblem of silence, a pledge of secrecy.

Since the days of the Renaissance, a common architectural motif has been the rose. Those who sat under it were regarded as confidants—that is, they were tacitly agreeing to hold in strict secrecy whatever they discussed while sitting "under the rose." Those who didn't want to keep a secret simply rose up and left.

## SULLEN

*See* SURLY

## SUNDAE

A *sundae*, as everyone knows, is a dish of ice cream with toppings such as syrup, fruits, nuts, and whipped cream. But what no one is sure of is where the word came from. Dictionaries note that its origin is uncertain. The best they can say about the word's history is that probably this rich dish was so named because it was originally sold only on Sundays.

H. L. Mencken in *The American Language* offers what is perhaps the most plausible theory concerning its origin. In the

1890's George Hallauer, a customer in an ice-cream parlor in Two Rivers, Wisconsin, feeling somewhat devilish, ordered chocolate syrup poured on his ice cream. The proprietor, E. C. Berners, thought the idea queer, but complied, and right then and there what has come to be one of America's favorite dessert dishes, the sundae, was born. Its fame spread rapidly. In nearby Manitowoc, George Giffy, who operated an ice-cream parlor, began to sell this new concoction—but only on Sundays. However, because his customers demanded it on other days, Giffy went along and sold daily what had come to be called a *Sunday*. Mencken concluded that the change in spelling from *Sunday* to *sundae* would forever remain a mystery. Anyone may tender a guess, of course, but never on Sunday.

## SUPERCILIOUS

A person who expresses disdain by elevating the eyebrows is, literally speaking, being *supercilious*. Meaning "arrogant" or "haughty," that word descended directly from Latin *supercilium*, which consisted of two parts: *super*, "over," and *cilium*, "eyelid." The implication was that a disdainful act needs not a word nor even a tilt of the nose—only a raising of the eyebrows to evince such indifference or scorn as to discourage social intercourse. *Supercilious*, as Opdyke pointed out, signifies "Olympian superiority that deserves ignominious debacle."

James Higgins' translation of *Junius' Nomenclator*, published in 1585, contained in print for the first time (according to the *OED*) the word *eyebrow*. It appeared in a definition of *supercilium*: "the ridge of haire above the eye lids on the eye browes." Today's dictionaries define *eyebrow* as the bony ridge that the hair above the eye grows on. Using the eyebrow superciliously has a meaning all its own.

## SURLY

The sentence "The surly villain was sullen" means that the rude scoundrel was gloomy. But not so in distant times. Then it would have had an entirely different meaning because, first, the word *surly* did not mean "rude, impertinent, or unfriendly" but "haughty, imperious, or lordly." An earlier spelling was *sirly*, literally "sirlike," which meant that a person's behavior was like that of a *sir,* a member of the nobility. Shakespeare, who used the term *surly* in its literal sense, advised: "Be opposite with a kinsman, surly with servants." Second, a *villain* was not a scoundrel or a criminal but a person attached to, or an inhabitant of, a farm. In feudal days villains were the tenants who lived on the grounds of the lord, a great landowner. The roots of *villain* can be seen in Latin *villa,* "a farmhouse." (A group of farms *(villas)* made up a village.) *Villain* gradually became a contemptuous name for a country dweller, a bumpkin, because rural people were regarded as simple-minded and boorish. The notion of untrustworthiness and wickedness arose in later years. Third, a sullen person *(sullen,* meaning "morose," "sulky," stems from Latin *solus,* "alone") referred to anyone who lived by himself and was thought to be lonesome. Today a sullen person may simply be nursing a grievance, and mumble: "I want to be alone."

## SURNAME

One might legitimately ask where one's own name came from. The answer depends on where he starts. Sir Galahad and Sir Launcelot of King Arthur's Round Table, for example, had no surname. Even long after the Norman Conquest, surnames were unknown in England. To help identify a Tom, Dick, or Harry, nicknames were used: Tom the tailor; Skinny Dick; Cross-eyed Harry. These were ekenames *(eke* meant "additional" or "extra," a name added to a given name). From the common use of an ekename the "n" of *an* became erroneously transferred, making it "a nekename"; whence, with a slight orthographic change, "a nickname."

When surnames originally developed, during the twelfth century, only the nobles used them. In fact, according to one conjecture, *surname* was first spelled *sirname,* which, in all likelihood, was merely a phonetic spelling. Then, in 1465, Edward IV decreed that all Englishmen had "to take unto them a surname." (Incidentally, the first known people to adopt more than one name were the Chinese. In 2852 B.C. Emperor Fushi ordered the use of family names.)

A surname (a family name or a patronymic) is, of course, an appellation that follows the original or first name. It is the second name, the one a person has in common with the other members of his family. According to another derivative version, a *surname* is the overname—a combination of French *sur* ("over") and English *name*, which would make it a half adoption and a half translation.

## SWAN SONG

> The jealous swan, against his death that singeth.
> —Chaucer, *Parlement of Fowler*

Legend dies hard—if at all. The belief persists that the mute swan (the only noise it ever makes is a hiss when venting anger) breaks its silence before death by singing a melodious song, its dirge. "This bird," according to Erman, "when wounded, pours forth its last breath in notes most beautifully clear and loud." No one has ever heard a swan sing, but poets have perpetuated this myth for so many centuries that the phrase *swan song* has come to mean the last effort of a poet, a writer, a musician, or a painter, just as it is the legendary last utterance of the dying swan. But the swan, so it is said, was not unhappy to die because, being sacred to Apollo, it knew that it was about to join the god it served. People, too, may associate music with death. In *Othello* appears this line: "I will play the swan, and die in music." From Byron's *Don Juan:* "There, swan like, let me sing and die." And from the *Merchant of Venice:* "He makes a swan-like end. / Fading in music."

## SYBARITE

About 720 B.C. Greeks immigrated to Lucania (a region in Southern Italy) and founded a city which they named Sybaris. Its inhabitants followed such a liberal policy of admitting people from all lands that the city flourished and was soon noted for its wealth and luxury. In fact, no other Hellenic city could compare with Sybaris in prosperity and splendor.

According to legend, a war arose between Sybaris and its neighbor, Crotona. Although the Crotonian forces were inferior, they were victorious and leveled Sybaris to the ground. This came about because the Crotonians exploited their knowledge of a weakness in the opposing army: the horses of the Sybarites had been trained to dance to the pipes. And so the

Crotonians marched in playing pipes: the horses began to dance, the Sybarites became confused, and the Crotonians vanquished their enemy. Someone might say, "That's really playing the horses."

The conspicuousness of the love of luxury and pleasure displayed by the citizens of Sybaris has led to the English word *sybarite*, a person devoted to excessive luxury and sensuousness—a voluptuary.

## SYCOPHANT

*See* TOADY

## SYMPOSIUM

If a man tells his etymologist wife that he's going to a *symposium*, she may rightly wonder whether he's going to do more drinking than learning. A symposium, as everyone knows, is a conference at which some topic of mutual interest is discussed. But originally a *symposium* was a merrier affair. It was a convivial gathering of the educated, usually held after dinner when the wine would flow as freely as the conversation. Literally, *symposium* (from Greek *syn-* (*sun-*), "together," and *posis*, "a drinking") means "a drinking together."

The title of one of Plato's works was "Symposium," a word adopted by English in the sixteenth century, hundreds of years after its coinage. In this work Plato lauds human relationships free of sexual significance and extols, particularly, the pure love of Socrates for young men.

Interestingly, *Plato* was a nickname; the real name of this great man was Aristocles. He was called Plato because he was broad-shouldered. (In Greek, *platus* meant "wide" or "broad," from which evolved Vulgar Latin *plattus*, in the sense "flat," and from which have come many English words, such as *plate, plateau,* and *platform*.) But for the nickname, love that transcends physical desires would be known, not as platonic love, but as aristocleonic love, a concoction of sounds that might turn some people off—or on.

## TABOO

That which is *taboo* is excluded from use, forbidden. The Tongan word *tabu*, meaning "sacred," spelled *taboo* in English, has, by extension, come to mean "prohibited." According to folk etymology, what is taboo must be ignored or avoided so as not to incur disaster.

The idea of hiding something that is taboo runs through many stories which have weaved their way through the generations. Perhaps the best known—certainly the most gruesome—is the legend of Bluebeard. The version most often given of this old tale concerns a Gilles de Retz, of Brittany, who in 1450 married and murdered six women in succession. On one occasion, according to this folktale, Bluebeard, who was about to leave on a journey, gave his seventh wife, Fatima, the keys to the doors of his castle, but told her that opening a particular door was *taboo*. Nevertheless, curiosity overcame her. She opened the forbidden door and discovered the bodies of her husband's six former wives. Bluebeard, upon his return, learned of her discovery through a telltale drop of blood on a key and planned to do away with her. Fortunately, she was saved by the timely arrival of her brothers, who promptly meted out to him the same treatment he had intended for his wife.

## TANTALIZE

The word *tantalize* goes all the way back to Greek mythology. It means "to hold out hopes or prospects that cannot be realized" or, as put by Dr. Johnson, "to torment by the show of pleasures which cannot be reached." The word is a lineal descendant of Tantalus, a Lydian king, who offended the gods by revealing secrets entrusted to him by Zeus. He was made to suffer, after his death, a most unusual punishment—the torments of continuous hunger and thirst. The king was placed up to his chin in the middle of a lake in the lower world. Above him dangled branches of luscious fruit, just out of his reach, and the waters always receded when he stooped to drink. Today's use of *tantalize* continues the same sense of frustration— to be teased with hopes of things that are ardently desired but ever unattainable.

## TATTOO

For those who wonder what the Military Tattoo (an annual Edinburgh concert) has to do with skin markings called tattoos, the answer is that there is no connection.

The tattoos that decorate the arms of some men (usually sailors) and a few women (the tattooed woman at the circus) with indelible patterns, pictures, and so forth, are created by rubbing pigments into the skin through small punctures (this *tattoo* is a Tahitian derivative from *tatu*, "to mark"). Tattoos were first observed in 1769 by Captain Cook, an English circumnavigator who was visiting the South Pacific.

In Medieval English, a tattoo signaled the closing of the barrooms. But it was then spelled *tap toe,* which meant to imbibing merrymakers that "the tap is closed"—that is, the beer tap. In those days pubs were frequented by soldiers after fighting hours (at sundown, armies put down their arms so that the soldiers could relax and sleep—fighting was more civilized then). At 9:30, the soldiers were recalled to their barracks (called First Summons) by the beating of drums. Not infrequently the summons would be ignored, whereupon a torch-carrying search party would seek out the carousing soldiers. When the barkeeps saw the torches, they would holler: "Tap toe," which translates into "Close the barroom!" Through normal semantic evolution, *tap toe* became *tattoo*.

The Military Tattoo (to rap on a drum is to tattoo it) is something quite different; it is a formal ceremony in which many uniformed bands participate and compete for prizes. The bands are judged on marching ability, the uniqueness and precision of formations, and musical prowess—in part on the tattooing of their drums.

## TAUTOLOGY

*See* REDUNDANCY

## TAWDRY

The odd evolution of some words makes one wonder how they came along as they did. For example, *tawdry*, which means "gaudy, worthless, cheap, and tasteless," is a slurring of St. Audrey, the name of a person once revered in Great Britain.

The story began in the seventh century with Etheldreda. According to one version she was a queen of Northumbria who forsook her husband and family for a nun's life; according to another, she was a Saxon princess who sought refuge behind a nun's veil to escape marriage. In any event, Etheldreda during her girlhood was particularly fond of wearing necklaces made of lace. Later in life she developed a tumor in her throat, which convinced her that this was God's punishment for the youthful passion of decorating her neck with worldly ornaments.

Etheldreda, whose name was anglicized as Audrey, was sainted. In her memory, a fair called St. Audrey's day was held annually until it petered out in the seventeenth century. At these festivities cheap jewelry and knicknacks were sold, but the most characteristic article for sale was a showy scarf, a local product called "St. Audrey's lace." These neckpieces were of poor quality, and as they became shabbier and cheaper as time went on, the word to describe them, and ultimately any worthless finery, was *tawdry*. Shakespeare in *Winter's Tale* presumably used *tawdry* in a different sense when the Shepherdess Mopsa said, "Come, you promised me a tawdry-lace and a pair of sweet gloves."

## TAXI

*See* BUS

## TELLER

A *teller* is someone who tells, a narrator. Or he may be an official who counts votes. But as used in this essay, a *teller* is a bank employee, a cashier who receives and pays out money. At the end of the business day, the teller counts his money to make certain it tallies with his records. The verbs *tell* and *tally* are associated terms, for the nub of their meaning is "counting," and that is the business of a teller (Anglo-French *tallier*). Money that was counted was *told,* a sense still evident in "There were five dollars in the till all told." To tell one's beads is in effect to count them, to say prayers serially as on a rosary.

To *tally* is to count or to reckon. A *tally* (from Latin *talea,* "stick") is a stick on which notches were made to reckon the accounts of the British Royal Exchequer. The stick was split down the center. One half was retained by the Exchequer and the other issued to the debtor. When the time arrived for a payment, the two halves were juxtaposed. If they "tallied," all was in order. The payment corresponded to what was due according to the tally.

Tallies were used from the time of the Norman Conquest to the reign of William IV when the system was abandoned because the storing of the sticks was expensive and cumbersome, especially since some of them exceeded eight feet in length. To destroy the tallies, it was decided to burn them in the stoves of the House of Lords. Two cartloads of tally sticks were wheeled up at six o'clock in the morning and dumped into the stoves. They were then set on fire—and so were the Houses of Parliament, which were completely destroyed.

## TEMPERAMENT

*See* COMPLEXION

## TENDERLOIN

*See* SIRLOIN

## TENNIS

Tennis is a game in which a ball is batted to and fro over a net. Some students of word derivations believe that the name of the game came from the call of the server, who shouted in French, "Tenez," meaning "Hold" in the sense of "Ready?" Others point to the fact that the covering of the first balls used in the game were made at Tinnis in lower Egypt, a name that sounds suspiciously like tennis. Hence, when someone says "Tennis anyone?" perhaps he doesn't realize that he's referring also to the hide of the balls. On the other hand, some etymologists contend that the name *tennis* was derived directly from the Arabic *tanaz*, meaning "to leap or to bound," which certainly is an activity associated with the game. Interestingly, the name of the game in French and Arabic sounds like English.

## TERMINUS

Logically this essay belongs at the end of the book, for it concerns the word *terminus*. Dictionaries define it as "the end of something" or "a final point or goal." Its capitalized form, *Terminus*, is a godly word referring to a Roman field deity who presided over boundaries and frontiers.

The worship of Terminus was said to have been instituted by King Numa, the second king of Rome, who ordered that all boundaries separating the lands of people be marked by stones consecrated to Jupiter. These boundary stones were so sacred that anyone removing even one might be slain with impunity. A Festival of Terminalia was held annually on February 23, at which time the boundary stones were crowned with garlands, and prayers and sacrifices were offered to the god. The festivities then ended with singing and merrymaking—with time out for love-making. Who knows, this last activity may have been what the people were praying for—their "final point or goal."

## TEST, TESTICLE, TESTIFY

A *test*, as all school kids know, is an examination given by a teacher. Of course, anything that is evaluated is "put to the test." But no matter how the word is presently used, its meaning has come far from its original definition.

According to Dr. Johnson's *Dictionary*, a *test* is "a cupel in which refiners try their metals." The word originated in Latin *testa*, meaning "earthen vessel" or "pot." When silver or gold was heated in a cupel or test, any impurities would be absorbed by the porous vessel, leaving pure droplets of the precious metal. From this practice grew the notion of "putting other things to the test" in a way suitable to prove genuineness, which might be through experiment, demonstration, or extensive experience.

The word that *test* suggests, about which there has been sly humor, is *testicle.* Many years ago the words may have been associated in some people's minds, first because they seem to have had the same root and, secondly, because of an associated experience. However, the parent of "test," as previously shown, was *testa;* of "testicle" (an entirely different root), *testis,* which means "a witness." A practice during the Middle Ages was for a witness to swear on the seat of his manhood (apparently women never served as witnesses). Of course the witness, while offering evidence was *testifying* (Latin *testis,* "witness," and *-ficari,* from *facere,* "to make"). In effect he was being examined or tested on his knowledge concerning a legal matter. But, as can be readily seen, the connection between the words *test* and *testify* is remote. In later years, in deference to one's sense of modesty, there were anatomical changes; oaths were taken by placing the right hand on the thigh and, still later, on the heart. Today the practice of religionists is to swear on the Bible and for non-believers to affirm.

Incidentally, from *testis,* in addition to *testify,* have come the English words *testimony, testator, intestate, attest,* and *detest.* This last, from Latin *de,* "down," and *testis,* "witness," originally meant to ask the gods to come down to bear witness against someone, to denounce; whence "to loathe."

## THUG

The only thing that the words *thief* and *thug* have in common, in addition to their first two letters, is that they suggest the felonious taking of what is not theirs. A thief may steal secretly or slyly—a sneakthief. He may pick a pocket. A thug is a different breed of animal; he is a hoodlum, a ruffian, a violent criminal. A thug feels no qualms about the physical injury he inflicts. The word *thug* was imported from the Hindustani *thag,* which means "thief." But these Indian thugs were not ordinary thieves. They were members of a North Indian religious society that waylaid wealthy travelers and then strangled and buried them, supposedly committing these heinous crimes in the name of their goddess Kali (after whom Calcutta was named).

Another import connoting slaughter is the word *assassin*. It refers to a member of an organized secret Persian group of murderers who also killed and plundered as a religious duty, frequently choosing crusading Christians as victims. Their professed purpose was to establish a Muslim empire. The word *assassin* originated in Islamic *hashshashin*, "hashish-users," for supposedly the members of this fanatical sect were so addicted. Science has now established that the drug rouses no desire for violence. The fanaticism that motivated these murderers must have come from another kind of religious fervor. (Some etymologists, relying on a report of Marco Polo, believe that *assassin* stems from Hasan, a Moslem leader who plied his followers with the drug whenever he desired them to assassinate someone. When they awoke from their stupor, he would direct them to the person to be disposed of, promising them rewards such as they had just dreamed of.) The meaning of *assassin* nowadays is restricted to the perpetrator of the deliberate murder of an important political figure—Presidents of the United States who were murdered are said to have been assassinated.

## THUNDER

> Thunder is good, thunder is impressive; but it is lightning that does the work.
>
> —Mark Twain, *Letter to an Unidentified Person*

Although the expression *thunderstruck* goes back for centuries, no one is known to have been struck by thunder. The fact is that thunder is a loud noise accompanying a flash of lightning; it is not a striking force.

From Old English *tunor* evolved Middle English *thunor*, later to become *thunder*. Why the *d* was added has not been established; perhaps to approximate more closely the sound of the growl or bang of the expanding air that frightens so many people. No doubt the supposed consequent effect of thunder instilled as much fear as lightning, even though the devastating effect of lightning on barns and other buildings was visible. As early as 1400 Maundev wrote: "We ware . . . stricken doune to the earth with great hidous blastez of wind and of thouner."

The fifth day of the week, Thursday, was named after Thor, the Norse god of thunder (in French, *jeudi,* "Thursday," honors Jove, also a god of thunder). Thor, it was believed, hurled thunderbolts at the earth. Jupiter, the Roman counterpart of the Greek Zeus, was depicted holding a scepter in his left hand and a thunderbolt in his right. Thunderbolts, of course, are mythological missiles. Shakespeare spoke of them in *Julius Caesar.* Brutus: "Be ready, gods, with all your thunderbolts, / Dash him to pieces!"

## TINKER'S DAMN

A person who thinks that something is worthless might say, "I wouldn't give a hoot for it," or "It's as phony as a plugged nickel," or "It's not worth a tinker's damn." A hoot, everyone knows, is a hoot owl's cry; a plugged nickel is not an American coin; but a question that might be raised is, What is a tinker? and why his damn?

A tinker, according to Dr. Johnson's *Dictionary,* is a "mender of old brass." Beginning with the Middle Ages, tinkers were itinerants who mended household utensils, primarily pots and pans. The name *tinker* is of uncertain origin but may be echoic of the tinkling sounds these menders made either as they beat their kettles to announce their presence in the neighborhood or as they worked on the housewives' utensils. From that *tink-tink* noise also came, it is believed, the verb and noun *tinkle.*

The second part of the phrase is more controversial because not even its spelling can be attested. One story is that tinkers were known to explode with foul language, frequently cursing with the word *damn* whenever their solder failed to hold. A more logical explanation is that tinkers, to make sure that the solder they were about to pour dried in place, would build a wall made of clay, beeswax, or pieces of bread around the hole to be filled. This dam (spelled with no *n*) would be thrown away after it had served its purpose, for it could not be reused and was utterly without value—it was not worth, so to speak, a "tinker's damn."

## TIP

It is often assumed that the word *tip*, meaning a gratuity, was derived from the initial letters of the signs "To Insure Promptness" posted over boxes in English inns and coffee-houses to remind guests to deposit coins that would ensure special service. This practice was said to be customary during the days of Dr. Johnson, although the word *tip*, in this sense, is not in his dictionary. Eventually the phrase on the boxes was abbreviated to TIP or TIPS.

This curious story has never been authenticated, however, and it is, in the opinion of linguists, pure folk etymology. Dictionaries note the origin of *tip* as uncertain because there is no record to substantiate its derivation. One suggestion made is that *tip* derived from *stipend*, whose stem was the Latin *stipendium*, "pay" or "gift." At least one can find a *tip* buried in it. Another notion is that *tipple*, "to drink," is the associated word. It begins with *tip*, and the sense of *tipple* prompts one to think of beverage money. In fact, the French equivalent of "tip" is *pourboire*, literally "for drinking," and the German, *Trinkgeld* ("drink money"). However, what should be borne in mind is that since one tips after service is rendered, it actually comes too late to ensure special attention.

## TITAN

A *titan* is a person of outstanding achievement or of tremendous strength or of colossal size. The White Star liner, the "Titanic," the largest ship afloat (45,000 tons) at the time it was launched, was appropriately named. Unfortunately, however, on its maiden voyage on April 14, 1912, speeding along at an unsafe speed of 22 knots, it struck an iceberg and sank in less than two and a half hours, with a loss of 1,513 lives; 711 passengers were saved.

Titans, according to Greek mythology, were monsters, the children of Uranus (heaven) and Gaea or Ge (earth). The early Greek poet Hesiod listed six male and six female Titans. Later authors listed others. In any event, Kronos and Zeus engaged in a struggle for supremacy of the world and the Titans sided with the former, who turned out to be the loser. After Kronos was vanquished, the Titans were confined to Tartarus, the infernal region where the wicked are punished.

M. H. Klaproth, a German scientist, who discovered *titanium* in 1795, so named the new element as "an allusion to the incarnation of natural strength in metal."

The adjective *titanic* (meaning "like a titan") was created simply to match *gigantic* (meaning "like a giant").

# TOADY

The English language has many synonyms for *sycophant* ("one who attempts to win favor or advance himself by flattering persons of influence"). Such a servile self-seeker may be called a bootlicker, flunky, lacky, fawner, apple polisher, backslapper, cat's-paw, yes-man, parasite, or toady. Take your choice.

The synonym that seems to have no bearing on flattery is *toady*. Yet it has come to mean a person who is an inordinate flatterer. This sense developed curiously many years ago during the period when country fairs were more prevalent than they are today. Mountebanks were common sights, hawking their wares, usually quack medicines they had prepared in their home kitchens. To demonstrate their magic powers of healing, and thus sell their remedies, they would have a lad pretend to swallow a toad (regarded as poisonous). The stricken assistant would immediately be given a dose of the life-saving medicine, and miraculously would recover and show no ill effects. The toad-eater, considering the service he performed, came to be looked upon as a "yes-man," a "hanger-on," one willing to do distasteful things for his master or, in the words of Henry Fielding in *Tom Jones,* "the most nauseous things that can be thought on." Hence the word *toady,* as in "to toady up to someone." Benjamin Disraeli, in *Vivian Grey,* said: "Sweet Reader! You know what a toady is?—that agreeable animal which you must meet every day in civilized society."

An ancient explanation of the derivation of *sycophant* is that it stemmed from the Greek *sukophantes,* "fig shower." (The significance of the phrase "fig shower" has never been made clear, according to Dr. Klein.) Its sense was "informer," one who denounced to officials any persons not paying the tariff on figs, a heavily taxed item at that time. But since these informants were playing up to the government, they were called government toadies. Although this has been well documented, some etymology spoofers believe that all this is simply a figment of someone's imagination.

## TOAST

Many a person who drinks a toast to someone's health must wonder what the word *toast* is doing in this pseudo-ceremony, since it involves no toast. Furthermore, a drink and a piece of toast seemingly have nothing in common anyway, yet years ago that was not entirely true.

One of the drinking customs that goes back more centuries than linguists can document is to put a piece of highly spiced toast into a glass of wine to add flavor to the drink. In the *Merry Wives of Windsor* Falstaff ordered Bardolph to fetch him a quart of sack and "put toast in't" to make the sack taste better. The word *toast* comes from Old French *toster,* "parch," which presumably was derived from Latin *tostus,* "parched or roasted."

In the early eighteenth century the custom of drinking a toast took a new twist. The toast was still drunk, but not, as today, to a member of the drinking party. Instead it was made to the health or honor of a popular or celebrated person, especially a beautiful woman, who might be completely unknown personally to the assembled group. This practice was helped along by Richard Steele's anecdote published in *The Tatler* (No. 23, June 4, 1709): "It happened that on a public day a celebrated beauty . . . was in the Cross Bath, and one of the crowd of her admirers took a glass of water in which the fair one stood and drank her health to the company. There was in the place a gay fellow, half-fuddled, who offered to jump in, and swore, though he liked not the liquor, he would have the toast (that is, the lady herself). He was opposed in his resolution; yet his whim gave foundation to the present honour which is done to the lady we mention in our liquor, who has ever since been called a *toast.*" Nowadays such a person, usually a popular actress or a fashion leader, may be known as "the toast of the town."

# TOBACCO

*See* NICOTINE

# TOUCHSTONE

A touchstone is a dark, flinty stone used to test the purity of gold and silver by the color of the streaks left when the stone is rubbed with either metal. Almost from the time of the discovery of this phenomenon, the word *touchstone* became equated with "test" or "criterion." The test may be made, figuratively, even in adversity. According to Beaumont and Fletcher's *The Triumph of Honour,* "Calamity is man's true touchstone."

In Ovid's *Metamorphoses,* Mercury changed Battus into a touchstone. Battus was metamorphosed because he saw Mercury steal Apollo's oxen. But to start at the beginning. Mercury bribed Battus to silence by giving him a cow, but later became fearful that he could not be trusted. To test him, Mercury garbed himself as a peasant and offered Battus a cow and an ox if he would divulge the secret. Battus could not resist so inviting an offer and told all. Mercury, thereupon, changed Battus into a touchstone as a punishment for his indiscretion, which undoubtedly made him testy.

# TRAGEDY

Strictly speaking, the word *tragedy* should not be used of personal misfortune but only of literary or dramatic works. Misfortune that befalls people may rightly be termed a disaster or a calamity.

The root word of *tragedy* is the Greek *tragos,* "goat," and *oide,* "song." Although no one knows for certain the equivalence of *goat song* and *tragedy,* it may relate to the Hebraic sacrifice of a goat called an escape goat. A similar sacrifice of a goat was a ritual associated with the god of the fields and vineyards, Dionysus. Just as the fate of the goat was death, so a tragedy would end unhappily. Another theory is that Thespis, a talented Athenian actor (actors are called *thespians* after him) once received a goat (the first Oscar?) as an award for his superlative performances. In any event, a tragedy is now defined as "a dramatic or literary work depicting a protagonist engaged in a morally significant struggle ending in ruin or profound disappointment."

The *protagonist* (Greek *protos*, "first," and *agonistes*, "actor") is the most important actor in a play or, by extension, the leading character in a novel, the one about whom the action revolves. Since there can be but one person who plays the leading part, it is incorrect to refer to *a* protagonist; it must be *the* protagonist. Also, since the *pro* in *protagonist* does not mean "for" (it is not a prefix), one should not assume that the protagonist is in favor of the role he is playing or that he approves of what he is saying. It may be very much the opposite; he may even be portraying a criminal, but he still remains the pivotal character.

## TRIVIAL

*Trivial* refers to something of no consequence. The word came from the Latin *trivium* through its adjectival form *trivialis.* Yet *trivium*, "a place where three roads meet," from *tri* ("three") and *via* ("way"), traditionally has been a word of great signification. In medieval schools the *trivium* (three roads of learning) was the name given the first three liberal arts—grammar, logic, rhetoric. With the passage of time the "academic" *trivium* was forgotten but not the "inconsequential" *trivial.* And that may be because of man's natural predilection toward gossip over learning. It has long been felt that gossips and idlers gather where roads intersect, since they make natural and convenient places to meet. What was usually discussed at these congregations was the commonplace, matters of little value, the gossip that one might expect to hear at *tri-viae*—the trivial.

## TURNCOAT

A *turncoat* is a traitor, a renegade. He is, figuratively speaking, willing to change his allegiance as quickly as one can turn a coat inside out. According to legend, that is exactly what the servants, farmers, and other hirelings of a manor who were compelled to ward off their master's enemies did to avoid capture. These make-shift soldiers were crafty. Although the outside of their coats bore their master's color, on the inside they had sewn in the enemy's color. If the battle seemed lost, they would, by simply turning their coats inside out, appear to belong to the winning side. They were real turncoats.

Another often-told story is of a certain Duke of Saxony and a Duke of Savoy whose coats bore the color of one country on one side and on the reverse, the color of another country. When they desired to show favor to a country, these Dukes would wear the color of that country on the outside.

A *turntail* is like a turncoat in that he runs away to protect himself, which does not necessarily prove him a coward. He may believe, in the words of an unknown author, "He that fights and runs away / May live to fight another day," or, as put by Paul Scarron, a seventeenth century French dramatist, "He can return who flies: / Not so with him who dies."

## TUXEDO

A man attending a formal affair today may wear a tuxedo and a black tie or a full-dress coat and a white tie. At one time, however, only the latter style was acceptable; in fact the tailless formal jacket was unknown until the 1890's. But that is getting ahead of the tale.

The Algonquian word for "wolf" is *p'tuksit* (pronounced with a silent *p*) and means "the animal with a round foot." From that Indian word a lake about forty miles from New York City came to be known as Tuxedo Lake, a rather good phoneticism. Much of the area surrounding the lake was purchased by Pierre Lorillard, and subsequently a fashionable and exclusive summer resort and residential community was developed called *Tuxedo Park*.

At one lavish affair, perhaps given by the Astors or the Harrimans, a brave aristocrat who disliked the formal "soup and fish" (the slang term for full dress attire) rebelled and wore a tailless jacket. The innovation was startling, but the shortened jacket became an immediate success. And quite naturally the new style was dubbed *tuxedo,* after the name of the place where the garment was first worn. Considering its ancestor—*p'tuksit*— it may be that many a dandy clad in dinner clothes is really a wolf parading as a social lion.

# 𝒰

## UMBRELLA

See PARASOL

## UMPIRE

See APRON

## UPPER CRUST

See HOBNOB

## UTOPIA

The utopian is the ideally perfect: it may describe a place or a state of things or an event or happening so satisfactory that it cannot be improved. In general usage, however, *utopian* has become a synonym for *impractical.*

Sir Thomas More in 1516 coined the word *Utopia* as a title for his two-volume book. The term is a composite of Greek *ou* ("no") and *topos* ("place"), which means "nowhere," an apt title, since the subject of the book concerns an imaginary island on which exists a perfect form of society, controlled solely by reason. *Utopia,* in translation, implies the unattainable, a dream world, in which communism is the cure for the predominating evils in public and private life. Private property and money are nonexistent. Gold is valueless (that is what the chamberpots are made of), and gems (diamonds and rubies) are used by children as toys. (Perhaps that is why Lord Macaulay once said: "An acre in Middlesex is better than a principality in Utopia.")

More, whose head was placed on the chopping block because he had refused to take the Oath of Supremacy in favor of the king, was supposedly as idealistic in the conduct of his own life as the life he pictured on the imaginary island of Utopia.

271

He was incorruptible. When someone tried to bribe him with a glove stuffed with gold, he returned the money, saying that he preferred unlined gloves. On another occasion, when proffered a valuable goblet, his Lordship immediately filled it with wine, drank to the briber's health, and then returned the empty vessel. The world could use More men like Sir Thomas.

# $\mathcal{V}$

## VANILLA

This is simply a history of the semantic evolution of some favorite flavorings. Foremost is *vanilla*, which not only adds flavor in its own right but also increases the strength of others that jiggle one's taste buds. The English word comes almost directly from the Spanish *vainilla*, which, in turn, was derived from the Latin *vagina* (a scabbard or sheath), so called because of the shape of the bean pods.

*Vanilla* originated in Mexico, where the Indians used it as an ingredient in *chocolate*, another Mexican word but one founded in the Aztec dialect. English borrowed it from the Spanish. Spelled *chocolatl*, it literally meant "bitter water" but came to mean "a food made by mixing the seed of *cacaua-atl* with those of a tree called *pochotl*." (This flavor would never sell at Carvel's!)

The word *cocoa* is a corruption of *cacao*, a tropical American evergreen tree from whose ground seeds the pulverized chocolate is made. *Coca* is the name of a South American shrub whose leaves contain cocaine.

The fruit of the palm tree, which yields a milky liquid and a flaky white "meat," was formerly known as *coco*. Now called *coconut*, it has been misspelled ever since the eighteenth century when, in Dr. Johnson's *Dictionary*, the articles on *coco* and *cocoa* were run together, apparently by mistake. Adding to the confusion, the *cacao seed* was formerly known as the *cacao nut*, which, once corrupted, became the *cocoa nut*. This term has now been replaced by *cocoa bean* to differentiate it from the fruit.

All this is enough to make one loco . . . or is it coco?

## VENTRILOQUISM

What is particularly interesting about *ventriloquism* is that, although today it is a medium of entertainment, superstitious ancestors thought it the practice of evil spirits. As Charlie McCarthy might say, "They all must have been dummies, like me." According to early belief, practitioners of this art were not to be taken lightly. They were thought to possess magical powers, perhaps even satanic. Thomas Blount in 1656 described a ventriloquist as "one that hath an evil spirit speaking in his belly," and in 1749 Charles Wesley asserted that "there was a compact . . . between the ventriloquist and the exorcist."

A *ventriloquist,* literally speaking, is "one who talks from his stomach," from Latin *venter, ventris,* ("belly") and *loqui* ("to speak"). The fact is, however, that a ventriloquist does not project speech from his stomach but achieves his illusion by slowing the escaping breath and squeezing the glottis. But how ventriloquists squeeze their glottises is something they don't talk about.

# VERMICELLI

The little worm (the kind seen on the front lawn or used for bait) has given rise to several English words—some not ordinarily associated with those wiggling creatures.

The Italian dish made of pasta strings smaller than those of spaghetti (the word *spaghetti,* from *spago,* literally means "strings") is called *vermicelli,* a diminutive form of Latin *vermis* ("worm"). The name *vermicelli,* since it sounds musical to the American ear, makes the dish inviting. Picturing a plate filled with cooked worms would not be so appetizing.

The brilliant scarlet red dye used by the ancients was made from the red body fluid of the cochineal insect. The name given the dye is not cognate with any color but with Latin *vermis,* "worm," the source of the dye; hence *vermilion.* (Caveat: *vermicelli* is spelled with two *e*'s; *vermilion,* with one.)

The English word that derives directly from Latin *vermis* is *vermin*—objectionable animals collectively, particularly disgusting insects. Figuratively an obnoxious person—a real creep— might be called *vermin.* And also figuratively speaking, the only worm a mother will tolerate in her home is her son the book- worm.

## VERNACULAR

When a person speaks in the vernacular, he uses the language of the common man rather than the more formal language of the intellectual elite. The word *vernacular* originated on an even lower social stratum, for it came from the word for "slave."

In ancient Rome a slave born in his master's house was called a *verna*, to distinguish him from one acquired in another manner. The adjective *vernaculus,* meaning "homeborn" or "native," acquired a variety of uses referring to things domestic. By the time the term *vernacular* was accepted into English, its meaning had once again shrunk; it then meant the native language of a country or the dialect of a region in contradistinction to the language of learned scholars (Latin).

In Medieval Latin the word *slave* was *sclavus.* During the Middle Ages herdsmen from East-Central Europe, known as Slavs, were subjugated by Germanic tribes, who then sold them into slavery. The word *slave* came to refer to enslaved Slavs, eventually to all persons considered another's property. In Italian, *sclavus* became *schiavo* and was used as a greeting "(I am your) slave"—an expression reminiscent of the obsolescent English complimentary closing, "Your most humble and obedient servant." In Northern Italy, a dialectal form of *schiavo* is *ciao* (pronounced "chow"), now a popular expression of greeting or farewell used by many peoples around the world.

## VILLAIN

*See* SURLY

## VIRTUE

If virtue is moral excellence or goodness, one wonders why men surrendered their exclusive right to that cardinal quality and permitted women to share it.

In very distant times *virtue* was an attribute only of men; it meant manliness, primarily signified by courage and daring, especially in war. The Latin *virtus* ("strength" or "courage"), which sired the English *virtue,* was itself sired by *vir* (Latin for "man"). Clearly traits that made heroes in battle were not exercisable by women, since they were not a part of the war machine.

With the passage of time, the sense of *virtue* came to embrace a sense of rectitude, moral conduct, and uprightness. And with its further extension to include women, its meaning reflected many other qualities of character, chiefly purity and chastity.

Today, although virtue may be possessed by anyone, men have tenaciously clung to one word stemming from *vir: virile,* which means "pertaining to, or characteristic of, a man." *Virilism,* on the other hand, another *vir* word, applies to women only. It means "having or exhibiting male characteristics," like a woman who has a masculine voice. Also *virago.* Although its current sense is "shrew"—a noisy, dominating woman—originally it referred to a woman of great size and strength, a so-called Amazon.

The phrase *by virtue of* does not imply moral excellence, but means "by reason of" ("He may command *by virtue of* his position.") A *virtuoso* is a prodigy, a master, or an expert in a particular field, but the term is most often used of musicians. *Virtue* has spawned many words with entirely different meanings. Restricting its use to one narrow sense is no virtue.

## VOLCANO

The similarity in spelling of *Vulcanus* and *volcano* can lead one to the correct conclusion that the word *volcano* was derived from the name of the Roman god of fire, *Vulcanus. Vulcan* (as he is known in English) was thrown into the sea by his mother because he was born lame. But Vulcan did not surrender easily. He thrived and eventually set up his metal workshop and became the armorer of the gods. He kept a forge in the bowels of the volcano Mt. Etna or in the volcanic islands of Lemnos (there are two versions).

Vulcan was bothered by amatory desires, not only his own but also his wife's. He was married to Aphrodite (the Roman Venus), the goddess of love and beauty. One day Vulcan learned that Aphrodite was disporting herself illicitly with Ares (the Roman Mars). He schemed to embarrass them by constructing an invisible net that descended around their bed during their love-making. While they were still embracing, Vulcan summoned the other gods to look and laugh at the guilty pair. What an ungodly X-rated scene!

## VOLUME

The commonest use of the word *volume* today is in reference to sound, as in "Please turn up the *volume*. I can't hear the announcement." That sense, however, is decibels apart from the word's original meaning, "a roll of papyrus."

In ancient days books were written on a substance made from the pith of the papyrus plant. For safekeeping and for transporting, the sheets (called *papyrus*) were rolled on a stick or spindle, a process the Romans spoke of as *volumen*, from the Latin verb *volvo*, "turn about," "roll." From *volumen* evolved Old French *volume*, which was absorbed unchanged into the English language in the fourteenth century and, by the sixteenth century, also came to mean "size or bulk" with reference to a book and then generalized to mean the space occupied by anything.

About the fifth century, papyrus gave way to parchment, a tough, durable substance (made from the skin of goats or sheep) that could be used on both sides and then folded. Although manuscripts are prepared differently today—they no longer are rolled or folded—the word for the finished product, *volume*, remains the same. (To speak volumes, of course, does not mean to speak about books but "to express much or to be full of meaning." When *volume* is used as here and as in the first sentence, in the sense of "fullness of sound," it also derives from *volvo*, "roll." The volume of sound is in effect "rolled out.")

# W

## WEDLOCK

Although ordinarily something that is locked up has been made secure, adding the suffix -lock to wed does not ensure the future security of the marital state. In fact, that lock does not refer to a latch or a padlock, in spite of John Ray, who, in *English Proverbs,* said, with tongue in cheek, "Wedlock is a padlock," or Byron in *Don Juan,* "And wedlock and a padlock mean the same."

*Wedlock* ("matrimony"), the only word in the English language still using this additive, originally meant "plighting one's troth." (*Wed* in Anglo-Saxon meant "pledge," and *lock* was *lac,* a suffix whose sense was "offering.") No longer, however, does *wedlock* suggest "the marriage," which Milton illustrated in 1643 in his *Doctrine and Discipline of Divorce:* "Where love cannot be, there can be left of wedlock nothing but the empty husk of an outside matrimony, as undelightful and unpleasing ... as any other kind of hypocrisy." Today *wedlock* most often appears in another unpleasing phrase, "born out of wedlock," which refers to a child born to an unmarried woman.

## WELCOME

A guest is made to feel wanted with the greeting "Welcome," a combination of the adverb *well* and the imperative of the verb *come.* The identical sense can be found in many languages; for example, *bienvenido* in Spanish, *bienvenu* in French, and *benevenuto* in Italian. Much closer in sound to the English is the German *willkommen.* A wanted guest is, of course, *well come* and therefore *welcome.*

A customary remark in early times, when someone was about to take leave, was "God be with you." This was later shortened to "good-bye" or, as now often spelled, "goodby," without the hyphen and without the *e.* Its actual spiritual sense is probably little thought of these days. (Spaniards still say *"Vaya con Dios,"* which means "Go with God," and occasionally the French, especially for a long leavetaking, say *"Adieu,"* which translates to the same effect, "to God.")

The word *farewell* is also a contraction. It stands for "fare thee well," meaning "travel well," but it no longer is a common acknowledgment of parting. Many young people use the childish *bye bye.* Another popular expression of leave-taking, *so-long,* may have come either from the Arabic *salaam* or from the Hebrew *shalom,* which means "peace be with you."

# WELSH

*See* SCOTCH

# WELSH RABBIT

Just as those who eat Yorkshire pudding know they're not eating pudding, so those who enjoy *Welsh rabbit* know they're not eating rabbit. This fanciful culinary dish, which first appeared in Wales about 1725, is a delicacy made of melted cheese and seasonings, served on toast, sometimes accompanied by beer or ale.

Many odd dishes have been jokingly given euphemistic names, *Cape Cod turkey* for *codfish,* for one. It is believed that the name *rabbit* was a lowbrow stab at humor—possibly by some unfortunate who couldn't afford meat and so called it *rabbit* to make the dish sound more appealing. The change from *rabbit* to *rarebit* has been credited to folk etymology. In any case, it is a corrupted form of *rabbit,* a corruption encouraged by the genteel. Obviously many restaurants find the term *Welsh rarebit* more palatable than *Welsh rabbit,* judged by the way they list this dish on their menus. That this change was unnecessary and foolish was underscored by H. W. Fowler's caustic comment: *"Welsh rabbit* [is a word that] is amusing and right, and *Welsh rarebit* stupid and wrong." Apparently restaurateurs don't read Fowler.

# WISEACRE

One may sensibly ask, Does the word *acre* in *wiseacre* refer to a measurement of ground? The answer is, it does not. The term comes from the Dutch *wijssegger,* which means "sooth-sayer." Since prophets were considered knowledgeable, it seemed logical to call them "wise," which is what *wijs* means. The *acre,* of course, was merely an adjusted pronunciation of the Dutch *segger,* "sayer." The term *wiseacre* today is used only contemptuously in the sense of "a wise guy," "a smart aleck," or "one who thinks he knows everything."

A story that made the rounds in the days of Ben Jonson is that, in reply to the boasting of a member of the landed gentry of his large estates, Jonson wryly commented, "What care we for your dirt and clods? Where you have an acre of land, I have ten acres of wit." Humiliated, the braggart mumbled, "He's Mr. Wiseacre."

## WITCH HAZEL

*Witch hazel,* as everyone who has been shaved by a barber knows, is a mild astringent applied to the face to sterilize cuts and nicks. The prickly sensation that follows is not the doing of witches, however. The lotion is made from the leaves and bark of the witch hazel plant (a shrub whose pod explodes when ripe) and a quantity of alcohol, a combination that makes the skin smart. The "witch" part of the name comes from the similar-sounding Anglo-Saxon *wice* and Old English *wic,* mean-ing "a tree with easily bent branches."

A tree that is closely associated with witches is the hazel tree (a member of the birch family), for it was supposed to have magical powers that could neutralize witches' spells. Also, it is said, divining rods made from this tree were used to discover underground springs that would be likely locations to sink wells. Some believed further that this wand could pick out criminals in a crowd of people and that it was a protection against evil forces. And then, too, carrying hazel nuts would prevent tooth-aches. (If not the tree of life, it must have been the tree of witchcraft.) The notion that the hazel tree was a "witch" tree could logically have come from Medieval English *wyche,* mean-ing, according to Dr. Klein, "a tree with pliant branches," of which the hazel was one, but especially the elm.

The theories behind the origin of the name *witch hazel* are interesting but hardly established—perhaps etymologists need an astringent to smarten them up.

# Y

## YANKEE

The question What is a Yankee? is answered differently by different people. To Europeans, a Yankee is a native or citizen of the United States. To most Americans, he is a descendant of Old New England stock. But to Southerners a Yankee is a Northerner—someone who comes from north of the Mason and Dixon line.

The origin of the term *Yankee* has been a matter of dispute among etymologists since the days of the Founding Fathers. Although no provable conclusion is available, some notions have been advanced that sound authoritative. However, many people have remained unconvinced. Perhaps (unless there is some lucky etymological find) it is best to consider its origin "uncertain" or "obscure."

The idea that enjoys the largest following is that Yankee came from Dutch *Jan Kees*—a dialectal variant of *John Kaas,* which literally meant "John Cheese," an ethnic insult for a Hollander (*Jan*—pronounced *Yahn*—was "John," and *cheese,* from the national product of Holland). Another notion espoused by some word historians is that New Yorkers, who disliked their northern neighbors, viewing them as country bumpkins, mockingly called them *Yankees.* But the English during the Revolutionary War extended the meaning further. They attached what was construed as a belittling tag to all residents in the northern territory, *Yankees*—and that became the British nickname for the colonists.

According to James Fenimore Cooper, Indians sounded the word *English* as *Yengees; whence Yankees.* In 1841 he appended a note in the *Deerslayer:* "It is singular that there should be any question concerning the origin of the well-known sobriquet of 'Yankee.' Nearly all the old writers who speak of the Indians first known to the Colonists make them pronounce 'English' as

281

'Yengees.' " But this corrupted pronunciation has not been otherwise substantiated. Other ideas abound—for example, that the word was derived from the Scottish *yankie*, "a gigantic falsehood," from Dutch *Jahnke*, a diminutive of *Jan*, or from Dutch *vrijbuiten*, "a freebooter" or "plunderer."

The War Between the States gave the word "Yankee" a derisive twist. The Confederate soldiers didn't call the Federal troops Northerners or Unionists but "Yankees," and, to underscore the lowest meaning of that term, they prefixed it with "damn." The Federal soldiers were not just "Yankees"; they were "damn Yankees."

Anyhow, when American troops go abroad, their allies take heart when they hear "The Yanks are coming," no matter what state they come from.

## YE

It is just as foolish to ask the pounding waves to be quiet as it is to ask people to change their pronunciation of *Ye*. Almost everyone pronounces it *yee*—Ye Olde Book Store, Ye Olde Tobacco Shoppe, Ye Olde Bread Basket. Yet its correct pronunciation is *the*. As the initial adjective in the names of some shops, *ye* may be called a fancy *the*. The opening line of the Mayflower Compact is "In ye name of God, amen." One should read it: "In *the* name of God, amen."

*Ye* developed, some say, as a printer's error. What was supposed to be set was a *thorn*, a character for *th*, which resembled the letter *p*. But the letter *y* was mistakenly used, and the error was continued by other printers. Another story is that, since the old English printers had no type for the symbol *th*, they used the letter *y*, its closest equivalent. But that form was not supposed to change the pronunciation; it was still to be pronounced *the*. Anyway, that's not the way *ye* sounds to most of *ye* good people.

*Z*

## ZANY

See JAZZ

## ZENITH

A person gazing straight up at the sky is observing the zenith, the point of the celestial sphere directly overhead. The word *zenith* did not follow a straight path into current English, however. In brief, it started with an Arabic phrase containing the word *samt* (the full phrase was *samt arras*, "way over the head"). This word was much abused. The *m* became *ni*—an easy mistake for a medieval scribe to make, especially in early script; the French spelled it *cenith* and the English *senyth* and then *senit*. From this came today's *zenith*.

Since, figuratively, *zenith* came to mean the nothing-beyond-which point, its meaning, by extension, became equated with *summit*, the highest point one can reach in any endeavor. Prospero, in Shakespeare's *Tempest*, spoke of *zenith* in this way when he said: "I find my zenith doth depend upon / A most auspicious star, whose influence / If now I court not but omit, my fortunes / Will ever after droop."

The antonym of *zenith* is *nadir*. It, too, originated in an Arabic word, *nazir*, which means "opposite." The nadir is the point directly under an observer's feet, the very opposite to the zenith. In a figurative sense, the nadir is the lowest point in anything. It may be the moment of greatest depression, misfortune, or adversity.

# Bibliography

Among the books consulted are those listed below. In addition, many other publications provided substantial material including encyclopedias, particularly *The World Book Encyclopedia* and the *Encyclopedia Britannica;* literary works, primarily those of William Shakespeare; the Bible; and books on quotations. Those who desire to pursue the study of the history of words will find pleasingly helpful the books that deal with word origins (and their titles distinguish them).

*American Heritage Dictionary of the English Language,* William Morris, Editor. Boston: Houghton Mifflin Co., 1976.

Bartlett, John, *Familiar Quotations.* Boston: Little, Brown and Co., 1980.

Bliss, A. J., *Dictionary of Foreign Words and Phrases.* New York: E. P. Dutton & Co., Inc., 1966.

Bremner, John B., *Words on Words.* New York: Columbia University Press, 1980.

Brewer, Cobham E., *The Dictionary of Phrase & Fable.* New York: Avenel Books, 1978.

Calvert, G. H., *Cortina Handy Spanish-English Dictionary.* New York: R. D. Cortina, Inc., 1980.

*Cassell's French Dictionary,* Dennis Girard, Editor. London: Cassell & Company, Ltd., and New York: Macmillan Publishing Co., Inc., 1962.

*Cassell's Italian Dictionary,* Piero Rebora, Editor. London: Cassel & Co., Ltd., and New York: Macmillan Publishing Co., Inc., 1967.

*Cassell's Latin Dictionary,* J. R. V. Marchant and Joseph T. Charles, Revisers. New York: Funk & Wagnalls Co. (undated).

Ciardi, John, *A Browser's Dictionary.* New York: Harper & Row, 1980.

Cirlot, J. E., *A Dictionary of Symbols.* New York: Philosophical Library, 1971.

Cotterell, Arthur, *A Dictionary of World Mythology.* New York: G. P. Putnam's Sons, 1980.

Espy, Willard R., *Thou Improper Thou Uncommon Noun.* New York: Clarkson N. Potter, Inc., 1978.

Evans, Bergen, *Comfortable Words.* New York: Random House, 1962.

Evans, Bergen, *Dictionary of Quotations.* New York: Delacorte Press, 1968.

Flesch, Rudolf, *The ABC of Style.* New York: Harper & Row, 1966.

Fowler, H. W., *A Dictionary of Modern Usage*. London: Oxford University Press, 1944.

Funk, Wilfred, *Word Origins and Their Romantic Stories*. New York: Bell Publishing Co., 1978.

Gayley, Charles M., *The Classic Myths*. New York: Ginn and Co., 1939.

Hoare, Alfred, *A Short Italian Dictionary*. Cambridge: Cambridge University Press, 1960.

Holt, Alfred H., *Phrase and Word Origins*. New York: Dover Publications, Inc., 1961.

Hunt, Cecil, *Word Origins*. New York: Citadel Press, The Wisdom Library, 1949.

Johnson, Samuel, *A Dictionary of the English Language*. London: Times Books, 1979.

Klein, Ernest, *Klein's Comprehensive Etymological Dictionary of the English Language*. New York: Elsevier Scientific Publishing Co., 1971.

*Larousse's French-English Dictionary*, Marguerite-Marie Dubois, Reviser. New York: Pocket Books, 1971.

Maleska, Eugene T., *A Pleasure in Words*. New York: Simon and Schuster, 1981.

Mathews, Mitford M., *A Dictionary of Americanisms*. Chicago: The University of Chicago Press, 1951.

Mencken, H. L., *The American Language*. New York: Alfred A. Knopf, 1937.

*Merriam-Webster Book of Word Histories*. New York: Pocket Books, 1976.

Nurnberg, Maxwell, and Morris Rosenblum, *All About Words*. New York: The New American Library, 1966.

Opdycke, John, *The Opdycke Lexicon of Word Selection*. New York: Funk & Wagnalls, 1956.

*Oxford Dictionary of English Etymology*, C. T. Onions, Editor. London: Oxford University Press, 1966.

*Oxford Dictionary of Quotations*, 3rd edition. New York and Oxford: Oxford University Press, 1979.

*Oxford English Dictionary*, James A. H. Murray, Editor. Oxford: The Clarendon Press, 1884.

Partridge, Eric, *Origins—A Short Etymological Dictionary of Modern English*. New York: The Macmillan Co., 1983.

Pei, Mario, and Salvatore Ramondino, *Dictionary of Foreign Terms*. New York: Dell Publishing Co., 1974.

Shipley, Joseph T., *Dictionary of Word Origins*. New York: The Philosophical Society, 1945.

Skeat, Walter W., *A Concise Etymological Dictionary of the English Language*. New York: Capricorn Books, 1963.

*Smaller Classical Dictionary*, E. H. Blakeney, Editor. London and Toronto: J. M. Dent & Sons, 1934.

Stevenson, Burton, *The Home Book of Quotations.* New York: Dodd, Mead & Co., 1967.

Stimpson, George, *A Book About a Thousand Things.* New York and London: Harper Brothers, 1946.

Strunk, William, Jr., and E. B. White, *The Elements of Style.* New York: The Macmillan Co., 1959.

*Webster's New International Dictionary of the English Language,* 3rd edition. Springfield: G. & C. Merriam Co., 1971.

Wentworth, Harold, and Stuart Berg Flexner, *Dictionary of American Slang.* New York: Thomas Y. Crowell Co., 1960.

*World Book Dictionary,* Clarence L. Barnhart and Robert K. Barnhart, Editors. New York: Doubleday and Co., 1983.

# Index